Public and Private Spaces of the City

Ali Madanipour

Routledge
Taylor & Francis Group

LONDON AND NEW YORK

First published 2003 by Routledge
11 New Fetter Lane, London EC4P 4EE
Simultaneously published in the USA and Canada
by Routledge
29 West 35th Street, New York, NY 10001

Routledge is an imprint of the Taylor & Francis Group

© 2003 Ali Madanipour

Typeset in Akzidenz Grotesk by Wearset Ltd, Boldon, Tyne and Wear
Printed and bound in Great Britain by TJ International Ltd, Padstow, Cornwall

100333674

British Library Cataloguing in Publication Data
A catalogue record for this book is available from the British Library

Library of Congress Cataloging in Publication Data
Madanipour, Ali.
Public and private spaces of the city / Ali Madanipour
p. cm.
Includes bibliographical references and index.
1. Space (Architecture)—Psychological aspects. I. Title
NA2765 .M25 2003
720'.1'9—dc21
    2002011015

ISBN 0-415-25628-3 (hbk)
ISBN 0-415-25629-1 (pbk)

Public and Private Spaces of the City

The subdivision of our social world and the spaces we inhabit into public and private spheres is one of the key features of how a society organizes itself. This affects individuals' mental state and experiences, regulates their behaviour, and superimposes a long-lasting structure onto human societies. This book sets out to find out how and why social space is subdivided in this way and to explore the nature of each realm as defined by spatial and symbolic boundaries.

To understand this dichotomous organization of space and society, the investigation is conducted along three scales: spatial scale (body, home, neighbourhood, city), degrees of exclusivity and openness (from the most private to the most public), and modes of social encounter and association with space (personal, interpersonal, impersonal). We start from the private, interior space of the mind and move outwards to the extensions of the body in space, the personal space. Then we visit the home, the domains of privacy, intimacy and property, followed by interpersonal spaces of sociability among strangers, communal spaces of the neighbourhood, the material and institutional public sphere and the impersonal spaces of the city.

As the shape of the city and the characteristics of urban life are influenced by the way public and private distinction is made, the role of urban designers becomes ever more significant. By establishing a flexible and eleborate boundary between the two realms, urbanism can be enriched, and the danger of encroachment by private interests into the public realm and the threat of public intrusion into the private sphere can be both minimized and carefully managed.

In writing this book **Ali Madanipour** drew upon his many years of research into cities, as well as teaching and professional practice in architecture, urban design and planning.

Contents

Acknowledgements

Chapters 5 and 7 contain material from the author's papers that were published in *Town Planning Review* (Vol. 72, No. 2, 2001) and *Environment and Planning B: Planning and Design* (Vol. 26, No. 1, pp. 879–91, 1999), which are used here with kind permission. The photograph in Figure 1.4 is by Simin Davoudi and in Figure 7.7 by Hamid Imanirad, used with their kind permission. Support material for the book was collected through many sources, including research projects and conferences funded by the European Commission; the UK's Economic and Social Research Council; the UK's Department of Trade and Industry; the British Council; Danish Building and Urban Research Institute; Aarhus School of Architecture and the Nordic Academy; Sharjah Municipality; Istanbul's Mimar Sinan University; Trabzon's Karadeniz Technical University; and the University of Newcastle upon Tyne. Special thanks are due to Simin and Suroosh for their continuous support.

Introduction

Have you ever felt the urge to look inside, when walking down a narrow street and passing in front of a door that is ajar or a window that is half-lit? Have you wondered what lies behind curtains that are drawn, gates that are shut, walls that are high? Have you thought about how objects, signs and symbols may invite you to one place and bar you from another? From inside the buildings, have you spent time standing in front of a window, watching the world go by from a detached, safe distance, or wishing to go to the open spaces outside, meeting your friends in public places or just joining the crowd of strangers?

On the one hand, if we monitor our individual everyday routines, one of the defining features of these routines is how we live in and pass through private and public spaces, and feel and behave accordingly. From the intimate space of the home to the interpersonal space of the school or workplace and the impersonal space of the busy city streets, we are located in different environments at each moment. Depending on our particular circumstances and our understanding of these environments, we feel and behave differently: from a place where we feel comfortable and relaxed to one where we feel the need to be careful and cautious. Many aspects of our mental and behavioural states at each moment, therefore, depend on whether we are on our own, with our intimate friends and relatives, or in the presence of strangers.

On the other hand, if we monitor the spaces of villages, towns and cities, we see how they are broadly structured around a separation of public and private spaces. It appears to be a defining feature of these settlements: how a society divides its space into public and private spheres, and how this division controls movement from one place to another and access to places and activities. This is almost a universal feature of cities, as cities of all cultures, at all historical periods, are organized along some form of public–private lines, although the nature of this division, the meaning of and relationship between public and private spheres vary widely. Ever since the rise of the city, with its division of labour and complex, stratified social and spatial structures, public–private distinction has been a key organizing principle, shaping the physical space of the cities and the social life of their citizens. The distinction between the home and the street that characterizes cities today can also be found in the Mesopotamian city-state of Ur more than four millennia ago. This suggests that there is a direct link between this distinction and the way human beings relate to each other in social environments. The way space is subdivided and the relationship between the public and private spheres in general are a mirror of social relations and a main indicator of how a society organizes itself.

The division of space and society into public and private spheres, therefore, affects individuals' mental states, regulates their behaviour, and superimposes a long-lasting structure onto human societies and the spaces they inhabit. Much of the research on how cities are structured, however, has focused on other issues. Some have studied the physical structures of the city, to understand the typology of buildings, or how the places, buildings and routes are shaped and used. Others have studied the forms of activity and functional organization in the city, to understand the patterns of land use and spatial structure. Other studies have concentrated on the patterns of social and cultural differentiation in the city, how uneven distribution of resources and economic and social polarization characterize a city or how different groups create different cultural identities in a city. The relationship between public and private lies at the centre of many such systems of stratification and classification, but is not sufficiently addressed by them. This book focuses on this important aspect of how the urban space is structured.

The book examines the constitution of the public and private spheres of society and the relationship between the two spheres, particularly as manifest in city spaces, where spatial and symbolic boundaries render visible a distinction that characterizes human societies across time and space. My central focus in this book is the concrete, physical space of human societies with its social and psychological significance, aiming to understand how and why this space is divided into public and private sections.

To be able to understand this division, however, it is important not to limit the investigation to a physical focus, as it soon becomes obvious that this division is a key part of the social life of human beings and is embedded in, and contributes to, the way people live together in societies. It is an integral part of how individuals see themselves and others, communicate with each other, divide their spheres of activity, and construct meaning. The nature of, and the relationships between, the public and private spaces of the city and the social and psychological meanings of these spaces are, therefore, the focus of the book. This book aims to investigate the nature of the two realms, the public and the private, by asking questions such as: How and why do we subdivide the city into the private and public spheres? What are its manifestations and meanings, especially as embodied in space? What does it tell us about our society and our selves?

To undertake this study, it has been essential to go through a journey of discovery in different places, different historical periods, and different disciplines that have addressed this division. The relationship between the public and private has overlapping economic, social, cultural and political dimensions and has a clearly visible physical manifestation, perhaps more than any other form of structuring the city. In economic terms, the private or public ownership of land and property determines the overall shape of the city. In political terms, the relationship between private and public realms was a formative notion in the development of modern democracies and continues to be a key governance concern. In cultural and social terms, the distinction between the public and private determines the routines of daily life and is crucial in the relations between self and other, individual and society. Each of these patterns of differentiation has been studied separately, or in collections of papers, but not necessarily through an integrated outlook and in relation to the structure of the urban space, a task that this book aims to undertake.

Many studies of public and private spheres have specifically focused on one or the other of these spheres. Studies of the home, for example, have emphasized the significance of privacy, while the urban design literature has focused on the public space. There seems to be a tendency for these and similar areas of literature to be mutually exclusive, each adopting a single focus and seeing the other sphere as outside their remit, or as a negative force that tends to encroach upon their chosen focus, and hence stressing the need to keep them apart. If we look at the world from inside the private sphere, we see the sense and the necessity of protecting a part of our life from the intrusion of others. When we look at the world from outside, from the public sphere, we see how it makes sense and how it is essential, to have a common ground where all can come out of their protected zones and communicate with each other. The public and the private, however, only make sense in relation to each other, as they are interdependent notions. This book adopts an integrated approach, studying the two spheres and their relationships, from a dynamic perspective. A dynamic perspective allows us to move between the two spheres, to look at the significance of each sphere on its own and as seen from inside of the other sphere, to deal with the interdependence of the two spheres.

A dynamic approach enables us to study space through a variety of scales and from a variety of angles, which are usually set within disciplinary and ideological territories, and helps us to engage in a dialogue that goes beyond static and narrowly partisan perspectives. Each of these approaches may have a unique perspective into the complex reality of the public–private distinction. They are, however, often incomplete: they can be either trapped in first-person narratives, as is the case with total reliance on phenomenological accounts of the world, or be left outside the complete picture by emphasizing the third-person, scientific views into socio-spatial phenomena. A dynamic approach would allow the investigation to be conducted from both a third- and a first-person perspective (Madanipour, 2001). It shows how the self is constructed at the intersection of biological and social processes, combining pre-linguistic and linguistic elements. It also shows how space is produced through a dialectic relationship between action and its context. It is important to understand the internal dynamics of actors, whether individuals or complex organizations, as well as the many-sided characteristics and dynamics of the socio-spatial contexts in which they operate. It is also important to see how their dialectic relationship affects and changes both actors and the multiple contexts of their action.

This book is part of a larger project of inquiry into cities. Earlier work had focused on the ways in which urban space is shaped at the intersection of political economy and cultural-aesthetic processes. These studies had concentrated on how urban space is structured along the lines of access to resources and of difference, which creates a fragmented mosaic of differentiation, polarization and social exclusion (Madanipour, 1996; 1998a; 1998b; Madanipour et al., 1998; Madanipour, 2001). This study now focuses on how urban space is structured along the lines of a key organizing principle of social life: public–private distinction.

A terminological clarification needs to be made at the start. I have used the term public *space* (and public *place*) to refer to that part of the physical environment which is associated with public meanings and functions. The term public *sphere* (and public *realm*), however, has been used to refer to a much broader concept: the entire range of places, people and activities that constitute the public dimension of human social life. Therefore, public space and public sphere are not coextensive; public space is a component part of the public sphere. The same distinction has been made between the private space and the private sphere. More detailed definitions of the terms private and public are given in Chapters 2 and 4.

The book is written to share the exploration of the public–private distinction in the city with the students and scholars with an interest in linking space and society. It targets those in spatial arts and sciences, including architecture, urban design, planning and urban geography, who are interested in studying urban space in the context of wider concerns, and those in social sciences and humanities, including urban sociology and urban studies, who have an interest in understanding the society through its spatial configuration. It is mainly focused on the contemporary Western city, but it travels to other times and places in search of the roots of ideas and practices and for finding out about comparable traditions. As such it uses social and historical research, attempting to take into account the temporal and spatial dimensions of public–private distinction. This book searches for frameworks with which public–private distinction in the city can be understood and represented. Its intentions, therefore, are to provide analytical insights, rather than providing a normative guide on how to design public and private spaces. However, it is hoped that the design and management of cities can be informed by the discussions and analyses presented in the book.

Rather than a dichotomous organization along the public and private lines, the book is organized along three scales, which form the bases of its investigations: spatial scale (body, home, neighbourhood, city), degrees of exclusivity and openness (from the most private to the most public), and modes of social encounter and association with space (personal, interpersonal, impersonal). We start from the private, interior space of the mind and move outwards to the extensions of the body in space, the personal space (Chapter 1). Then the spaces of privacy are discussed (Chapter 2), followed by the spaces of intimacy (Chapter 3). The three spaces of body, private property and home constitute the spatial core of the personal private sphere. We then move outside to the interpersonal public realm, starting from the interpersonal spaces of sociability among strangers (Chapter 4), and the communal spaces of the neighbourhood, the spaces of familiarity (Chapter 5). This is followed by the impersonal public space, where the material and institutional public sphere (Chapter 6) and the impersonal spaces of the city (Chapter 7) are studied. Some of the main discussions are brought together in a concluding chapter (Chapter 8).

Chapter 1
Personal space of the body

The core of the private sphere is the sphere that is closely associated with the human body. In this chapter, we focus on the body: its inner space of subjectivity as well as the psychological-physical space which is body's extension to its immediate surroundings. We will search for the implications of such divisions as between inner self and others, between personal and interpersonal, for an understanding of the division between private and public spheres. We also look at how some non-Western cultures approach the notion of the self and the private space of the body.

The division of urban space into the public and private is a physical manifestation of the relationship between private and public spheres in society. In turn, these spheres are one reflection of the deeper level relationship between the individual and society, between the self and the other. This chapter focuses on the debates about this relationship between self and other. This will provide a first step in our investigation into the relationship between the private and the public, as it examines how individuals relate to themselves and to the world around them. It then discusses how different modes of analysing this relationship have produced different approaches to urban space and to the demarcation of the public and private spheres within it.

We then move out of the interior space of the body to the outside world, to find out how public and private spaces are constituted around the body. A major form of space, which lies at the heart of private sphere, is explored. It is personal space, a socio-psychological, invisible, and yet physical personal space around each individual, which others may not enter without consent. We explore the nature and dimensions of this personal space and the role it plays in the constitution of the private and public spheres.

INNER SPACE OF THE SELF AND OUTER SPACE OF THE WORLD

To understand the relationship between the public and the private realms, we have to start from one of the most fundamental divisions of space, that between the inner space of the self and the rest of the world. It is a commonly held belief that the mind is the innermost part of a conscious human being, his/her most private space.

The public domain, whether on television screens or in the middle of streets, appears to be accessible to all, while the inner world of the mind is clearly beyond such access. An individual's thoughts, feelings and desires can all be kept secret inside a box, the inner space of the mind, or be made public when it is felt appropriate to do so. The mental world of consciousness becomes the most basic manifestation of privacy because it is the realm which only one individual is aware of and has access to. I may not have complete control over my mental state but it is still best known to me and not to others. It feels to be outside the material world and as such beyond the reach of anyone else.

For some, this private space is where they can take refuge from the outside world, to relax, to make sense of the world, or to feel in control. In contrast, some may feel trapped inside this private space, unable to reach out, while others may be afraid of entering it, preferring to spend their time always in the company of others, for fear of turbulent feelings, bad dreams, or boring loneliness. The distinction between the private and public, therefore, starts here, between the inner space of consciousness and the outer space of the world, between the human subject's psyche and the social and physical world outside. The way we make this fundamental distinction has a direct impact on all forms of institutionalized public–private distinctions in our lives.

The discussions of the relationship between the two realms of the inner self and the outer world often revolve around two foci: the relationship between body and mind and the question of autonomy of the self. Each of these two themes has emerged first as a general classical notion, to be later challenged and altered through critical responses.

MIND AND BODY

To study the distinction between the inner and outer realms, it is essential to study the characteristics that distinguish them from each other, the borders that separate them and mediate between them, and the relationships between them. The inner space is seen to be the non-physical, soft space of thoughts and feelings, which grasps the world but is distinctive from the hard physical reality of the outside. This apparently common sense contrast formed the basis of what is now termed Cartesian dualism. For Descartes, the mind (a term he used interchangeably with 'soul') is essentially non-physical and has a real distinction from the body (Cottingham, 1992b: 236). Descartes argued that the essence or nature of the mind consists of thinking and it is free of place or material things: '. . . this 'I', that is to say, the mind, by which I am what I am, is entirely distinct from the body' (Descartes, 1968: 54). Descartes was working within a religious as well as scientific frame of discussion, in a period dominated by sceptical arguments, prevalent among them Montaigne who wrote of 'the soft pillow of doubt' (Koyré, 1970: x). Descartes, however, was searching for certainty in knowledge. He aimed to put to one side all that he had been taught and tried to find a solid, rational foundation for his philosophy, which he found in thinking: 'I think, therefore I am' (Descartes, 1968: 53). The theme of the self thus became the central theme of modern philosophy since Descartes (Scruton, 1996: 481). The shape that Descartes gave to this theme four centuries ago has framed the discussion ever since.

As with any other form of public–private distinction, this separation of the inner and outer space relies on a boundary, which in this case is the human body. It feels that the mind is hidden in the head, but understands the world through bodily senses and can communicate with others through gestures, patterns of behaviour, and language, i.e. through the body. The non-physical, inner, private space of the mind is thus highly dependent on the body to grasp the physical, outer space of the world. In other words, the body mediates between the states of consciousness and the world. The body is the boundary between the two realms. It is the medium through which the two realms are related to each other (Figure 1.1).

Many commentators have since questioned Descartes' dualism, so that many today would identify themselves as anti-Cartesian (Cottingham, 1992a: 1; Žižek, 1999). Cartesian dualism has been criticized on the ground that it separates the mental from the physical and the 'inner' mental states from the 'outer' circumstances (Scruton, 1996: 48). Criticism of dualism often leads to some form of materialism, widely held by philosophers today, which rejects the possibility of the existence of consciousness outside the physical world. While dualists stress that the mental is irreducible, the tendency of the materialists is to get rid of the mental phenomena and reduce them to some form of the material or physical (Searle, 1999: 46–9). Even those who reject such reductionist materialism, stress that consciousness is a biological process taking place in the brain (Searle, 1999: 53).

Criticisms have also come from scientists, who argue that clinical observations have shown how drugs, head wounds and strokes change the state of the physical brain, which in turn changes the way people think and feel. This has made it difficult to accept the separation of a physical brain from a mental mind (Greenfield, 2000: 56). For the neuroscientist Susan Greenfield, the mind is the personalized brain (2000: 57). As we grow, networks of cells are formed, reflecting the individual experiences, which turn a generic *brain* (with its one hundred billion neurons) into a personalized *mind*. Consciousness is thus deepened as these agglomerations imbue each conscious moment with meaning (p. 164). For her, the mind and the self are synonymous terms: 'After all, if *mind* is the personalization of the brain, then what more, or what less, could *Self* actually be?' (pp. 185–6).

1.1 The first boundary between the public and the private worlds is the human body, separating an inner self from the outside world (Paris, France)

But the brain does not work in isolation. It is 'in constant two-way traffic with the rest of the body' (Greenfield, 2000: 174). The integration of the body and mind leads to an understanding of how the mind is open to the influences of the body. This is particularly discussed in psychoanalysis, which posed a challenge to the classical notion of a pure mind disengaged from the body. Sigmund Freud (1985) investigated into the nature of, and the conflict between, conscious and unconscious contents of mind.

> Normally, there is nothing of which we are more certain than the feeling of our self, of our own ego. This ego appears to us as something autonomous and unitary, marked off distinctively from everything else. That such an appearance is deceptive, and that on the contrary the ego is continued inwards, without any sharp delimitation, into an unconscious mental entity which we designate as the id and for which it serves as a kind of façade – this was a discovery first made by psychoanalytic research ... But towards the outside, at any rate, the ego seems to maintain clear and sharp lines of demarcation. (Freud, 1985: 253)

The unconscious contents are desires and wishes, which function to obtain immediate satisfaction, with an energy coming directly from the primary physical
instincts. There is no coordination or organization here, as each impulse seeks satisfaction independently of all the rest, to the extent that opposite impulses can
flourish side by side. This, however, stands in sharp contrast with the more social
and critical mental forces, which adapt to reality and avoid external dangers.
Dreams are the outcome of such a conflict between the primary unconscious
impulses and the secondary conscious ones (Strachey, 1985: 19–20).

The theories of Freud, with their precursors in early German idealism and in
Nietzsche, develop a psychological critique of the subject, which is associated with
a major intellectual current challenging the classical concept of the human subject
(Honneth, 1995: 261). This was in fact decentring the subjects, who were often
unaware of their unconscious and whose coherence and integrity, therefore, was
now being questioned (Rosenau, 1992: 44–5). These discoveries show how the
contents of the mind are diverse, conflicting and not transparent to the individual.
They also show how the relationship between the inner space of the mind and the
world is not necessarily logical and rational, but can be pre-linguistic and conflict-
ual. All this contradicts those who believe that 'everything specifically human in man
is *logos*. One would not be able to mediate in a zone that preceded language'
(Bachelard, 1994: xxiii).

An implication of psychoanalytic findings for the public–private distinction is
to see how there is a deeper level private space that is not accessible even to the
individual who is its container. It might be said that the realm of unconsciousness is
the innermost, and hence the most private realm of an individual. There may,
however, be some problems with this argument, as public and private are clearly
categories shaped by the exertion of various degrees of control, by the individual
and by the society. That which lies outside access cannot be easily classified as
public or private. But if it is taken to be a part of an individual, in the same way as
any of the body organs are, then it falls within the private realm of an individual, but
perhaps not in a privileged position above others.

Psychoanalysis was based on a belief in the liberatory powers of reason and
the possibility of authority of the subject. If the unconscious desires are known and
brought to consciousness, e.g. expressed through words, then the pathological
consequences of the conflict between conscious and unconscious can be
addressed. As a result, the subject can take charge and become autonomous. The
fact that the subject's mind was not transparent to him/her did not deny the subject
the possibility of achieving such transparency.

But where does that leave the body in our analysis of the public and private
realms? Does it belong to the public or the private sphere? It is clear that the

patterns of access to the body and to the streams of consciousness within it are quite different. One is more accessible than the other and is hence less private. Whereas the body can be seen and touched by others, the mind is hidden, with a mental world that seems to be entirely within the private control of an individual. While access to the body is possible for others, access to the mental world is the privilege of the subject. Even when people share their minds and bodies in intimate relationships, there are always parts of the mind that are kept apart, consciously or otherwise. Therefore, the body, like any other boundary between two realms, finds an ambiguous role: it belongs to both spheres. On the one hand, it is the generator and the container of the inner space of consciousness and can be identified with it. On the other hand, it is one among many objects that make up the world. As we shall see later, the way this boundary, the public face of a human being, is treated is central to the way societies are organized.

Thus the investigations of philosophers, scientists and psychoanalysts have shown how the body and the brain work together in generating an inner realm of consciousness. The close integration of consciousness and the body shows how the working of the physical brain and the unconscious impulses generated by the body can directly shape the streams of consciousness, undermining the classical notion of a mind separated from the physical world of the body and in command of its realm. This poses a critical challenge to this most basic form of distinction between private and public realms. The unconscious and the consciousness, the mind and the body, as deeper manifestations of private and public realms, appear to have far more connection and continuity with each other than the simple distinctions suggest.

AUTONOMY OF THE SUBJECT

Another aspect of the relationship between inner self and outer world, closely related to mind-body dualism, is the question of individual autonomy, or in other words the question of power. The classical notion of the self that emerged in the Enlightenment presented it as 'a stable centre incorrigibly present to itself and negotiating with its surrounding world from within its own securely established powers of knowing and willing' (Dunne, 1996: 139). It is in relation to this notion of the individual that the realms of the private and the public have been understood and shaped (Figure 1.2).

According to Cartesian dualism, the subject is identical with his/her mind, and has a 'privileged', first-person view of it (Scruton, 1996: 48). This view was developed and radicalized to intensify the first person authority. One form of radicalization of Cartesian dualism was idealism. It was rejected by Hume, who

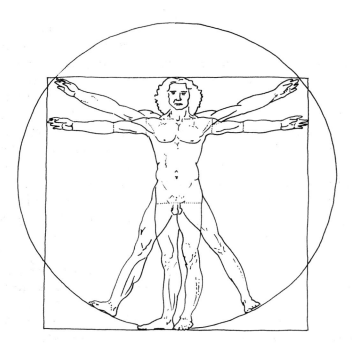

1.2 An independent self as 'a stable centre incorrigibly present to itself and negotiating with its surrounding world from within its own securely established powers of knowing and willing' characterized the modern world

argued that when we have separated the mind and its ideas from the world, the result is that all that we have access to, or can accept to exist, is our own ideas (Politis, 1993). A major criticism of dualism and idealism came from Kant in his major work *Critique of Pure Reason*, who argued that 'the world and how the world appears to us in experience are not two distinct things but two sides of one thing' (Politis, 1993: xxx). Kant argued for 'the transcendental unity of consciousness' (Kant, 1993: B131). All the representations of the world that I receive are, or can be, connected to each other. I can call them my representations for I can comprehend them in one consciousness; 'otherwise I would have as many-coloured and various a self as are the representations of which I am conscious' (Kant, 1993: B133). Understanding, he argued, 'is nothing more than the faculty of connecting *a priori*, and of bringing the variety of given representations under the unity of appreception. This principle is the highest in all human knowledge' (Kant, 1993: B133–5).

Another form of radicalizing Cartesian thought has been phenomenology, as developed by Edmund Husserl at the beginning of the twentieth century (Schutz, 1962: 102), starting a major philosophical tradition, through Heidegger and

Merleau-Ponty, among others. With the help of philosophical doubt, Husserl aimed to show the implicit presuppositions that the sciences use in their analysis of the world. The Cartesian philosophical doubt was to be radicalized by two tools: 'phenomenological reduction' and 'intentionality'. Phenomenological reduction used the technique of 'bracketing', which means concentrating on the contents of mind by leaving aside the world around us. In other words, 'putting the world in brackets', focusing on 'the universe of our conscious life, the stream of thought in its integrity, with all its activities and with all its cogitations and experiences' (Schutz, 1962: 104–5). The second tool was to make a distinction between the act of thinking and the object of thought, linking them through 'intentionality'. This means that every thought has an intentional character: it is the thought *of* something. 'There is no such thing as thought, fear, fantasy, remembrance as such; every thought is thought *of*, every fear is fear *of*, every remembrance is remembrance *of* the object that is thought, feared, remembered' (Schutz, 1962: 103). By using these two tools of analysis, the objects I see around me 'are no longer the things of the outer world as they exist and as they really are, but the phenomena as they appear to me' (Schutz, 1962: 106).

This first person viewpoint and the possibility of autonomy of the subject were criticized in the twentieth century by a language philosophical critique of the subject, as developed by Wittgenstein, on the one hand, and by Saussure, on the other (Honneth, 1995: 261–2). A major critic of the first-person view of the world is Ludwig Wittgenstein, whose 'private language argument' has been summarized as follows:

> It says: Stop looking for foundations for your beliefs and step out of the first-person viewpoint. Look at your situation from outside, and ask how things must be, if you are to suffer from these doubts and uncertainties. You will find that one thing at least is true: that you speak a language. And if that is true, it must be possible for others, too, to learn your language. If you can think about your thinking, then you must be speaking a public language. In which case, you must be part of some 'public realm', in which other people could wander. This public realm is no fiction of the demon, but the fundamental reality. (Scruton, 1996: 54)

David Hume had earlier questioned the validity of a claim to construct an error-free principle. Now in the 'post-Wittgensteinian world', it was not possible to step outside history and culture; the emphasis was on the realization that human knowledge operates only within social and linguistic frameworks (Cottingham, 1992a: 2).

The language critique seemed to lead to the elimination of the subject 'in every sense of the word' (Lefebvre, 1991: 61), to the extent that subject becomes merely 'a position in language' (Derrida, quoted in Rosenau, 1992: 43). As a result, a major line of postmodern thought has argued for the decentring of the subject (Rosenau, 1992: 42–61). This was influenced by Nietzsche, who equated the death of the subject with the death of God, which was applauded by Foucault as getting rid of human subject as the centre of representational thinking and discourse (Schrift, 1996: 328). Structuralist and poststructuralist thought was not convinced of the authority of individuals and attributed the authorial stance to social structures and systems. According to Pierre Bourdieu (2000), the elementary, or original, form of scholastic illusion is that the world is an object placed before a self-conscious, perceiving subject who can take it in with a single gaze. As individual speech depends on a pre-given system of linguistic meanings, it is concluded that the human subject cannot constitute or exhaust meaning, as was presented by the transcendental notion of the self (Honneth, 1995: 261). The authority of the subject has been undermined through seeing the subject as no more than a cog in the linguistic wheel, uttering words and sentences of a public language which is not of their making. In social sciences, these approaches have been employed to show that the agency of the individual is shaped and severely constrained by the forces of the social.

These studies, therefore, question the classical notion of autonomous individuals in command of their faculties and of their environment, by showing how individuals are influenced by social forces, as represented by language. The public realm takes precedence over the individual, whose autonomy in society and even control over mental states and thought processes are considered as illusory.

Authority of the subject is also undermined through science, which insists that what individuals describe about their circumstances is limited and unreliable, therefore in need of objective validation or rejection. Descartes' first-person perspective, as adopted by phenomenologists, entails that '*I* describe in a monologue (which I let you overhear) what *I* find in my conscious experience, counting on *us* to agree' (Dennett, 1993: 70). This critique has shifted the emphasis away from the first-person to a third-person view. The third-person perspective is the method of sciences, attempting to look from outside, unconvinced that such monologues can be verified by objective methods (Dennett, 1993: 70). But emphasizing a third-person viewpoint makes it difficult to explain the human subjectivity. John Searle (1999: 50), a leading contemporary philosopher, argues that the third-person viewpoint tends to reduce consciousness to 'the behaviour of the body, to computational states of the brain, information processing, or functional states of a physical system'. This, however, cannot account for consciousness, which is 'an inner, subjective, first-person, qualitative phenomenon' (Searle, 1999: 50). That is why attempting to reconcile the two becomes tempting. One example is Daniel

Dennett's heterophenomenology, with the ambition of offering 'a method of phe-nomenological description that can (in principle) do justice to the most private and ineffable experiences, while never abandoning the methodological scruples of science' (Dennett, 1993: 72). The search is ongoing among philosophers for an account that can integrate the mind and body and explain the mental states to be simultaneously phenomenological, functional and physiological (Nagel, 1998a).

SELF AS EMBEDDED AGENCY

Thus the influences of the forces of the physical body and of the social world on the human subject have come to be widely acknowledged. Two major groups of responses to these critiques of the classical notion of the self can be identified. On the one hand, some argue for a further radicalization of these criticisms, to deny the possibility of a knowing and willing subject altogether, as reflected in the work of poststructuralists, especially deconstructionists (Valdés, 1991; Honneth, 1995). Another group of responses try to integrate the two strands of criticism to develop a revised notion of the self (Taylor, 1989; Castoriadis, 1991; Honneth, 1995; Dunne, 1996).

Despite strongly rejecting Cartesian dualism, the argument for radicalizing the decentring can be seen as a new version of this dualism, as it emphasizes the mental and linguistic, and undermines the physical and biological, effectively creat-ing a new divide. Those who emphasize language cannot account for the connec-tion of the flow and exchange of ideas with the biological body, the 'practical and fleshy body' (Lefebvre, 1991: 61). Radicalizing the decentring of the subject leads to the realm of dualism and idealism, where physical and material are separate and the contents of the mind are the main reality. If these contents are the product of the outside influences, as it can be widely shown in human practices, then there is no centre to the subject. But a counter-argument can be made by asserting the connection between the biological and psychological and the existence of an agency, an empirical, embodied subject who performs the task of making connec-tions between these outside linguistic and cultural influences and who *creates* new combinations. Language is not a static, outside megastructure, as portrayed by these critics. It changes both in form and content through its dynamic use by its speakers and through its changing relationship with the real world of facts and events. It is essential to question the idealized image of the individual and see its fragmented, incoherent reality. But its empirical existence and its practical and political agency cannot be denied. As every individual is different from the other, the theme of difference, which is so essential in postmodern thought, in this way contradicts another of its main themes, the decentred subject.

On the one hand, seeing the world only through the eyes of an individual creates a collection of fragments with large gaps in the middle. On the other hand, seeing the individual as entirely driven by the public realm of the social is undermining the subjective and biological authority of the individual. It is at the intersection of the biological and social that the individuality of a human agent is constructed. The interaction between these two realms makes humans what they are. Wittgenstein's private language argument can debunk the myth of the might of individual mind working independently of others and of the language with which it works to construct its thoughts. But this realization of the interdependence of thought processes, which are essentially social, should not mask the reality of the biological individuals, each with their own, different empirical and biological make up, each responding and adjusting, in their own way, to the social environment with which they interact. However much the contents of consciousness are interrelated and interdependent in human societies, there is no escape from the fact that individuals exist as separate biological entities, engaged in independent life processes. This whole empirical unit is what the self is. Unlike Greenfield's personalized brain, the self should be taken to be the personalized body, or embodied mind, as consciousness is closely related to the state of the body as a whole and its evolving experiences.

The self of a person is constructed at the intersection of biological and social processes, combining pre-linguistic and linguistic elements. Pre-linguistic elements are biologically inherent in the body, such as the feelings of hunger and thirst, which humans share with animals. If a person is brought up apart from any other humans, s/he may not have a language for communication, but will definitely have the biological processes of an individual. So empirically, s/he has a self, which will have developed in relation to the world around her/him, even if this is not a linguistic relationship. On the other hand, the linguistic elements, from common sense to scientific knowledge, are constructed through living in a human society, and therefore are socially constructed. The subject's authority comes from a combination of biological individuality and the ability to make connections between, and creative interventions in, the flows of ideas and practices.

The problem with the third-person perspective is that it may undermine the voice of the individual. It can therefore be less democratic if the voice of the individual is not heard, dismissed as unreliable fiction. The first-person account can be in this sense more democratic, but only if it links with other accounts, if an intersubjective bridge is made. In other words, the first- and the third-person viewpoints are both essential ingredients of the relationship between the inner self and the outer world. The third-person perspective might be interpreted as the tyranny of the 'other' against the 'self'. However, the biological processes and common sense have always put the centre of the world within the self, with the 'other' as the marginal and secondary.

For the first-person viewpoint, the private inner realm is a sphere only to be known and accessed by the subject, explored through introversion and contemplation. The public becomes the inter-subjective sphere, where subjects meet and communicate. On the other hand, for the third-person viewpoint, the public sphere is the starting point, where the frameworks of individual consciousness are set. The private sphere becomes an individuated portion of that public realm, constructed through publicly available tools of language and culture. As it is not possible to abandon the insights of each perspective, it is essential to develop a dynamic perspective, which allows us to use both these viewpoints to find complementary accounts of public–private distinction. While the first-person account can provide insights into the way public and private spheres are experienced, the third-person account provides an external view into how individuals and groups construct and behave according to such a distinction. The inner space of the self, therefore, is a site where constantly shifting bodily experiences and interpretations of the world are generated, where some of these leave a mark strong enough to shape the next wave of experiences and interpretations. From outside, however, the self is far more stable, an active agent within a social world involved in making connections and undertaking actions, in response to the external frameworks and stimuli. Without moving between the interior and exterior realms, it would be impossible to understand and explain the two realms sufficiently and realize the extent of their interdependence.

The story that emerges so far is that the Western Enlightenment battled against the strong forces of the unknown to establish a normative notion of the self that could see, know and act with utmost confidence. The fault lines in this confidence, however, have appeared, as the influence of natural and social forces on the individual have been acknowledged. Understanding these limitations does not, however, necessarily lead to an inevitable and extreme scepticism, but can be mobilized to develop a more realistic and refined notion of the self. The classical notion of the individual was a normative notion, rather than an empirical reality. But it was embedded in, and had profound impacts on, the way Western societies were organized. Indeed its emergence was embedded in a long historical process in Western Europe between c. 1300 and c. 1800. As its unintended consequence, this process produced the modern European state on the one hand and the notion of the modern individual on the other (Coleman, 1996: ix) (Figure 1.3).

The bid to autonomy by Renaissance humanism and modern Enlightenment was itself set against the religious medieval worldview, aiming at liberating humans from the tyranny of traditions. The new bid to contextualization, however, is a

1.3 The modern notion of the autonomous individual in the West emerged through a long historical process between 1300 and 1800 (Florence, Italy)

reminder that, although worthwhile, such liberty is limited and only operates within social and biological frameworks of which it is a part. The notion of public and private should be studied in the light of this classical notion of the self. An autonomous self is seen to be in control of a private realm, but also in communication with others who are in control of their private realms, to constitute a public realm that was beyond private control. The critiques of philosophy of language and psychoanalysis introduced a degree of realism and contextualization: to show the extent of to which the self was under the influence of its physical body and its social environment. These challenges have paved the way for the emergence of new notions of the self, by showing an individual that is free to act but is also embedded in a physical and social context, with a far less degree of control than was idealized by earlier generations. The inevitable outcome of such realism appears to be the need to search for new, more contextualized notions of the self and of public and private realms.

INDEPENDENT AND INTERDEPENDENT SELF

Cartesian dualism was a new formulation of a view that goes back to ancient times. The dichotomy of body and soul that Plato developed had a deep influence on the development of Western thought. Dualism has also been present in many cultures. For the ancient Zoroastrians, and the Manicheans and others who were influenced by them, the world was a battlefield between the forces of good and evil, and the role of humans was to take the side of the good and fight the evil. For the ancient Egyptians, creation of a cosmic order which separated humans from the chaos of nature around them was a key concern, while for the ancient Chinese the dualism of Yin and Yang underlay the dynamic of all phenomena. An essential ingredient of the major monotheist religions that emerged in the Middle East was a clear separation between the natural and supernatural.

The self has been seen as the central theme of Hindu thinking, as the 'essence' of Hinduism has been the quest for enlightenment and the perfection of the human person. The concern has been with a metaphysical and religious self, drawn from elite Brahmanic traditions, as opposed to an empirical self that is often denigrated (Morris, 1994: 70). Whereas the phenomenal, material self is associated with the body, the inner, spiritual self is an individuated form of the absolute (Brahman) and is formless and immutable. As particularly emphasized in Vedanta, salvation lay in the detachment of the individual from the phenomenal world (Morris, 1994: 76–9). Buddhism, on the other hand, categorically denied the existence of soul or self within the body, and saw the world as impermanent and in continuous flux. The main difference between Indian and Chinese thought was their different emphases on the spiritual and social. In Hindu thought, personal development takes place outside the material world, as the spiritual had the highest value. In the Chinese humanist tradition of Confucianism, in contrast, the self was essentially located within a social context, and self development meant establishing successful, hierarchical relations with others (Morris, 1994). In Iran, the strong influence of mysticism with its doctrine of unity of existence promoting the unification of the self and other, together with the divine nature of the Islamic law and the despotic nature of politics, were thought to have led to conformity and the non-development of an independent self, as it emerged in the modern West (Ahmadi and Ahmadi, 1995).

Modern Western culture is often characterized by the notion of an independent person who has broken free from the constraints of society and nature, while the rest of the world is characterized by sociocentric, holistic notions of the self

(Morris, 1994). To describe the non-Western notion of self, the term 'interdependent self' is used, where the boundaries between individuals are fuzzier and they are more dependent on group characteristics (Moghaddam, 1998: 59) (Figure 1.4).

In non-Western traditional cultures, it is argued, the human subject is far more constrained by society and nature and the notion of an independent self is not developed. For example, Louis Dumont identifies two conceptions of the individual in two modern and traditional societies:

> (1) The empirical agent, present in every society, in virtue of which he is the main raw material for any sociology. (2) The rational being and normative subject of institutions: this is peculiar to us (modern society) as is shown by the values of equality and liberty. As opposed to modern society, traditional societies which know nothing of equality and liberty as values, which know nothing, in short of individual, have basically a collective idea of man. (Dumont, 1970: 9)

As Morris shows, this notion, which Dumont develops for India but also generalizes to all pre-capitalist societies, is not true in the case of many communities in

1.4 The term 'interdependent self' is used where the self is considered to be located within a social context, where the boundaries between individuals are less sharply drawn (Shanghai, China, photo by Simin Davoudi)

India, with their emphasis on individualism and egalitarianism (Morris, 1994: 92). The main shortcoming of such interpretations, it can be argued, is that they equate the normative concepts of a society, as devised by its elite, with the way it actually works. In many cases the normative religious systems were devised to control the inherent individualism of the members of society. It is, therefore, this individualism which can be regarded as the empirical reality and not the pure spiritualism or sociocentrism that many elites have devised in response with the intention of controlling it.

Furthermore, as we saw earlier, the notion of independent self has been criticized by many writers, who have emphasized that the self is 'both embodied and embedded within a nexus of relations' (Morris, 1994: 17). Hallowell, for example, argued that the development of self, mind and personality was 'fundamentally dependent upon socially mediated experience in interaction with other persons' (quoted in Morris, 1994: 7). The notion of individual that emerged in the modern West was a normative paradigm, helping to socialize male, bourgeois individuals in such a way that they could cope with the break from religious rules and traditions, from society and nature. It was hoped that they could then engage in a free exchange of ideas, goods and services and in accumulation and consumption of wealth. This normative paradigm was a liberating innovation that unleashed energies capable of transforming the world. What was gradually realized, however, was that this was not an innate condition but a coping mechanism, and that a complete break from society and nature was impossible.

The systems of dualism were indeed systems of classification and clarification, which could be achieved by a degree of abstraction and simplification. This made the world understandable to humans, and provided moral support for their action. This need for clarity and support has continued to this day. There is at the same time a rising recognition that reality is formed of many shades rather than merely two colours, and that action in a complex world would need a more complex system of support. As women have argued, dualism often finds a gendered meaning, in which roles and symbols are assigned to men and women, with the outcome of subordinating women. For environmentalists, the dualism of society and nature leads to the subordination and degradation of nature. Postmodernists, in developing a new normative paradigm in opposition to the modern independent self, have reverted to interdependence. The postmodern selves are thus, according to one commentator, similar to the modern females. They are 'relational, interdependent citizens'; rather than 'the application of pre-existing codes', their 'ethical guides develop out of commitment to others' (Buker, 1999: 97).

THE SOCIO-PSYCHOLOGICAL PERSONAL SPACE

Between the interior space of the body and the space that finds architectural and geographical expression, there is one layer that is invisible and mobile. This is personal space, which is the space around the body. Earlier in this chapter we saw how the realm of the mind is considered the innermost private realm. The extension of this subjective realm is the realm of the body, the space associated with the body. While the mental realm is hidden from all, the body constitutes the realm that is potentially accessible and makes up the realm of behaviour and social interaction. It is here that a physical boundary between the self and the other is articulated, where a fundamental ingredient of the public–private relationship develops.

Personal space is the space that a person and the others observe around his/her body, as the extension of the body (Figure 1.5). It is a space that is emotionally charged and helps regulate the spacing of individuals (Sommer, 1969: viii). As Sommer (1969: 26) puts it: 'Like the porcupines in Schopenhauer's fable, people like to be close enough to obtain warmth and comradeship but far enough to avoid

1.5 Personal space is defined as a small but invisible protective sphere or bubble that individuals maintain around them (Dortmund, Germany)

pricking one another.' The term personal space also refers to the spaces that are personalized by people who inhabit them and the processes through which this personalization occurs (Sommer, 1969: viii).

The theme of personal space was a key concern of the anthropologist Edward Hall, who discussed the cultural dimension of using and interpreting space by different people (Hall, 1959; 1966). Hall classified interpersonal relationships, and following that the spaces among individuals, into four categories: intimate, personal, social and public. The distances observed in each category depended on the desired mode of communication, which he believed to be the core of culture. For Hall, personal distance, a term originally used by Heidegger, was 'a small protective sphere or bubble that an organism maintains between itself and others' (Hall, 1966: 112). Two types of personal distance could be identified. The first was a close phase, i.e. one and a half to two and half feet (45 to 75 cm), which is the distance one can hold or grasp the other person. The second is the far phase, i.e. two and a half to four feet (75 to 120 cm), which is the arm's length, or the 'limit of physical domination in the very real sense' (Hall, 1966: 113). With a proper understanding of the spatial behaviour and needs of people in general and their variety among different cultures, he argued, city design can create congenial environments for diverse urban populations and avoid 'the many crimes against humanity' that were committed in the name of urban renewal (p. 122).

The social and environmental psychologists such as Sommer (1969) and Altman (1975) followed him by analysing the notion of personal space within a framework of environment and behaviour research. Sommer (1969) tried to find a social scientific, functionalist foundation for making design decisions, moving away from the pure aesthetic considerations and visual thinking of the designers. He rejected the notion of architecture as 'hollow sculpture or timeless unchanging form whose existence is an end in itself' (Sommer, 1969: 4). Instead, he stressed that the personal expression of the architect must yield to the functions that the building serves (p. 5).

Altman's argument (1975: 3) was to see privacy as a central regulatory process through which access to a person or group is controlled. The desired level of privacy is achieved through mechanisms of personal space and territorial behaviour. Crowding and social isolation are the causes and symptoms of failing to achieve a desired level of privacy. Privacy is defined as 'an interpersonal boundary-control process, which paces and regulates interaction with others' (Altman, 1975: 10). There is a direct link between the permeability of this boundary and the levels of privacy that can be achieved.

Empirical studies followed, which showed how the intrusion and surveillance of personal space can lead to significant degrees of stress and to withdrawal behaviour among individuals (Greenberg and Firestone, 1977). These studies tested how different groups observed a personal space or felt when their own personal space was intruded by others. These were measured for different races (Bauer, 1973), different sexes (Harris *et al.*, 1978; Sinha and Mukerjee, 1990), different levels of self esteem (Stratton *et al.*, 1973), different levels of cultural adjustment (Roger and Mjoli, 1976) and different conditions of density and crowding (Harris *et al.*, 1978). Personal space was almost exclusively dealt with by the psychologists (Altman, 1975: 2). A generation later, it appears that the notion of personal space is a standard one, appearing in dictionaries and textbooks of social psychology (Moghaddam, 1998), as well as in environmental psychology (Bell *et al.*, 1996; Veitch and Arkkelin, 1995).

Personal space is a subjective space around individuals, as it is not visible or real. It is at the same time objective, in the sense that the individual and the others around him/her seem to agree in observing it, although they may disagree on the methods of this observation and the size of this personal space. The individual protects it and the others avoid invading it. Getting very close to a complete stranger often has the result that the stranger will move back to keep the distance. It is a piece of private space that individuals carry with them around wherever they go. That is why it is called 'portable territory' (Sommer, 1969: 27). It is this space in which individuals perform their social acts, where they feel safer and in control of their bodies. Social interaction in the public sphere therefore takes place from across personal spaces. Intersubjective relationships depend on the safety and security that the observation of subjective spaces bring about for those involved.

Behaviour in bus stops and underground stations shows how the establishment of personal space is a complex relationship between the patterns set by the first individuals to arrive, their number and the number of subsequent arrivals, and the size of the space. The distance that the first few keep on the platform may be as large as 3 to 4 metres. As new passengers arrive, they may follow this pattern until the linear space of the platform appears to be full. From this moment on, the distances observed grow smaller and new adjustments are made. The extreme conditions of adjustment emerge when large crowds wait for buses or trains, effectively reducing the personal space to a minimum, which may be even smaller once inside the vehicle. This shows how in a short period of time the size of personal space is established and adjusted. In a busy bus or underground train, when people have to be very close to each other, the barriers may have to come down, as everyone is aware of the inevitability of crowding. But as soon as a person can have some control on the surrounding environment, the personal space will be observed. In this sense, personal space is a sign of control, a sign of power over one's environment, which is part of a general sense of psychological wellbeing.

Personal space provides a person with a location in the world and is a barrier that distinguishes and protects individuals from the outside world. It is part of a repertoire of a person's protective and communicative measures, such as body gestures, clothing and speech. In our analysis of public–private spatial relations, therefore, personal space is another layer of privacy, beyond which the less private, or public domain lies. Beyond the private personal space, the space of others lies, including the public space. Personal space is less private than mental space, but more private than the intimate space of the home. When the home is the living place of a single person, the boundaries of personal space may be extended so that the two overlap, for the space of the home and personal space of the body become one and the same. But when the home is shared with other members of the household, the space becomes more stratified to create zones of comfort and privacy for household members. Here some areas at some times may become the extended personal space and the rest of the home negotiated, interpersonal space.

The layers of privacy that ensure self protection go on to larger scales and higher complexities. In a sense, the individual can be seen to be situated at the core of a multi-layered shell, surrounded by an onion-shaped structure of layers of protection. The private realm can therefore be interpreted as webs woven around the human being, to ensure self protection, reproduction, and confidence for communication. The shape of society, however, is not necessarily a large number of well protected multi-layered units of this kind. Individuals live in a particular social context, where their location and protective layers of privacy makes sense. The social realm is one that manufactures these layers and can change, suddenly or through time, their shape and composition, to enable individuals to live together in a society. Even though a person gradually weaves around him/her these layers of protection as s/he grows older and higher in status, they are not necessarily invented by individuals. These layers are tools that the society creates and makes available to its members, which they can personalize and use as they develop and socialize. Evidence for this is that these protective layers are recognizable only by those who have been socialized in the same way. Anyone outside the social norms could violate these norms by not seeing them or by not acknowledging them. Invading armies and thieves do not take account of these protective layers and can puncture them sometimes with such ease that what looked impenetrable becomes invisible, as if evaporating into air.

DIMENSIONS OF PERSONAL SPACE

The observation of personal space is closely related to the situations in which social encounter takes place (Bell *et al.*, 1996) and a number of factors, such as age and development, gender, personality factors and cultural differences (Altman, 1975: 67ff).

The size of personal space is related to the real or perceived role and status of the individual in society, as well as other individual differences (Bell *et al.*, 1996). It grows with age, sense of confidence and independence, and also with a sense of vulnerability and fear. The perception of personal space is different for the observer and the observed. Depending on their circumstances, they may observe different sizes of personal space around a person. This gap can only become clear when an individual's personal space is tested or invaded.

The size of personal space, i.e. the distance we maintain between ourselves and others, is determined by its two functions of protection and communication (Figure 1.6). The amount of space that could allow these functions depends on the situation in which individuals interact with each other, as some relationships and activities require more distance from the others (Bell *et al.*, 1996: 278). Social interaction with friends or those perceived to be similar to the person lead to closer distances, as there is an expectation of fewer threats (Bell *et al.*, 1996: 282). The communication function of personal space is maintained by choosing closer distances, which convey information to the liked others that the person is attracted to

1.6 The size of personal space, i.e. the distance we maintain between ourselves and others, is determined by its two functions of protection and communication (London, UK)

them and expects to communicate intimate sensory cues to them (Bell *et al.*, 1996: 282).

The provision of furniture appears to institutionalize personal space. The seats on the bus or in the classroom show how the space is equally divided into small territories for functioning in a particular way. This may differ when different status levels are incorporated into the space arrangements, as in the plan of air-planes, in which the first class and economy class passengers have completely different allocations of personal space. The division of space for use is reflected in land-use zoning or in lot subdivisions supported by property rights.

The effects of controlling interpersonal distance in various professional situ-ations are well known. For example in classrooms, closer distance between a teacher and a student or appropriate seating arrangements can affect learning pos-itively. The appropriate distance between doctors and patients can also have a positive impact on their communication. Group processes can be influenced by 'sociopetal' spacing, which brings people together, or 'sociofugal' spacing, which separates people (Bell *et al.*, 1996: 289). Simple examples of these two situations are when chairs are so arranged that group members face each other, or are arranged in a row. Individuals who are placed in a central spatial orientation where others eye them directly can become influential in a group process through their location (Bell *et al.*, 1996: 290).

Research has shown that individuals maintain a larger personal space when rooms are smaller in size, or are narrower in shape, and, for men, when ceilings are low. Furthermore, people seem to require larger personal spaces when placed in the corner of a room than in the centre, when seated than standing, when indoors than outdoors, and in crowded than uncrowded conditions. These preferences seem to reflect differences in availability of escape; we are content with less space when we know we can get away (Bell *et al.*, 1996: 286–7).

Too much or too little personal space, i.e. when we are forced to interact with another person through 'inappropriate' distance, has a negative impact on indi-viduals and their interaction. This may be creating overload, stress, arousal and anxiety, loss of privacy, negative attributions and inferences in communication, and fear and discomfort. The response in ongoing interactions can be lower attraction, negative inferences and compensatory and coping behaviours, such as changing the distance, eye contact or body orientation. In the case of invasion of an indi-vidual's personal space by a stranger, the individual may decide to leave or to perform coping reactions of various kinds. When personal space is invaded by unwelcome outsiders or unexpectedly, the individual reacts negatively and defen-sively. The reaction to the invasion of privacy varies. Individuals seem to be more tolerant if approached from the side rather than front. They would be more tolerant if they are extroverts rather than introverts, and friends rather than strangers. It appears that males are alarmed by the face-to-face positioning of a stranger who invades their personal space, but not affected by an adjacent invasion. The situation appears to be the reverse for females, who react negatively to the invader who sits next to them, but are not affected by one who sits across from them. Males and females also show difference in their spatial behaviour when they are invading others' personal space. One study suggested that females find it easier to invade the personal space of someone who is smiling rather than displaying a neutral face, while for the male the reverse was true (Bell *et al.*, 1996: 290–301).

In law, minor invasions of personal space are often tolerated, as they are so frequent that 'it is to the mutual advantage of all to allow them to proceed without hindrance' (Epstein, 1998: 188). The body is where the boundaries of the self start and end and where the boundary is crossed by contacts such as touching of another person. The general doctrine of 'privilege' covers accidental contact in crowded places and friendly touching. Only when contact becomes malicious or dangerous does the privilege ebb away and we start thinking in term of tort remedies for physical invasion. In general, however, social conventions are the basis for dealing with invasions of private space.

> The conventions here are strong; and regardless of background and circumstance, we all understand the rule that requires us to respect the 'space' of others, even though no visible fences do, or could, mark the boundary between persons. (Epstein, 1998: 188)

INDIVIDUAL AND CULTURAL DIFFERENCES

Personal space grows with age, as young children do not observe it at first. According to Sigmund Freud (1985: 254), 'An infant at the breast does not as yet distinguish his ego from the external world as the source of the sensations flowing in upon him. He gradually learns to do so, in response to various promptings.' The process through which the ego detaches itself from the outside world is a process of discovery of the 'objects' outside the ego, and learning how to differentiate between internal feelings and external objects. Therefore, while 'originally the ego includes everything, later it separates off an external world from itself' (Freud, 1985: 255). As their brain cells multiply and their spatial cognition develops, children find the ability to navigate the world, to represent it by various means, and to interpret and use it in more complex ways (Stiles-Davis *et al.*, 1988; Butterworth, 1977). Gradually a boundary is drawn between the self and the other. As they develop a sense of the self, an awareness of social codes and of possible dangers around them, they start wearing a protective personal space to keep a distance from the stranger and work out an appropriate distance from the familiar (Figure 1.7). The management of the distance becomes a key part of the child's social skills. Research has shown that after age six until adulthood, children's preferred interpersonal distance grows with their age. Around the age of puberty, adult-like norms are exhibited. In parallel, the distance adults maintain with children grows larger as the child's age increases (Bell *et al.*, 1996: 285).

As children grow into socialized adults, their observation of personal space will depend on their gender and sense of vulnerability. A woman may be more alarmed if her personal space is invaded by a stranger than a man, an old person more than a young one. But research seems to suggest that males maintain larger personal space zones than females and that people generally keep greater distances from males than females. Females interact at closer distances with liked others and female–female pairs maintain closer distances than male–male pairs

1.7 As children develop a sense of the self, an awareness of social codes and of possible dangers around them, they start wearing a protective personal space to keep a distance from the stranger and work out an appropriate distance from the familiar (Bergen, Norway)

(Bell *et al.*, 1996: 284). The picture, however, is not so clear and varies with age and ethnic and cultural background (Altman, 1975: 74–5), as well as with 'hormonally determined sexual receptivity' (Bell *et al.*, 1996: 284). Overall, research has shown that women show more tolerance for distances that are inappropriately close to them (Bell *et al.*, 1996: 301).

The impact of personal differences on the observation of personal space is undeniable. As individuals respond differently to social stimuli and are socialized in different environments and conditions, they may adopt different approaches to personal space. These differences can range from personality variations to personality disorders. An introvert individual, for example, is likely to observe a larger personal space and be more defensive of the invisible bubble than an extrovert one. Similarly, those who are prone to anxiety place greater distances between themselves and others. In the case of those with personality disorder and psychological problems, research has shown that they have a wider variation in the distances they keep from others. While some keep a larger than normal distance, others observe smaller distances. Other research on prison populations showed that prisoners classified as aggressive or violent may have a less permeable self/other boundary (Altman, 1975). Those with higher esteem or more in need of affiliation have shown the need for smaller personal space than those with low esteem or low in need for affiliation (Bell *et al.*, 1996: 286). Personal space grows with social status, as the people in higher social ranks are always expected to keep a larger distance. Not only they seem to do so, but also do the others, who show 'positive deferential behaviour' towards them (Bell *et al.*, 1996: 302).

Part of the variation in personal space boundaries among these different groups refers to their own characteristics. Part of the variation, however, lies in the reaction of the others to them. As such, personal space and the observation of distance in social interaction relies on a set of mutual actions, performed through various signs, to set a self/other boundary. Some studies show that people maintain a greater distance from those who are labelled to have a social stigma, such as amputees, epileptics and mental patients. Among them, greater distances were kept from those with invisible stigma, such as epileptics and mental patients, than those with readily observable stigma, such as amputees. According to Altman, 'to understand personal space mechanisms, we must move in directions that account for the joint regulation of boundaries by both partners of an exchange' (1975: 72). It is important, at the same time, to link this joint regulation of boundaries to the social and environmental contexts in which the exchange takes place and the location of individuals in these contexts. The impact of past experiences on an individual should also be mentioned. If past experiences lead a person to the belief that one is in control of a situation, then he or she feels more secure at close distances with strangers than if the past experiences led to the belief that events were beyond the control of the individual (Bell et al., 1996: 285).

The existence of personal space is a social institution and depends on the norms of that society, the social positioning and life stage of the individual, and the complexity of the environment. It is a social institution in the sense that the observation of personal space depends on the perceived sense of the self and of the appropriate behaviour in public places. In some countries (e.g. the traditional Middle East), two male friends may walk hand in hand in the street without any sexual connotations or causing any social objections as they are displaying their friendship. A male and female, however, may avoid walking hand in hand in public, as they will be making a display of an intimate, possibly sexual relationship, which goes against social norms. In the West, however, these two patterns of behaviour will be interpreted completely differently, with different social meanings and expected reactions. Researchers compared Arabs and Americans in their use of space, taking into account the angle of orientation, touching, physical contact, thermal and olfactory cues, and voice behaviours (Watson and Graves, 1966). In this project, Arabs were found to show more direct face-to-face orientation, less distance between each other, more touching, more direct visual contact, and greater voice loudness. These findings may show, as Moghaddam would argue (1998: 59), an interdependent notion of the self among Arabs, as compared to the independent notion of the self among Americans. At the same time, while these findings and similar studies (e.g. Hall 1966 on the French, English, German, Japanese and Arab differences) point to the diversity of behavioural patterns among different cultures, they help construct stereotypes of different peoples, disregarding the immense range of behaviour within these national groups.

Several people can share their personal spaces to establish a shared private space in the middle of public space. This is exemplified in the meeting of a group of friends in the middle of a street, or in a restaurant, where the table provides a focus for a private sphere to be established in the middle of what otherwise would be a public arena. Establishment of such a shared private space means opening up the personal space to people who qualify as friends or associates. This forms a group space, which is protected by the group and the others in the same way as a personal space would be observed. A study of invading group space found the group to show the same compensatory reactions to avoid invaders as does an individual (Bell et al., 1996: 302).

PERSONAL AND INTERPERSONAL

The early studies by environmental psychologists on spatial behaviour, in particular personal space, territoriality and privacy focused on the psychological function of control or personal defence, which limited the development of research in these areas (Bonnes and Secchiaroli, 1995: 83). Spatial behaviour has been analysed to show that people tend to maintain greater distances when the physical space of the environment is very tight, and when they are engaged in competitive rather than collaborative relations (Bonnes and Secchiaroli, 1995: 84). Much emphasis has, therefore, been put on personal space in a negative capacity, as a reactive dimension of privacy, which ensures the individual's sense of control.

Personal space is, however, an aspect of the individual which cannot make sense in the absence of the others. Personal space, therefore, is an aspect of interpersonal relationships. Indeed it is possible to define its existence only in the presence of others, in the interaction between at least two persons (Bonnes and Secchiaroli, 1995: 84). What appears to be an invisible bubble around an individual is in fact a dimension of interpersonal communication, as Edward Hall (1966) had articulated. The private sphere that the personal space defines, like other aspects of privacy, makes sense only in relation to others. As soon as we have moved our investigation into public–private relationships outside the body, we are engaged in studying interpersonal relationships. This is why the size and functions of personal space vary according to interpersonal situations, whether positive and collaborative, or negative and competitive.

The psychologists' insights into human use of space have been deep in parts and limited in others. One psychologist has criticized the discipline's theoretical and methodological limitations for failing to see the larger picture (Liben, 1988: 167). Individual investigators may gather highly restricted and reliable data, but these are not integrated, leaving a complete picture of the subject beyond comprehension (ibid.). Despite recent trends in employing interpretive and qualitative research, researchers into person–environment relationships continue to use the traditionalist positivist methods of measuring person–environment relationships with the aim of making some prediction about human behaviour (Walsh et al., 1999). The functionalist viewpoint of research seems to analyse human behaviour without paying much attention to the first-person viewpoint of interpretive narration of human subjectivity and experience, or to the wider contexts in which these behaviour patterns are originated and performed.

The environmental psychology's approach to personal space focuses on individuals (as distinct from groups or societies), and hence sees privacy as a key requirement of individuals and crowding as a violation of this privacy (Sommer, 1969; Altman, 1975). While this approach was useful in discussing the notions of personal space and privacy, its lack of balance with public requirements, as opposed to private needs, made these views rather limited. A look at the environmental psychology handbooks (Bell et al., 1996; Veitch and Arkkelin, 1995; Walsh *et al.*, 1999) shows much emphasis on personal and private engagement with, rather than on public dimensions of, the environment.

In a sense the emphasis on personal space has been a sign and a consequence of a growth of individualism. As we discussed earlier in this chapter, an independent sense of the self is promoted by Western culture, which in turn expects the individuals to be endowed with their own personal space. In cultures where an interdependent sense of the self prevails, the observation of personal space is widely different.

The growth of studies on personal space in the postwar period, especially in the USA, was parallel with the major process of suburbanization in which the middle classes withdrew from the city to live in the suburbs, where they could live at low densities, high levels of privacy and the possibility of maintaining substantial personal spaces. As the energy crisis of the 1970s, the consequent environmental concerns, technological change and economic transformation promoted city living, it was essential that the debates enter a new phase. While the environmental problems continue to be a major concern, the energy crisis seems to have been either forgotten or its impact on spatial behaviour considered as limited. The suburbs keep expanding as the widely available fossil fuel makes car travel easier than ever before. The only serious deterrent to many motorists seems to be traffic congestion. The need for privacy, which was being met in the expanding suburbs, was to be balanced with the need for public areas, which could be found in towns and cities. A new balance between public and private needed to be discussed in order to make city living viable. Some works that analysed public spaces of cities and societies, rather than personal spaces of individuals, can be seen as attempts in this direction (e.g. Altman and Zube, 1989).

Personal space is invisible and portable. When extended and institutionalized, it takes the legal form of property or the intimate form of the home, which are fixed forms of private sphere and territoriality. However, there are mobile forms of personal space that can be identified. An extension of personal space that can take a physical shape is the motor car, which in a sense is the ultimate portable territory (Figure 1.8). As we sit inside a box moving across the urban space, we carry around with us a personal space. The inside of this box is visible to others, but it is not often accessible to them. The car is the private domain of its passengers. The public road is then sometimes carpeted by private boxes. The prevalence of cars in the city has historically reduced pedestrian safety and comfort. It has generated a fast and dangerous movement of large objects in straight lines, to the detriment of the slow moving pedestrians with their more limited use of space and at time meandering routes. The personal space of the pedestrian was a small space around the body, which was now enlarged to the moving glass and metal

why car, no bus?

1.8 Cars are mobile personal spaces, an extension of private space into the public space (Los Angeles, USA)

box of the car. The possibility of communication and sharing of personal space, as it can happen in a face-to-face meeting, is thus reduced as communication from across these boxes can mainly be visual. The barriers between individuals in the public space of the city is therefore not the observation of an invisible space around them. The barrier is now both the speed with which they pass through the city and the physical container which they inhabit in their passage. Driving a car is 'a way to feel social without having to be social' (Kuipers, 2002). It allows its passengers a safe distance from others while going through a cinematic experience: a visual contact with passing scenes, where the viewer can remain detached from the unfolding story.

LOCATING THE INDIVIDUAL IN SOCIAL SPACE

The notion of personal space is one that *locates* an individual in the physical world. Its significance lies mainly in how it marks out a personal territory, enabling the individual to develop a sense of identity and engage in the rituals of communication and recognition. To make sense of the personal space, therefore, we will have to see it as part of a person's location in social space. In solitude, the mysterious personal space appears to lose sense or significance, as it comes alive only at the level of interpersonal relationships. But many attributes of the individual, which found expression in his/her personal space remain the same, even in solitude. How do we analyse personal space as such a location in social and physical space?

The biological body of the individual is situated in a place, occupying a position in physical space and social space. Pierre Bourdieu defines this place, this *topos*, as 'the site where a thing or an agent "takes place", exists, in short, as a localization, or relationally, topologically, as a position, a rank in an order' (2000: 131). This distinction therefore refers to the individual's place both as a location in physical space and a position in social space (Figure 1.9). The relationship between the two is often direct and mutual.

When the position of the individual in social space is marginal or precarious, the result is social exclusion, where access to resources, to decision making, and to shared experiences is limited (Madanipour, 1998a). This may lead either to entrapment or to withdrawal into a deep and dark private sphere, as in mental and social isolation, or to being deprived of privacy, as in homelessness and imprisonment.

1.9 The city is a social world in which individuals are located, physically and socially (Lisbon, Portugal)

Bourdieu hesitates to use the term 'individual' and rejects the notion of an individual separate from the social world. Following Heidegger, he rejects perceiving the body 'from the outside' as a 'most naive kind' of materialism (Bourdieu, 2000: 132), and a 'typically scholastic viewpoint' (p. 133). Instead, he insists that the body is 'open to the world, and therefore exposed to the world, and so capable of being conditioned by the world, shaped by the material and cultural conditions of existence in which it is placed from the beginning' (p. 134). The individuation of the body is therefore the result of going through a socialization process, where social relations have shaped the singularity of the self. This process is one in which we acquire practical knowledge through learning with our bodies. The past experiences of the social agents, in the form of systems of schemes of perception, appreciation and action, are inscribed in their bodies, enabling them to perform acts of practical knowledge. The individual is a 'habitus', by which Bourdieu means 'a system of dispositions' (p. 130), 'a socialized biological body', which is at the same time 'the social, biologically individuated through incarnation in a body' (p. 157).

Social space, according to Bourdieu (2000: 130), is 'the locus of the coexistence of social positions', which forms the basis of the viewpoints of its occupants. Social space, he maintains, 'tends to be translated, with more or less distortion, into physical space, in the form of a certain arrangement of agents and properties. It follows that all the divisions and distinctions of social space (high/low, left/right, etc.) are really and symbolically expressed in physical space appropriated as reified social space . . .' (Bourdieu, 2000: 134). This system of positions, this habitat, is in a dialectical relationship with a system of dispositions, the habitus. This dialectical relationship means a mutual relationship between the individual and society, not dissimilar to the structure–agency dialectic that Giddens (1984) describes.

The personal space, both as the invisible bubble that locates the individual and the position in social hierarchies, can therefore be analysed in this light, without necessarily accepting the premise that rejects the notion of individual. The way an individual is brought up and is socialized largely shapes his/her treatment of personal space. This includes the way the body performs its actions, including gestures, performances and the observation of personal space, among others; this is largely determined by the past histories of a person, which are inscribed in the body. These are deeply ingrained features and are not easy to change, as psychoanalysts may hope, by bringing them to consciousness. Such change needs sustained training to make any long term impact. 'While making things explicit can help', Bourdieu rightly asserts, 'only a thoroughgoing process of countertraining, involving repeated exercises, can, like an athlete's training, durably transform habitus' (Bourdieu 2000: 172). As living organisms, however, we are also aware that our habits and positions are changing constantly, sometimes as a result of conscious attempts and at other times as a result of adjustment to particular external constraints. The limitations of the notion of habitus, therefore, can be also seen in this light, that human agency is capable of changing the script ingrained on his/her body, rather than being entirely a prisoner of these inscriptions. Accepting the social space as if it were the weather, where nothing can be done but to adjust, or seeing it as an overarching umbrella over existence, where it cannot be changed, are potentially the sources of other analytical limitations.

CONCLUSION

All forms of private and public distinction are directly related to the fundamental distinction between the inner self and the outside world. The notion of the self, as developed in modern Western Europe, has been a central theme of the way public and private realms are defined and organized. The self was non-physical and autonomous, providing a first-person view of the world that could know and act with confidence. As against this formulation, a number of critiques have caused major changes in the conceptualization of the self. The physical and mental dimensions of the individual human being are closely linked; the impulses of the body and the forces of the social world influence and shape the contents of the mind; and the first person's authority is doubted by a scientific or literary third-person viewpoint. A new concept of the self emerges as an empirical unit at the intersection of biological and social processes and of first-person and third-person views of the world. The human subject has privileged and exclusive access to a realm of consciousness, which is the ultimate private realm of an individual. As the contents of this realm are not under full control of the subject, it appears that the subject is a mere spectator in this private realm. But the ability to make connections and take action entitles the subject to be understood as an agency, albeit to a limited degree and always at interplay with the biological and social frameworks of which the subject is a part. Both the inner self and the outer space of the body are mainly constructed through interaction with others. The privacy of these spaces, therefore, are not innate but a result of social process and exchange.

The inner space of the body (that which is contained within the skin) is closely associated with personal space (the immediate space around the body). Personal space is often closely related to the realm of privacy as its essential ingredient. It provides an invisible and portable protective layer for an individual, ensuring the desired level of privacy and freedom from outside intrusion. With closer inspection, it becomes clear that it is equally a constituent part of the public realm. It is the building block of social encounters, where individuals regulate their interaction through maintaining the appropriate distance from one another in interpersonal communication.

Personal space, therefore, is as much for protection as for communication, as much a part of the private sphere as it is of the public realm. It is as much determined by the personal as it is by the interpersonal dimensions of life in society.

Personal space observation is directly related with a growing sense of individualism, and as such is present more strongly in the cultures that have nurtured individual autonomy and independent sense of the self. The significance of personal space, therefore, is that it not only denotes an individual territory, but also a portion of the group space. It is established only in the context of social encounters, rather than being an absolute territory. Its features are mainly based on how they have been acquired by individuals, depending on their personal differences as well as their social and cultural contexts. It is a dynamic, ever changing sphere that evolves, expands and contracts according to the situations in which individuals find themselves.

Chapter 2
Exclusive space of the property

In the last chapter we studied the private sphere as the hidden space of consciousness that lies inside the body, and the personal space as an invisible and portable space around the body. In this chapter we move our analysis one step further, to study the visible and stationary space of private sphere: the private property. The space here is hidden behind fixed, often visible boundaries and is protected by the owner and the others as sanctioned by law. If personal space was a socio-psychological and interpersonal space of protection and communication, private property is an institutional and legal entity, which combines personal and impersonal dimensions. While our last chapter drew on philosophy, anthropology, and social and environmental psychology, this chapter will have to venture also into legal and political theory, in search for a better understanding of the private sphere.

In this chapter, we explore the relationship between individuals and physical space, searching for the psychological and political–legal significance of private space. The chapter starts by searching for a definition of private sphere and private space. Then it moves on to the notions of territory and territorial behaviour, which humans share with animals in extending their control over physical space, to control access to a particular area. This is followed by an investigation of the institutionalized control over space, which is formalized through law and protected by physical boundaries. Here the discussions about privacy and private property show the significance attached to the protection of a private sphere for individuals. The chapter ends with a discussion of boundaries, as the means with which physical space is subdivided into public and private.

DEFINING THE PRIVATE SPHERE

Definitions of the word 'private' are often coupled with, and rely on, the meaning of the word 'public', so that one word does not appear to make sense without the other. The origins of the word go back to Latin, where *privus* meant 'single, individual, private'. Living a private life could denote a negative meaning and a sense of loss, as *privare* meant 'bereave' and 'deprive', while *privatus* meant 'withdrawn from public life, peculiar to oneself, a man in private life'. This negative interpretation seemed to be a definition that was produced from the perspective of those engaged in public life looking into the private realm. Hannah Arendt, for example, saw private life in a deeply negative light, to the extent that for her, the private person 'does not exist', with actions which remain without significance or consequence to others (Arendt, 1958: 58). A life mainly lived in the restricted sphere of the household, as historically it was for women, therefore, was not worth living.

> To live an entirely private life means above all to be deprived of things essential to a truly human life: to be deprived of the reality that comes from being seen and heard by others, to be deprived of an 'objective' relationship with them that comes from being related to and separated from them through an intermediary of a common world of things, to be deprived of the possibility of achieving something more permanent than life itself (Arendt, ibid.)

As against this condemnation of living a private life, there are those who see it as an essential part of human life.

> Privacy permits people to share intimacies and ideas on their own terms, and thus establish those mutual reciprocal relinquishments of the self that underlie the relations of love, friendship and trust.... The right to privacy is thus an inescapable aspect of our humanity. (Krattenmaker quoted in Silver, 1997: 43)

In modern usage, the word's meanings, according to the Oxford English Dictionary, are mainly adjectives describing people, places, or activities. When the word refers to a person, its meanings include: 'not holding public office or an official position; of or pertaining to a person in a non-official capacity; not open to the public; restricted or intended only for the use of a particular person or persons; that belongs to or is the property of a particular person; one's own; of, pertaining to, or affecting a particular person or group of people, individual, personal; peculiar to a particular person or persons; particular, retiring; reserved; unsociable; formerly also, secretive'. When, on the other hand, the word refers to a service, business, etc., it means: 'provided or owned by an individual rather than the State or a public body; (of a system of education or medical treatment) conducted outside the State system and charging fees to the individual concerned; of or pertaining to such a system; kept or removed from public view or knowledge; not generally known; secret; confidential, not to be disclosed to others'. It also means 'without the presence of another person or persons, alone; privy; enjoying another's confidence, intimate'. When the word is used to refer to a place, it means 'secluded, unfrequented, affording privacy'.

Private sphere, therefore, is a part of life that is under the control of the individual in a personal capacity, outside public observation and knowledge and outside official or state control. It follows that private space is a part of space that belongs to, or is controlled by, an individual, for that individual's exclusive use, keeping the public out. Much of the private sphere unfolds in private spaces, although it can also go on outside private territories, such as in a public library or in a park, which is a part of private life played out in a public place.

THE RIGHTS OF PRIVACY

The notion of privacy has been hard to define and a wide range of analytical approaches have tried to clarify it (Wacks, 1993). The 'archetypal' complaints in law about privacy have been about 'public disclosure of private facts' and 'intrusion upon an individual's seclusion, solitude or private affairs' (Wacks, 1993: xv). The common definitions of privacy, according to the Oxford English Dictionary, are 'the state or condition of being withdrawn from the society of others or from public attention; freedom from disturbance or intrusion; seclusion; absence or avoidance of publicity or display; secrecy; a private or personal matter; a secret'. But the wide range of social, political, economic and legal implications that result from this range of meanings are by no means unproblematic. Issues as different as the rights of women (especially abortion), the use of contraceptives, the freedom of homosexuals, the right to obscene or pornographic publications, and the problems associated with AIDS continue to be debated all around the notion of privacy, without a clarified conception of what privacy means (Wacks, 1993).

The conceptual ambiguity is particularly felt within legal circles, where it is not even safe to assume that the courts have an adequate conception of privacy (Parent, 1983: 325). A private sphere may be established through social norms and its violation may not be as severe as breaking the law. Some invasions of privacy may be considered bad manners but not subject to legal consideration. For example, if someone is sitting in the park reading a book in a clearly private mood, this means the person has established a private sphere and does not wish to be disturbed. But approaching that person and asking a question, or even making noise nearby does not break the law. How can the law protect privacy when a clear definition may not exist?

One conception of privacy sees it as the right to be let alone (Ernst and Schwartz, 1962), and the right to privacy as 'the most comprehensive of rights' (Brandeis, quoted in Parent, 1983: 321). Towards the end of the nineteenth century, in a famous essay, Warren and Brandeis proposed what is considered to be the original legal formulation of privacy (Wacks, 1993: xi). They argued that the intensity and complexity of the modern life have made it necessary for individuals to have some retreat from the world, as the intrusion of privacy has subjected the modern individual to mental pain and distress (Parent, 1983: 320).

The right to privacy is, therefore, according to Abe Fortas, a former member of the US Supreme Court, 'the right to be let alone; to live one's life as one chooses free from assault, intrusion, or invasion except as they can be justified by the clear needs of the community living under a government of law' (quoted in Parent, 1983: 318–19) (Figure 2.1). Another, related, conception of privacy sees it as freedom from unwarranted government intrusion. Parent argues that these definitions confuse privacy with liberty, which is freedom from external restraints such as those imposed by the government. He criticizes Altman's definition of privacy as a form of control over access to the self, or other definitions that see privacy as control over personal information or sexual matters. Instead, he narrows down the definition of privacy to 'the condition of not having undocumented personal information about oneself known by others' (Parent, 1983: 306). The 'right to privacy' is,

2.1 One conception of privacy sees it as the right to be let alone (Barcelona, Spain)

therefore, considered to be at its core related to 'protection against the misuse of personal, sensitive information' (Wacks, 1993: xii). Privacy should not be, Wacks argues, confused with autonomy or freedom.

Defined in this way, privacy may have a clearer legal definition, but the impact of privacy on space may be somewhat limited. Another definition by Gavison (quoted in Wacks, 1993: xiii), sees privacy as 'limited accessibility', with three independent but related components: secrecy (information known about an individual); anonymity (attention paid to an individual); and solitude (physical access to an individual). When any of these areas is violated, a loss of privacy occurs, which is distinctive from an infringement of the right of privacy. This broader notion of privacy addresses some of the social and psychological forms of violation of privacy, as well as addressing the issue of space, where ensuring privacy may have a spatial dimension. The definition is limited in that it cannot be applied to certain conditions. It is objectionable to have attention focused upon us, or to be subjected to uninvited intrusion into our solitude. But when these happen in public space, we cannot claim that privacy has been lost in a legal sense.

The discussion of privacy as a condition addresses what it means to have privacy. There is also a discussion about privacy, which sees it in a normative light, as privacy rights. The most influential formulation of these rights has been made in the Universal Declaration of Human Rights proclaimed by the General Assembly of the United Nations on 10 December 1948. According to the Article 12 of this Declaration:

> No one shall be subjected to arbitrary interference with his privacy, family, home or correspondence, nor to attacks on his honour and reputation. Everyone has the right to the protection of the law against such interference or attacks. (quoted in Neill, 1999: 20)

Articles 9 and 10 addressed freedom of thought, conscience and religion and freedom of expression. Article 8 provides:

> 1. Everyone has the right to respect for his private and family life, his home and his correspondence.
>
> 2. There shall be no interference by a public authority with the exercise of this right except such as in accordance with the law and is necessary in a democratic society in the interests of national security, public safety or the economic wellbeing of the country, for the prevention of disorder or crime, for the protection of health or morals, or for the protection of the rights and freedoms of others. (quoted in Neill, 1999: 20)

In English law, a general right of privacy has not been recognized, although sub-stantial protection has been given to the defence of a person's reputation and piecemeal protection of privacy has developed. Privacy rights have traditionally been associated with property and land, and so issues of trespass and nuisance have been addressed in the law. Also addressed are issues of harassment, breach of confidence, defamation and malicious falsehood and data protection (Neill, 1999). Several codes of practice have also addressed the concerns for privacy. The Press Complaints Commission, which deals with complaints against the press, addresses privacy in one of its clauses in this way:

> 3. Privacy
> 1. Everyone is entitled to respect for his or her private and family life, home, health and correspondence. A publication will be expected to justify intrusions into any individual's private life without consent.
> 2. The use of long lens photography to take pictures of people in private places is unacceptable.
> Note – Private places are public or private property where there is a reasonable expectation of privacy. (quoted in Neill, 1999: 15)

The *Code on Fairness and Privacy* by the Broadcasting Standards Commission shows a similar concern:

> 14. An infringement of privacy has to be justified by an overriding public interest in disclosure of the information. This would include revealing or detecting crime or disreputable behaviour, protesting public health or safety, exposing misleading claims made by individuals or organizations, or disclosing significant incompetence in public office. Moreover, the means of obtaining the information must be propor-tionate to the matter under investigation. (quoted in Neill, 1999: 16)

Some experts, therefore, believe that English law now requires a general law regarding the protection of privacy. This law, it has been suggested, could revolve around protecting 'the freedom to preserve the privacy of personal information which is confidential' (Neill, 1999: 22).

For Thomas Nagel (1995) the private space, as the space of freedom of choice for individuals, is closely related with human rights, while public space is equated with scrutiny and control. As usual, the two are set at the two ends of a spectrum, dependant on each other: 'Of course any issue of individual rights depends on there being, at least in the offing, a contention that something or other is the public's business and subject to public control' (p. 94). Nagel defines rights as 'universal protections of every individual against being justifiably used or sacrificed in certain ways for purposes worthy or unworthy' (p. 85). These are aspects of being a member of the moral community. Human rights can be defended on an instrumental basis: that they are vitally important in fostering happiness, self-realization, knowledge and freedom. Nagel, furthermore, argues for the intrinsic value of human rights, as a non-derivative and fundamental element of morality. 'The real test of a belief in human rights is whether we are prepared to insist that they be respected even in the service of worthy causes' (p. 86). In this case, when a person is tortured or shot for demonstrating peacefully, what really matters is the particulars of the treatment, rather than the economic performance or popularity of the regime that was responsible.

Human rights are moral rights, which are purely normative rather than necessarily institutional. An individual who is in the possession of human rights has, therefore, the status of 'inviolability' (p. 89). However, 'to be inviolable does not mean that one *will not be violated*. It is a moral *status*: It means that one *may not* be violated in certain ways . . .' (p. 89). The way this moral status is expressed may vary depending on the circumstances, which could range from economic development to racial, religious and ethnic conflict. But the issue remains the same whenever the scope of individual rights is being determined in the context of the circumstances:

> What kind of force may be used against people, and for what reasons? The limits always represent a balance between collective goods and individual independence, but every morality should accord to each individual some substantial space of personal independence, immune from coercion by the will of others. (p. 94)

It is therefore important to defend the privacy of individuals as part of their basic human rights, which includes choice in a number of directions such as the search for cosmic or religious meaning or in choices of personal pleasures, sexual fantasies and non-political self-expression. These, Nagel argues, should remain a matter of private choice, shielded from the control and scrutiny of public space, in the same way that the more basic human rights should be protected. In the relationship between the sexes, which is an important aspect of the public space, it is important to realize that a 'psychic jungle of private worlds' exists, which should not be treated as a public space with its expected controls and accommodation (p. 104). While personal liberties and human rights are on the same side, public control and state interference are on the opposite side. The 'main contemporary threat to human rights', therefore, is the 'radical communitarian view that nothing in personal life is beyond the legitimate control of the community if its dominant values are at stake' (p. 106).

What is promoted, therefore, is the need for catering for the plurality of human society within an enlarged private sphere and for keeping the already crowded public space free from disruptive material, such as public debate and media interest in the sexual conduct of public figures, past and present. The task should be, Nagel (1998b) argues, to maintain civility and concealment, which would keep both the disruptive material out of the public arena and protect private life from the crippling effects of the external gaze (Figure 2.2). However, we might ask, how far is it is possible to maintain this distinction, to protect the private space when for some people, such as the homeless, no such privacy exists?

THREATS TO PRIVACY

The notion of personal space is part of an understanding of the private realm, which sees it as an essential ingredient of human life. The concern for privacy and the need for protecting it are, therefore, often set against the fear of its violation by

2.2 The balance between the public and private spheres in the city helps to maintain civility and concealment, keeping the disruptive material out of the public arena and protect private life from the effects of the external gaze (Naples, Italy)

Beijing   decentralization

intrusion and loss of control. In the nineteenth and twentieth centuries, the fear of overcrowding was a major concern, as cities grew by attracting large numbers of incomers and, in some places and periods, by high birth rates. Many studies were conducted to relate overcrowding and crime. The modernist planning promoted a reduction of overcrowding in the cities. What was promoted was a decentralization of the cities, so that overcrowding could be tackled. The city of London after the last world war, for example, was to be decentralized, relocating a large number of its population from the central areas to the peripheral new towns (Abercrombie, 1945). Enjoying the support of both public and private sectors, a process of suburbanization was in full force in this period in Britain and the United States. Many studies of privacy and the fear of overcrowding took place in this period. The impact on the spatial configuration of the cities was phenomenal, as the cities were decentred and spread in all directions to avoid the harms of overcrowding.

Suburbanization was in a sense a new pattern of consuming space, which allowed the middle class households to have larger personal and intimate territories. At the same time, this fear of overcrowding was parallel to the fear of the poor and racially different people. The postwar history of American cities shows how fast a part of the city could lose its white population once the black residents moved into an area (Keating and Krumholz, 1999). While a crowd of similar people had been tolerated in the past, the crowds of different people and the accessibility of cars and federal subsidies all made it possible for large numbers to flee the city and its supposed overcrowding.

As new technologies have despatialized some aspects of urban life and excluding social practices have kept the undesirables out, new concerns for privacy focus on access to information, alongside the traditional concern for access to places. A brief look at the titles of publications on privacy shows the rising significance of access to personal information, especially in the context of new information and communication technologies (e.g. Diffie and Landau, 1998; Norris, 1999; Garfinkel, 2000).

The distinction between the public and the private is everywhere around us, from our daily routines of living and passing through different shades of private and public spaces, to patterns of behaviour which we perform in accordance with the character of these spaces. In the newspapers and on television screens, we see and hear a constant tension between what may or may not be defined as public or private, from the images of what happens in the private lives of fictional characters to the reports on the factual behaviour of public figures in private. This is a tension that we observe all around us, the distinction between the public and the private being one of the key lenses through which we see and interpret our daily lives.

The distinction goes back very far in human societies everywhere. But modern technology has changed the way privacy and publicity are practised and protected. In the not too distant past, privacy could be secured through the physical barriers of walls and doors, and the spatial limitations dictated by being in a particular place at a particular time. Almost all you could hear or see was limited to this local, everyday experience, which was bounded by limitations of space and time, of being here and now. Hence the walls and gates could regulate the publicity and privacy fairly effectively (Figure 2.3). Some of what happened behind the walls could be known to the outsiders, but only those who lived locally, in the same street or village. It could spread farther, albeit very slowly and in distorted forms, only if the person involved was very significant.

Now, it is possible for photographs to be taken from inside the private sphere, voices listened to by electronic devices, communications to the outside world tapped, details of personal information known, without setting foot behind the walls and doors. Furthermore, all this could be broadcast around the world at the click of a button. The law does not seem to protect individuals against many forms of such intrusions, as shown by a case in court, in which it was argued by the judge

2.3 Walls and gates have always been used to regulate the relationship between two parts of space (Cardiff, UK)

that if a person's address is known locally, it could well be made more widely known by the national media (Parsons, 2001).

Not only can the private sphere be violated in this way, it is also a common phenomenon that the public sphere is crowded with material that would normally be regarded as private. Even at the heart of one's private sphere, for example, there seems to be no escape from being bombarded by details of the private affairs of a public figure or a celebrity entertainer. Meanwhile, the media are often run by commercial organizations in need of making profit through maintaining the audience's interest. Hence the emphasis on stories with human interest dimension, hence the encroachment into private life even when not justified.

The extended power of the mass media, through the use of advanced technologies such as satellite communications, may be a welcome development. No more, it is argued by the media, can the authorities in brutal regimes or the misconduct of public officials in the more democratic ones be hidden from the eyes of the citizens. The free media constructs a strong public sphere in which such misconduct is discussed and revealed. These extended technological abilities give the media the power to rival, and even override the traditional democratic institutions. Discussions in front of television cameras can become more important than those in Parliament, the leaders of the political parties much more important than the local representatives, who may be from outside the area and even unknown to the voters. Politics could be more scrutinized by powerful media, counterbalancing the powerful political parties. At the same time, politics seems to be ever more limited to a dialogue between two sets of large and powerful organizations, political parties and the media, bypassing the voters who appear to lose interest or be marginalized.

It might be said that not everyone is equally suffering from the new, technologically enabled forms of intrusion into their private lives. Those who live in poverty do not seem to attract media attention and are therefore spared from such intrusions. At the same time, the poor are heavily monitored in their private lives, living in public housing areas supported by public funds and social benefits, managed and handled by public officials, and watched by surveillance cameras in public places. Here too, private lives are monitored by outsiders, to the extent that the more affluent might find difficult to bear.

This dramatic change in the nature of the public and private realms and how new technologies can transform them in new ways does not mean that the traditional spatial distinctions are obsolete. The private sphere continues to be mainly defined in spatial terms and protected by spatial means. Private property is still the bastion of privacy, and the despatialization of the public sphere does not take away the significance of the public places of the city.

TERRITORY AND TERRITORIALITY

The continuous exertion of control over a particular part of physical space by an individual or a group results in the establishment of a territory. Territoriality, as closely associated with this process, has been defined by environmental psychologists as 'a set of behaviours and cognitions a person or group exhibits, based on perceived ownership of physical space' (Bell *et al.*, 1996: 304). Ownership is mainly understood to be the legal entitlement to controlling a property. It is also possible to establish territories without legal ownership, e.g. the area an office worker occupies and treats as personal territory, even though it would legally belong to someone else. Indeed there may be many layers of control, leaving each layer with a different sense of territory: from one who owns the land, who may be different from the one who owns the building, from the one who owns the company, from the managers and section managers who are in charge of all or a particular part of an office, to the one who works in a particular office, or even the one who frequently visits the office and thus feels a sense of belonging there. There is a hierarchy of power and control involved. But wherever their location in the hierarchy, these individuals will all feel a sense of territoriality, a degree of ownership and control over the physical space.

This is a sense of territoriality that has been derived from emotional attachment and familiarity, as well as from the more abstract forms of control through monetary, legal and institutional power over space. Territory is considered to be used as an 'organizer' of activities, by allowing us to anticipate the types of people and forms of behaviour in different places, and so plan accordingly for our daily lives (Figure 2.4). Furthermore, territory provides feelings of distinctiveness, privacy and a sense of personal identity (Bell *et al.*, 1996: 306). According to Altman (1975; Bell *et al.*, 1996), three forms of territory can be identified, depending on the duration of occupancy, the cognitive impacts on the occupant and the others in generating a sense of ownership, the amount of personalization, and the likelihood of defence when violated. A primary territory, such as home or office, is perceived to be owned by the occupant and others relatively permanently. It is extensively personalized and the owner has complete control over space, finding intrusion a serious matter. The second territory, such as a classroom, has a moderate level of control, as the occupant does not own the place and is considered as one of a number of qualified users. These users may personalize the place to some extent during their period of occupancy, which gives them some power over the space. The third level is public territory, such as an area of beach, where the degree of control is low, and difficult to assert. The occupant is one of a large number of possible users. It can be personalized in a temporary way and there is little likelihood of

2.4 Territories are established, through signs and physical boundaries, to control behaviour in space, as this system of traffic restriction exemplifies (Cambridge, UK)

defence. These three forms in turn help individuals meet their needs by choosing the appropriate territory for their activities.

As territorial behaviour is performed by both humans and animals, some researchers believe that human territoriality is instinctive, driven by a need to claim and defend territory in a world where space is limited and relationships are determined through conflict over resources. Others, however, argue that people learn their sense of territoriality through their past experiences and their culture, which show them the social significance of space. There are also those who see territorial behaviour as the outcome of an interaction between social and biological processes: while territoriality, particularly in its elementary forms, is driven by instinct, its intensity and more complex forms are regulated through social frameworks (Bell *et al.*, 1996: 305–6).

This interaction between instinct and learning takes us back to the discussion in Chapter 1 on the biological and social forces shaping human mind and behaviour. The establishment of a territory may be the drive that we share with animals for our survival. The way this territoriality takes shape and is translated into physical space, however, varies widely, as evidence of the impact of culture and civilization. The private sphere has many more layers of social significance than the instinctive territoriality. This interplay between the biological and social leads us to Freud's analysis of private property as a channel for controlling aggression.

Sigmund Freud rejected the communist demand for the abolition of private property (as discussed later in this chapter) not on economic grounds but on psychological ones. He could not agree with the communist belief that the human nature is essentially good but has only been corrupted by the institution of private property. 'In abolishing private property we deprive the human love of aggression of one of its instruments, certainly a strong one, though certainly not the strongest' (Freud, 1985: 304). By limiting aggression, which is an essential part of human nature, and directing it towards the outside world, humans are able to channel their instincts for constructive purposes. By abolishing private property, aggressiveness will not disappear, as the communists hoped; aggressiveness predates property ownership, as evident from early childhood and early periods of human civilization. (pp. 303–4).

Research into the relationship between aggression and territory shows that territory may serve either as an instigator to aggression or as a stabilizer to prevent aggression. Where territories are not yet established or disputed, and when the boundaries between territories are ambiguous rather than well drawn, both humans and animals show evidence of increased aggression. On the contrary, established territorial boundaries have a stabilizing effect in reducing hostility among neighbours. The environmental psychologists argue that the importance of these research findings has not been recognized by design professions. For the residents of institutions, such as mental hospitals, homes for the elderly, residential rehabilitation settings and prisons, the ability to establish territories (such as bringing personal possessions and personalizing an area, which is often not allowed) has led to an improvement in the social atmosphere of the ward. Also the clear demarcation of houses was found to have a positive impact on reducing burglaries (Bell *et al.* 1996: 312–20).

PRIVATE PROPERTY

In the previous chapter, we saw personal space as a relationship of control over one's body in social interactions. In this chapter, we study this relationship of control with physical space in establishing a more permanent, stationary private sphere. While the private sphere may start from the person's mind and extend to the personal space of the body, it is in private property that it finds a strong, socially acknowledged expression. The self and the personal space may be seen as deeper, softer parts of the private sphere; it is only in private property that the private sphere finds a hard-edged embodiment. In the discussions about public and private spheres, the private sphere is often represented by private property, which is the historically established, spatial form of an individual's sphere of control. Through the control of its boundaries, individuals regulate their social interactions, and the balance between being on their own and being with others, both in space and in time (Figure 2.5).

Private property combines personal and impersonal dimensions of dealing with space. For the one who owns and controls it, it is an outlet for exertion of power and attachment of emotions. As such it becomes one of the most widely used vehicles of psychological development, expression of personal identity, and empowerment in social networks. At the same time, it is an abstract commodity, exchanged in the market and regulated by law. Such institutionalization by the state and the market gives private property an impersonal dimension, as it is treated like any other commodity, which can be exchanged in the market without personal and emotional attachment.

Discussions about whether or not to own property, how to regulate individuals' claims to the resources of the earth, how to exert control over property and protect it from the intrusion of others or to share it with others have been a key theme in utopian ideals as well as (and clearly linked with) developing new systems of government. The provision and protection of private sphere is the cause of endless debates. According to the legal theorist Richard Epstein,

2.5 Private control of property gives the individual the right to exclude all others from a particular part of space (Dublin, Ireland)

more private, more public ~~less private, less public~~

> The right of an owner of property to exclude all others from his property is one of the most prized – and most feared – rights any civilization can confer on its members. From one point of view, a system that creates this right also allows individuals to harness their talents and to develop natural resources under their control, both to their maximum extent. But from another vantage point, the right to exclude is condemned as snobbish or nettlesome behaviour that inconveniences or harms people left on the outside looking in. (Epstein, 1998: 187)

Private property ownership is seen as a sign of economic stability and even wealth, which, as Arendt reminds us (1958: 64), Proudhon associated with theft. Before the modern age, however, property was a condition for the membership of a free society. It provided a root, a location from which a person could enter the public realm. Unlike the modern form of property, which is easily exchanged in the marketplace, the ancient property was a precondition for the elite's membership of the community. To own property then meant 'to be master over one's own necessities of life and therefore potentially to be a free person, free to transcend his own life and enter the world all have in common' (Arendt, 1958: 65).

The classic discussions of private property go back to the disagreement between Plato and Aristotle. Plato raised the position of property to that of the body and mind, to form a triad. For each, there was a pernicious state and a branch of expertise to deal with it. For mind it was immorality, which needed administration of justice; for body it was sickness, which needed medicine; and for property it was poverty, which needed commerce (Plato, 1994: 55–7). Plato's utopian republic was to be run by an elite group of propertyless guardians (Plato, 1993, Chapter 5). None of these rulers, who had to go through vigorous training and to live a puritan life, was allowed to have any private property, 'except what is absolutely indispensable' (p. 121). This would mean that their living quarters and their property in general would not interfere with their ability to carry out their duties. Plato's fear was that,

> If they do come to own their own land and home and money, they will be estate-managers and farmers instead of guardians; they will become despots, and enemies rather than allies of the inhabitants of the community ... With private property, they will be racing ever closer to the ruin of themselves and the whole community. (p. 122)

This denial of property ownership, however, was limited to the ruling guardians and did not extend to the rest of the community, who could own estates and enjoy the benefits of private property (p. 122). Morality in this utopian community, Plato argued, was 'keeping one's own property and keeping to one's own occupation' (p. 142).

Aristotle, in his Politics (II v), objected to this scheme as unrealistic, arguing that 'the general principle should be that of private ownership', which would ensure increased effort in looking after property (Aristotle, 1992: 114) and would give 'an immense amount of pleasure' both in enjoying its benefits and in helping friends, strangers and associates (p. 115). Without private property, he argued, 'no man will be seen to be liberal and no man will ever do any act of liberality; for it is in the use of articles of property that liberality is practised (p. 115).

Aristotle (1992) argued against seeking excessive unity and emphasized the need for private property and for acknowledging the difference among citizens. He suggested that 'the greater the number of owners, the less respect for common property' (p. 108). As if describing a public housing estate in the second half of the twentieth century, Aristotle wrote: 'People are much more careful of their personal possessions than those owned communally; ... the thought that someone else is looking after (common property) for them tends to make them careless of it' (ibid.). He therefore defended the private ownership of property, but held that its use could be communal (pp. 113ff).

In the modern period, the debate starts in the seventeenth century with John Locke, who argued for a natural right of property ownership, which lies outside social contract and cannot be negotiated. He held nature to be common and private property to be a consequence of investing human labour on the common property.

> Though the earth and all inferior creatures be common to all men, yet every man has a property in his own person; this nobody has any right to but himself. The labour of this body and the work of his hands are properly his. Whatsoever, then, he removes out of the state that nature hath provided and left it in, he hath mixed his labour with, and joined to it something that is his own, and thereby makes it his property. (Locke, 1976: 15)

The difference of value on everything, then, was the result of human labour. Without human labour, the value of land 'would scarcely be worth anything' (p. 23). This principle may apply to the sparsely populated countries and the frontier lands. But what about the highly populated countries where people are engaged in trade and commerce and live under a government? The appropriation of common land by individuals, Locke believed, was not jeopardizing the right of others, as the wealth of all increased by such appropriations: 'he who appropriates land to himself by his labour, does not lessen but increase the common stock of mankind' (p. 20). Furthermore, the limit to this appropriation of nature and the common property was to be set by the needs of the individual and the consent of the others. Here the principle was that 'no one can enclose or appropriate any part without the consent of all his fellow-commoners' (p. 18).

Locke's belief in the natural right to property was rejected by Rousseau, who saw property ownership as a legal right. Rousseau saw private property as the source of inequality and war (Rousseau, 1968: 56), which needed to be brought under the control of a legal framework set by society. For him, 'all legitimate authority among men must be based on covenants' (p. 53). Individuals convert their independence into political and legal freedom by entering a social contract. The core of this contract is the notion that,

> Each one of us puts into the community his person and all his powers under the supreme direction of the general will; and as a body, we incorporate every member as an indivisible part of the whole. (p. 61)

The property rights of individuals, therefore, became 'always subordinate to the right of the community over everything' (p. 68). Without this subordination, Rousseau argued, 'there would be neither strength in the social bond nor effective force in the exercise of sovereignty' (p. 68). In this way, the lands of the private individuals are united and contiguous to become public territory. By this he did not mean to leave private property under the control of the sovereign or deprive the individual of them. '[O]n the contrary', he argued (p. 67), 'it simply assures him of their lawful possession.'

For Hegel, protection of private property through the administration of justice was one of the main 'moments' of civil society (Hegel, 1967: 126). He associated private property closely with personal freedom, believing that 'in the last resort no community has so good a right to property as a person has' (p. 236). Property ownership allowed a person to translate his/her freedom into an external sphere, in the realm of 'things' over which humans have 'the absolute right of appropriation' (pp. 40–1). Beyond catering for our needs, private property is an essential part of an individual's freedom,

> If emphasis is placed on my needs, then the possession of property appears as a mean to their satisfaction, but the true position is that, from the standpoint of freedom, property is the first embodiment of freedom and so is in itself a substantive end. (p. 42)

Indeed property for Hegel is the 'means through which I give my will an embodiment' (p. 236). As the embodiment of personality, property, therefore, has a central place for the sense of the self, where the individual's will is related to the objects of the world (pp. 45–6). This relation takes place in three stages: taking possession of the thing (which can be directly grasping it, by forming it, and by marking it as ours), using it, and alienating it (p. 46). Through our control over private property, then, we find an outlet for our will to relate to the world and, as a result, find an expressive satisfaction and a sense of personal freedom and development. Hegel, therefore, argued in favour of the institution of private property as an expression of individual self. This was criticized by Karl Marx as causing alienation rather than realizing the individual self (Scruton, 1996: 434–5).

Marx's formulation was completely opposite of Hegel's. In the *Communist Manifesto*, Marx and Engels (1930: 25) argued that 'The history of all human society, past and present, has been the history of class struggle.' In the contemporary period, it was a struggle between the bourgeoisie and the proletariat, i.e. between capital and wage labour. The antagonism between capital and labour revolved around property. Labour created capital, which was the property that in turn exploited labour (p. 44). For in the bourgeois society, 'those who work do not acquire property and those who acquire property do not work' (p. 46). Capital was 'a collective product', 'a social force', which was only possible to result from the joint activities of all the members of society (p. 44). But it was owned by a minority, who thus deprived and alienated the workers from the outcome of their own labour. The result has been a society in which private property has already been abolished for nine-tenths of the population (p. 46). The communist answer to this problem was to dismantle the private ownership of property: 'Communists sum up their theory in the pithy phrase: the abolition of private property' (p. 43).

Through their choice of words, from the very beginning of their communist manifesto ('A spectre haunts Europe, the spectre of communism.') to the phrases where they spelt out their vision of utopia, Marx and Engels were in a combative mode, wishing to frighten their opponents. This is particularly acute when private property is addressed: 'In a word, you accuse us of wanting to abolish *your* property. Well we do!' (Marx and Engels, 1930: 46). They were engaged in a war, mainly fought over private property. All arguments against such abolition were rejected on the basis that these arguments (such as those in favour of individuality, liberty, culture, right etc.) were themselves the outcome of bourgeois property relations (p. 47). 'When you speak of individuals you are thinking solely of bourgeois, of the owners of bourgeois property. Certainly we wish to abolish individuals of that kind!' (p. 46).

Marx (1974, originally 1859) analysed the historical processes of property transformation. At the stage of primitive accumulation of capital, the individual private property that is based on the labour of its owners (which was the foundation of petty industry) is dissolved. A process of centralization ensures that capital is accumulated in the hands of a few. Here, private property is capitalistic, 'which rests on exploitation of the nominally free labour of others, i.e. on wage-labour' (p. 714). Labourers are thus turned into proletarians, while their means of labour is transformed into capital. The next phase comes when this centralization of the means of production and socialization of labour become incompatible with their capitalist framework. 'The knell of capitalist private property sounds. The expropriators are expropriated' (p. 715). Rather than re-establishing private property for the producer, a 'socialized property' is created (p. 715). The outcome of this explosion is 'individual property based on the acquisitions of the capitalist era: i.e. on co-operation and the possession in common of the land and of the means of production' (p. 715).

The heated debates and class wars of the nineteenth century continued to dominate the twentieth century, in the form of the Soviet experiment and the wars and tensions that it caused, and also in the general improvement in the working conditions of the workers in the West. But, with the collapse of the Soviet empire and its rapid and troubled return to private ownership, has the debate on private property ownership disappeared? Maybe it was a leftwing preoccupation that has subsided with the failure of communism to materialize? With the economic restructuring in the West and the privatization of government assets in many parts of the world, the debate indeed has entered a new phase. The balance between public and private ownership continues to form a central part of the quest for social justice and ideal forms of government.

According to Jeremy Waldron, one of the key themes of liberal thought in the twentieth century has been 'whether it is possible really to enjoy civil liberties and political freedoms as they are traditionally understood, without also enjoying a fair degree of material security' (Waldron, 1993: 5). It is not, therefore, as the libertarian Nozick (1974) had suggested, to hold that private property ownership has an unquestionable priority over the material needs of the large number of the poor. The case that Waldron puts forward is to argue for welfare rights in connection with the more traditional rights of human beings. For him, 'the logic of welfare rights is not "Please let me sleep on your land", but rather "How dare you erect fences around land that people may need to sleep on?" ' (Waldron, 1993: 20).

Even those who promote the idea of limited government and the reduction of controls on private property accept that there is a need for a limit also on the individual's control of resources. Even those who promote laissez-faire, with its rejection of constraints on individual liberty, private property and free contract, seem to agree on the necessity of a mixture of public and private engagement in social life, searching for appropriate roles for markets and governments (Epstein, 1998: 3–8). The fault lines between these different shades of opinion, however, appear when the optimum balance between the two is sought, where the boundaries between the public and private are to be drawn. As ever, this line is a contested and hotly debated boundary.

BOUNDARY AS A MEANS OF SUBDIVIDING SPACE

Public and private spheres in the city entirely depend on the boundaries that separate them. Both for those who defend the private sphere from public intrusion and those who defend the public sphere from private encroachment, the erection of boundaries signifies an act of delimitation and protection. This boundary, which regulates concealment and exposure, plays a significant part in human societies. According to Nagel (1998b: 3), 'The boundary between what we reveal and what we do not, and some control over that boundary, are among the most important attributes of our humanity.' This boundary between the public and the private faces two directions: on the one hand it keeps the disruptive material out of the public arena and, on the other hand, protects private life from the public gaze.

The separate identities of the public and private realms mainly result from the construction of the boundary between them; if the boundary is removed, how can a distinction be made? The character of each side depends, to a large extent, on the way this boundary is articulated, as much as the configuration of what lies behind the boundary (Figure 2.6). To study these boundaries, it is essential to know how they are constructed, what they are made of, what they are meant to signify, and how they relate to the spheres that lie on either side. There may be no intrinsic qualities to the subsections of the space. It is only the way this space is subdivided through boundaries that creates its character. A new housing estate that is developed on an open field, for example, establishes a series of physical boundaries and assigns meaning to these subdivisions. These qualities and characters, therefore, are constructed through the process of boundary setting, which is a form of definition. By defining space, enclosing it within boundaries which separate the public and the private, the social relations take a spatial form; a concrete and relatively fixed representation of constantly changing social phenomena.

From this perspective, city building is essentially a boundary setting exercise. The space of the city is shaped by many forms and levels of boundaries, each with

2.6 Boundaries are systems of signs which symbolize the separation of two realms. The character of each side depends, to a large extent, on the way this boundary is articulated (Los Angeles, USA)

multi-level configurations and meanings. It is a process through which space is constantly divided and reshaped in new forms. A living city witnesses, throughout its history, constant change in its spatial configurations, shaped by changing boundaries which define and redefine areas to have different functions and meanings, such as those expressed in public or private distinction.

In ancient Greece, the law was identified with the boundary line that separated one household from the other. This was an actual space, a no-one's land, which separated the two properties, as the two buildings were not permitted to touch. The notion of the law and the hedge were closely associated with each other for the Greeks, whose word for law, *nomos*, derived from *nemein*, which meant to distribute, to possess (what has been distributed), and to dwell (Arendt, 1958: 63). The law of the polis, the city-state, was quite literally a wall, which enclosed a number of households living in a political community. The Greek word *polis*, the Roman word *urbs*, the German word *Zaun* and the English word 'town' all originated from the notion of a 'ring-wall', a 'circle', a surrounding fence. This was also the case in ancient China, as we shall see in Chapter 7. The Romans even had a god for the boundary, Terminus, whom they revered highly (Arendt, 1958: 63–4). It was the boundary that demarcated a notion of household and group of households who formed a town or a city. The separation of public from private, an essential part of the constitution of society, depended on the erection and protection of boundaries.

> What prevented the *polis* from violating the private lives of its citizens and made it hold sacred the boundaries surrounding each property was not respect for private property as we understand it, but the fact that without owning a house a man could not participate in the affairs of the world because he had no location in it which was properly his own. Even Plato, whose political plans foresaw the abolition of private property and an extension of the public sphere to the point of annihilating private life altogether, still speaks with great reverence of Zeus Herkeios, the protector of border lines, and calls the *horoi*, the boundaries between one estate and another, divine, without seeing any contradiction. (Arendt, 1958: 29–30)

The barriers between the two realms are used to shape social relations and spatial arrangements. These boundaries are rooted in particular social and historical contexts. They are controlled by society, through peaceful means or forced agreements, and have evolved and transformed throughout history to create particular forms of distinction. Remove this distinction between the public and private spheres and you have reshaped the entire society, as the communists believed they could do. The Berlin Wall separated two worlds from each other on the basis of their approach to private property (Figure 2.7). On the eastern side of the wall, there was a world in which private property was confiscated in the name of public interest. On the western side, there was a world in which private property was the foundation of social relations. The fact that people on both sides of the wall helped demolish it showed that such strict separation was not tenable and that this was an imposed boundary restricting the personal freedoms of most inhabitants of the city. The freedom of movement that the wall prevented was closely associated with the different approaches to the private control of space.

The same dynamics of the social realm may apply to the political realm. In liberal democratic politics, the existence of a dividing line between the public and private realms is a normative notion, where it is important for all to see that the line is kept clear. Nolan's report on Standards in Public Life (Nolan, 1995), a report commissioned by the British Prime Minister to investigate the conduct of public officials, for example, rejects the notion of 'grey areas' as 'a rationalization of morally dubious behaviour' (p. 16). The report defines seven principles of public life: self-lessness, integrity, objectivity, accountability, openness, honesty and leadership

2.7 The Berlin Wall separated two worlds from each other on the basis of their approach to private property (Berlin, Germany)

(p. 14). Selflessness refers to the main boundary between the public and private realms: interest. Holders of public office are expected to take decisions on the basis of public interest and not their own financial or material gain. They should have the honesty of declaring their private interests. Integrity refers to the same boundary, as it asks public officers to avoid putting themselves under any financial or other obligation to outside individuals or organizations that might influence their decision-making. Objectivity asks them to make their choices on merit, when making public appointments, awarding contracts and recommending individuals for rewards and benefits. Holders of public office are expected to be open about, and accountable for, their decisions and actions. They should give reasons for their actions, be prepared to submit themselves for appropriate scrutiny, and should promote and support these principles by leadership and example. The seven principles, then, seem to refer to separation of public and private interests as well as openness and accountability. The boundary between the public and private realms, therefore, is constructed through insisting on separation of interests and keeping the public realm accountable to all and open for scrutiny.

The boundary between the public and the private, as any other form of boundary, is an expression of a power that can subdivide space, give its subdivisions different meanings, and expect the others to share these meanings by believing in them. While the construction of such boundaries was crucial in the development of national states, they were not all successful enterprises. Many ethnic and linguistic communities, for example, are divided by national borders. For them, the narratives of nationalism that have legitimized the national borders make less sense than for the majority ethnic and religious groups who established these narratives. From the subdivisions inside the home to those at international levels, the establishment of a boundary signifies the power of defining space, and as such will have those who are satisfied by boundaries, as well as those who are discontented. The way forward could not be to abolish all distinctions and boundaries to create a formless chaos, in which the weak will suffer most; but to create sufficient flexibility to allow a dialogue between what is inside and what lies outside, and to allow the possibility of redrawing boundaries always to exist.

BOUNDARY AS A MEANS OF COMMUNICATION

As much as it is a means of separating the two realms and protecting them from each other, the boundary is indeed a site of interface and communication between them. A gate in a wall is the starting point of both the interior of a house and of the outside world of the street. At times, therefore, a boundary is part of both sides of the divide or of none, as it forms a threshold. The boundary can find an ambiguous character, which in some circumstances may be welcome, as it can promote permeability and social interaction. In the articulation of spatial boundaries, there may be an emphasis on creating links between the two realms, so that social interaction and vitality can be generated in urban space. A prime example of such an articulation is provided by the colonnades that line streets and squares (Figure 2.8). Another example is the front porch of a house, which turns the boundary of the private sphere into an area of interaction and communication. In the final analysis, however, the definition of the public and private falls on the question of ownership. The boundaries are created to separate the space owned and controlled by individuals from those beyond such control and under the control of the society as a whole.

The differentiation between the different sides of a property is one of the main tools for defining the character of the public and private spheres. Whereas the front of a house, for example, provides a public face for the inhabitants, the back of the house may be its less desirable, more private façade, where the quality of material is inferior, rubbish bins are kept and, in the past, the coal was kept or the horses passed through. On the contrary, the public face of the building has the best building materials and quality of craft, and is kept cleaner and for more general purposes.

While liberal politics promote a normative separation of the public and private realms, the actual circumstances of public life have created conditions of increased ambiguity. The boundary between the two realms is actively made ambivalent, so that public–private partnerships can be formed to undertake a range of activities. The working methods of public organizations are transformed to be made similar to the private sector, to increase efficiency and flexibility. The boundary between public and private spaces is made ambivalent so that social encounters are encouraged. At the same time, the two realms are kept apart, so that private interests do not undermine public interest and the public realm does not intrude in the private sphere. The ambivalence between the two realms is, therefore, at once seen as positive and negative. It becomes the task of the boundaries to articulate this apparently impossible coexistence of ambivalence and clarity.

The more ambiguous and articulate the boundary, the more civilized a place appears to be. When the two realms are separated by rigid walls, the line of interaction becomes arid, communication limited, and the social life poorer for that. Fortresses that sit on hilltops and are protected by high walls are the extreme cases of attempting to control relations between the two realms. Many may treat their homes in the same way, seeing them, as the proverb has it, as their castles, which implies the control of boundaries by force to protect them from the invasion of others. Large institutions in cities, such as shopping malls, department stores, banks etc. are new forms of these fortresses, where large numbers of people are

2.8 The articulation of spatial boundaries, as exemplified by colonnades and front porches, promote interaction between the private and public spheres and the boundary becomes a means of communication (Paris, France)

admitted inside but the boundaries of these institutions are carefully controlled. These are private properties that are defended against possible intruders and undesirables, creating a managed environment, where entrances and exits are clearly inviting but the rest of the boundaries left potentially similar to a fortress.

We keep the public and private separate, for very few of us would wish to live in an undistinguishable common space. But the main point is that separation of public and private is not often, and should not be, treated as a black and white distinction. Especially in space, the lines that divide the two are porous and ambiguous. This may not be the case in law, where private properties are clearly protected by documentation and the support of the legal system. Ambiguity occurs in practice, where the boundaries are frequently crossed for a variety of purposes.

The parcels of land are clearly delimited and protected by law, which also describes the conditions under which access to private property can be secured (Aldridge, 1997). The landowner is not under a general legal duty to erect fences along the boundaries of the private property, apart from certain circumstances (Aldridge, 1997: 60). In general, however, the clarity that fences create are thought to generate better neighbourly relations, as the famous phrase by Robert Frost in 'Mending Wall' puts it, 'Good fences make good neighbours' (quoted in Aldridge, 1997: 1).

Libertarians, such as Nozick (1974), emphasize the centrality of boundaries, demanding for protecting them vigorously and guarding them against boundary crossings by individuals who may invade the space of others. In practice, however, boundaries are not so rigid, but rather 'semipermeable' (Epstein, 1998: 187). In everyday practice throughout history, many instances can be found where boundaries are crossed by the agreement between neighbours. The boundaries between agricultural fields in the Middle Ages, for example, were subject to negotiation for shared use of space to allow the plough to turn round. Another example is the general duty of each neighbour to provide lateral support for the land of the neighbour, e.g. by not digging out land adjacent to the boundary, which would have resulted in the subsidence of the neighbour's land. Also the so-called rule of 'live and let live' means that 'all individuals have to put up with a certain amount of noise and interference from their neighbours, on condition that the neighbours reciprocate in kind' (Epstein, 1998: 191). These and other similar circumstances show how property boundaries are legally protected but crossed by agreement, making them semipermeable. Epstein (1998: 190) suggests a general approach:

> The best way to approach a boundary is to endow it with a certain presumptive validity, and then to identify the circumstances in which its strictness can be relaxed to the mutual advantage of the parties on both sides of the line. Paradoxi-

cally, a world with semipermeable boundaries can strengthen the institution of private property.

As we saw from the psychologists' research into territory, the separation of territories into public and private is not absolute and can vary according to the number of people involved, the size of the place and the length of occupation, in other words depending on the conditions of society, space and time. Public and private territories become shades rather than dichotomies, their boundaries socially constructed and permeable rather than sacred and natural. In law and politics, however, there is demand for the clarity of these boundaries and the maintenance of the dichotomy, as a means of protecting the individual. The social and psychological shades of understanding and action in the lived world are here taken to be inappropriate in a normative, ideal framework of public–private separation. In this context, Epstein's suggestion is a compromise between clarity and ambiguity, between ideal and existing distinction between the two realms.

INTERDEPENDENCE OF THE PUBLIC AND THE PRIVATE

At its core, the relationship between the public and private goes to the heart of a key concern of social philosophy: the relationship between the individual and society. The public–private relations address the desired balance between the two and whether and how each can and should establish a distinctive realm. On the one hand, the question is: How can a realm be established that caters for the cultural and biological needs of a social individual to be protected from the intrusion of the others? On the other hand, the question is: How can a realm be established that caters for the needs of society and be protected from the encroachments of individuals?

This formulation has led to a normative tension between two camps. On the one hand there are those who argue for expanding the realm of the individual, promoting various forms of individual freedom and arguing for limiting the sphere of the public control. For example, mass media and new information and communication technologies are seen as capable of endangering the values of privacy and identity for individuals (Post, 1989). Liberalism, indeed, 'may be said largely to have been an argument about where the boundaries of [the] private sphere lie, according to what principles they are to be drawn, whence interference derives and how it is to be checked' (Lukes, quoted in Wacks, 1993: xii). On the other hand, there are those who promote expanding the public realm, with stricter and more far-reaching public controls (e.g. Etzioni, 1995). One version of the gap between these views is reflected in the tension between libertarians and communitarians.

Depending on the side of the argument, public and private spheres can be defined in a positive or negative way. If the aim is to protect privacy, it finds a positive value and publicity needs to be kept at bay as a negative force. On the other hand, when private interests are on the offensive, the protection of public realm gives it a positive value and assigns a negative interpretation to the private sphere. This tension can be traced back to the emergence of the nation state and theories of sovereignty in the sixteenth and seventeenth centuries, when the idea of a distinctly public realm emerged (Wacks, 1993: xi; Habermas, 1989). To counterbalance this development, there was at the same time a concern to delineate a private sphere free from the encroachment of the state.

Understanding the interdependence of the notions of public and private poses a major challenge to urban design. Is urban design taking properly into account the private sphere and its significance, or is it mainly emphasizing the public realm embellishment without due consideration as to what lies behind the boundaries that enclose it (Figure 2.9)? Is a lack of attention to private sphere part of a new form of specialism, a division of labour between the architect and the urban designer? Urban design itself emerged partly as a response to the neglect of public realm. Is it now focusing too narrowly on elements of public realm so that it neglects the private realm and its importance? Or is it taking private sphere for granted, that it will be looked after by private interests? In any case, the public and the private can only exist as an interrelated set and any design effort that does not see them in this close interdependence runs the risk of being limited and ineffective.

CONCLUSION

Private space is an individuated portion of social space, a part of space that individuals enclose to control for their exclusive use. It provides a physical home for the body, with its mental or portable personal spaces that were discussed in the previous chapter. This control offers humans social and psychological wellbeing by giving them an outlet for exerting their will on the outside world, to express and tame their aggression, and to find a location in the social world. The control of enclosed, private space offers the individual an ability to communicate with others through becoming a means of expression of their will, identity and power. It also offers them the ability to be let alone by being protected from the intrusion of others. The establishment of a private sphere offers the individual the ability to regulate the balance of concealment and exposure, the balance of access to oneself and communication with others. Major moral problems arise, however, when the creation of a private sphere of their own is not possible for some while others

2.9 Is urban design taking properly into account the private sphere and its significance, or is it mainly emphasizing the public realm embellishment without due consideration as to what lies behind the boundaries that enclose it? (Aarhus, Denmark)

expand theirs relentlessly. This is when private sphere is no longer a response to a basic social and biological need.

The boundaries that separate the two realms are the most visible spatial manifestation of this division of social life. Architectural and geographical articulation of the boundary is thus the embodiment of a divide, the signifiers of a social organization. The challenge of boundary setting, i.e. the challenge of city building, is to erect the boundaries between the two realms so that they combine clarity with permeability, acknowledging the interdependence of the two realms, and supporting both sides of the boundary.

We saw in the last chapter that a new notion of the individual was needed, one in which the autonomous self was seen to be constructed by the forces of the social and biological and that universal norms were needed to be exposed to a critique of difference. In this chapter, we have followed this line to see how the relationship between individual and society is regulated by the designation of public and private spheres and by the construction of boundaries between them. In this sense, the critique that was needed has been built into this structure of the public and private, each limiting the other by articulating conditions in which they can flourish and limits beyond which they may make no more sense. A critique of the private from the viewpoint of the public, and at the same time a critique of the public from the viewpoint of the private are essential ingredients of a constantly readjusting relationship between the individual and society.

Chapter 3
Intimate space of the home

In this chapter, we look at the home, which is widely considered to be the symbol and materialization of private realm. This will be done through two different but intertwined dimensions, which look at the interplay of inside–outside and the dynamics of the inside of private space. First, the home is the private intimate space that is separated, and protects its members, from the public impersonal outside, as reflected in the social institution of the household and the historic process of the rise of the modern family. Second, the inside of the home is also a socio-spatial world in which changing interpersonal relations and physical configurations mean privacy can be a complex and contested notion, as reflected in the changing shape of the family and interior space of the home.

THE SYMBOL OF PRIVACY

Home is the spatial unit that combines a number of traits of private sphere, as we have so far discussed. It provides personal space, a territory, a place for being protected from the natural elements, as well as from the scrutiny of others, a location in the social world to engage in social life, which is socially acknowledged and legalized. In addition to being a haven for the individual, it is also a place for a social unit, which has for long been the family. It is therefore also a place of living for a handful of people in a close, intimate relationship (Figure 3.1). It provides a small group with a territory, which has historically been essential for the reproduction of the species, to accommodate biological life processes, as well as a place which is meaningful and satisfying to the psychological needs of individuals. As such, the home epitomizes private sphere, even though it is not the only form of private sphere possible. The realm of the household and the home is the institutionalized arena of privacy.

Home has been praised as the key node of society, as the place where identities are shaped and memories are rooted. It is a centre of intimacy. Intimacy, as Nagel asserted, 'creates personal relations protected from the general gaze, permitting us to lose our inhibitions and expose ourselves to one another' (1998b: 5). According to Saunders (1990: 311),

3.1 Home is the symbol of privacy, a place where a handful of people live in a close, intimate relationship (Trabzon, Turkey)

The home is a core institution in modern society. It shelters the smallest viable unit of social organization – the household – and basic patterns of social relations are forged, reproduced and changed within it. It is the place with which individuals can most readily identify and it easily lends itself to the symbolic expression of personal identity. It offers both physical and psychological shelter and comfort. It is the place where the self can be expressed outside of social roles and where the individual can exert autonomy away from the coercive gaze of the employer and the state. It is the private realm in an increasingly public and intrusive world. For many of us, its integrity is of the utmost value in our lives.

The significance of the home goes beyond its role as the physical shelter for protection from the elements and its basic functions of providing a place for rest. It has been endowed with psychological significance, with meaning that is deeply rooted in the human psyche. Bachelard, for example, searches for a meaning of the house, where the 'warm substance of intimacy resumes its form' (Bachelard, 1994: 40). The house is, as he reminds us, essentially a geometrical object and as such invites us for a rational analysis. He insists, however, that 'Inhabited space transcends geometrical space' (p. 47). As such, understanding it requires new tools and approaches. To do this, he uses a phenomenological approach in conducting an inquiry into the poetic images of the house, to enable him to go beyond what the scientist, the psychologist and the psychoanalyst can provide. He offers to 'read the house' or 'read a room', as they are 'psychological diagrams that guide writers and poets in their analysis of intimacy' (p. 38). Poetic image is, he maintains, 'a sudden salience on the surface of the psyche' (p. xv), 'independent of causality' (p. xvii), which means it cannot be understood rationally, but only through a phenomenological investigation.

In his investigation, he finds the house a nest for daydreaming, a shelter for imagining, emphasizing the significance of space for imagination and intimacy. Bachelard sets out to analyse the house as an 'intimate space', by which he means 'space that is not open to just anybody' (p. 78). The house, through providing a place for daydreaming, becomes 'one of the greatest powers of integration for the thoughts, memories and dreams of mankind' (p. 6). According to Bachelard,

If I were asked to name the chief benefit of the house, I should say: the house shelters daydreaming, the house protects the dreamer, the house allows one to dream in peace. Thought and experience are not the only things that sanction human values. The values that belong to daydreaming mark humanity in its depths. (p. 6)

The inside and outside, as manifest in the internal space of the house and the external space of the world, form a dialectic of division (pp. 211ff). On the one hand, there is the intimate interior, which is concrete and secure, even though it can be also claustrophobic. On the other hand, there is the undetermined space of the outside, which is vast and free, but also possibly agoraphobic.

The main purpose of space is to contain compressed time (p. 8). A large number of our memories, therefore, are 'housed' and to the parts of the house, especially the one we were born in, we go back in our daydreams all our lives (p. 8). The spaces of the house and its corners, such as its cellar, garret, nooks and corridors, can be analysed through the images of the house provided by the poets. The analysis of the images, however, should not lead to verifying them: 'To verify images kills them, and it is always more enriching to *imagine* than to *experience*' (p. 88).

There seems to be a number of untold and unexamined parameters underlying Bachelard's analysis of the house. Like other phenomenologists (and for that matter like Saunders, from whom the previous quotation is reproduced here), Bachelard emphasizes the individual, the first-person narrative rather than the voice of one who lives among others, especially in the interpersonal intimacy of the house. His phenomenology is that of a person who is born in a house (rather than in a hospital) and grows up there (rather than moving around from place to place), showing a degree of stability and continuity (rather than constant change), a period of long residence (rather than a highly mobile existence) that allows one to develop slowly a deep attachment to a place. Furthermore, this is an imaginative person (rather than a practical one), a person with happy memories of this place (rather than distressing memories of dysfunctional relationships) so that one wishes to daydream about it, rather than suppressing it into a black hole in the unconscious. Added to these is a nostalgia about the house, as the city-dwelling analyst is deprived of living in a house, as Bachelard must have felt: 'In Paris there are no houses, and the inhabitants of the big city live in superimposed boxes' (p. 26).

The home, therefore appears to be a point of reference through which the individual finds a place in the world, as testified by the vast literature produced on the subject. Considering this, however, we may wonder about the position of the homeless. How do people who are deprived of this point of reference navigate their world?. How far is the right to privacy, as mentioned by the Universal Declaration of Human Rights, which we saw in the last chapter, accessible to them (Figure 3.2)?

3.2 If the home is the point of reference through which individuals find a place in the world, how do the homeless navigate the world and what rights of privacy do they enjoy? (Los Angeles, USA)

HOME AS A HOMOGENEOUS PRIVATE SPACE?

The question of public–private relationships in dwellings is often seen as the way the house as a private realm is separated from the outside world. The house is controlled by the household as its property, owned or rented, and thus is separated from what is beyond the household's control. What is within this boundary is considered a private realm, as established by various legal and cultural boundaries.

The way dwellings relate to each other and to the streets and open spaces are essential features of a housing layout, in which the problems of maintaining an optimum level of privacy is raised. For a long time, the houses in their settings were given a different treatment on their front and back elevations. The front elevation was considered a public elevation and therefore received all the attention in details and ornamentation. The back elevation, however, was built with cheaper materials and belonged to a private realm. These different treatments were extended to the front and back gardens, where different levels of attention and maintenance may be noted. The Essex Design Guide, for example, stressed the distinction between the public and private zones of the house in its setting: in the public zone, the living room should be given a reasonable degree of privacy; in the private zone, however, a high degree of privacy is required for living rooms and an outdoor sitting area (Essex County Council, 1973: 29–34).

Houses can be seen as distinctive spaces in which individuals come together in intimate relationships, claiming the control of these spaces for privacy and comfort. These individuals, even though small in number, form an interpersonal forum that is less private than their own private worlds, creating a combination of private, semi-private, and at time even semi-public spaces. Therefore, the relationship between them takes various forms and, subsequently, the space they use for these relationships takes various degrees of privacy. According to the criteria of access, agency and interest (Benn and Gaus, 1983), it might be shown that the public parts of the house are accessible to, run by, and in the interest of, all the members of the household, as distinctive from the individuals' private rooms that are often controlled by them.

Also, the public realm of the outside finds its way inside the house in the form of visitors, some of whom are closer to the householders than others. Both these internal and external contacts and relationships mean that the dwelling is not an entity entirely cut off from the outside world. It is possible to trace a continuum of relationships from the most private to the most public, all within a realm that is often considered private. From the front of the house, which is its most public point, an entrance leads to the public parts of the dwelling. The entrance is controlled by the residents and is the gateway between the enclosed realm of the interior and the world outside. The public parts of the house, such as the living and dining rooms, are those spaces where all the residents have open access and communicate with each other and with visitors. The private rooms, such as bedrooms, which are often separated from the public parts by doors, distance, or by difference of levels, are on the other hand the private realm of the individuals often not easily accessible even to the other members of the household. These spaces create a continuum in which each space can be slightly more or less private than the others. However, the two ends of this continuum are entirely separated from each other: bedrooms are as far as possible from the entrance.

The form of the relationship between the public and the private, and the concepts of privacy and control of space may vary due to the cultural and behavioural patterns of the household. Depending on whether personal gratification and reinforcement of self-identity are at the core of behaviour mechanisms, or preference for the group is dominant, habits and forms of use of space vary (Howel and Tentokali, 1989). In all cases, however, a distinction appears to be made between private and public at home, even though this may not be institutionalized by phys-ical forms and functional allocation.

The existence of a continuum shows how the organization of space inside the house is influenced by the way it relates to the outside world, to the public domain (Figure 3.3). This is also evidence of how it is not possible to see the house as an entirely private space, as it is organized with two distinctive characters. First, it is expected to be open to the outside world in a controlled way. Second, it is meant to be suitable for communication between residents, which can have a public dimension, especially as the number of residents increases. Both of these characteristics, it may be argued, have existed ever since human beings have claimed or built spaces as their dwellings. It is a well known, although not always well observed, principle in housing design to be aware of this variety in the degree of privacy and its requirements to provide comfortable and useful spaces.

In each period, however, the relationship between the public and private inside dwellings has taken a different form. To understand the contemporary rela-tionship of these two, it is necessary to look at the way the house developed during modern times. The way the social structures, especially the household's configura-tion, and the house types have transformed are of particular interest in this investi-gation. More specifically, the modern process of functionalization of space has had a central role in redefining the interior space of the dwellings, whereby private and public realms have been gradually separated in specified spaces, creating a new set of relationships inside the house.

THE BIRTH OF THE INTIMATE SPACE

The origins of the modern family house can be traced back to the medieval bour-geois house. The poor, in town or in countryside, lived in very bad conditions, without sanitation or water, with almost no furniture and few possessions, well until the beginning of the twentieth century. That is why the concepts of home, family, as well as domesticity, comfort and privacy are seen as the principal achievements of the bourgeois age. The merchants and tradesmen, who lived in walled towns and were relatively free from the power of feudal lords, had a different pattern of life from the rest of society. '[U]nlike the aristocrat, who lived in a fortified castle, or the cleric, who lived in a monastery, or the serf, who lived in a hovel, the bourgeois lived in a house' (Rybczynski, 1986: 25).

In the Middle Ages and long afterwards, there were no boundaries between professional and private life (Ariés, 1973: 354). Working and living were combined in the typical bourgeois townhouse of the fourteenth century, where living quarters consisted of not a series of rooms but a single large chamber, a hall. This was a

3.3 The organization of space inside the house is influenced by the way it relates to the outside world, to the public domain (Aarhus, Denmark)

place with only a few pieces of furniture, which would be moved around to make possible cooking, eating, entertaining guests, conducting business, and sleeping. In the absence of restaurants, bars and hotels, the home was a public place, a meeting place for a range of activities, as well as a residence for a large household, which could include employees, servants, apprentices, friends and protégés (Figure 3.4). Life was, indeed, 'lived in public' (Ariés, 1973: 392). The notions of privacy, function and comfort as understood today did not exist. The density of society, where people lived and worked together in houses that were open at all hours to the visitors, left no space for the family as a separate entity and privacy was virtually unknown or impossible to find. Places and events had meaning, which included functions, but also other attributes such as beauty, age, style, etc. A medieval house, like church bells, swords and cannons, was given a name and thus was personified, a practice which has continued till now but has now largely been overtaken by numbers, which offer anonymity and represent economic rather than emotional value (Rybczynski, 1986: 25–35).

The change in the concept of family can be analysed, as Ariés (1973) does, from the changing attitude to children. In the Middle Ages, children were mixed with adults from an early stage. Children from all classes were sent out to other families, to work as apprentices, to learn good manners and skills. The relationship between parents and children was thus limited, as the family was a moral and social reality, rather than a sentimental one. The extension of school education from the fifteenth century started to change all that, and the modern notion of family emerged, which placed the child at its centre. With school education, starting with the middle classes, theoretical education replaced the old practical apprenticeships and the parents could keep their children near home and establish stronger sentimental relationship with them. As a result of this rising tide of intimacy, the concept of equality among children developed, as against the supremacy of the eldest son.

Between the end of the Middle Ages and the seventeenth century, a major transformation of the family took place. Rather than being sent away, children found a central place in the family. They became an indispensable element of everyday life, where concern for their health, education and future life was a central theme. Despite these changes, the house was still the centre of dense relations with the rest of society. The big house of the middle-class family was a centre of *sociability*, open to the obtrusive world of friends, clients and servants.

In seventeenth-century France, therefore,

Material success, social conventions and collective amusements were not separate activities as they are today, any more than professional life, private life and social life were separate functions. The main thing was to maintain social relations with

3.4 The origins of the modern family house can be traced back to the medieval bourgeois house, which worked as a public place, a node for a range of activities, as well as a residence for a large household, which could include employees, servants, apprentices, friends and protégés (Oxford, UK)

the whole of the group into which one had been born, and to better one's position by skilful use of this network of relations. To make a success of life was not to make a fortune, or at least that was of secondary importance; it was above all to win a more honourable standing in a society whose members all saw one another, heard one another and met one another nearly every day. (Ariés, 1973: 363)

As a result, a great emphasis was placed on friendship and on sociability, on how good manners (or 'civility' as they called it) should be learned and how conversations be conducted. What mattered was the reputation of a person and therefore mastery over communications with others.

Alongside the appearance of the modern individuated self after the Middle Ages, the house changed from a node in public life to a setting for the development of the private life of the individual and the nuclear family. As a typical bourgeois house in seventeenth-century Paris shows, space was subdivided into a larger number of rooms. Even though most activities continued to take place in a large room, a *salle*, a move towards concern for privacy can be detected, especially in separating the servants from the masters. The bourgeois house was becoming primarily a residence, separated from the place of work. It was a more private place, although privacy inside the home remained relatively unimportant. In larger houses, for example, there were no corridors and each room was connected to the next, so that all traffic (family members, guests and servants) had to pass through every room to get to the next. Here the house was transformed into a setting for social theatre, a stage, where appearances mattered more than privacy (Rybczynski, 1986: 38–41).

By the eighteenth century, however, the modern family is born, i.e. parents and children who are happy to live as a group separated from the rest of society. The isolated group of parents and children opposes the society and invests all its energy on helping the children to rise in the world as individuals (Ariés, 1973: 389–90). A private space was created for the emerging family, through the rearrangement of the house, reform of manners, and exclusion of others. The rooms multiplied, connected now through corridors and specialized to cater for different functions. Manners were reformed, so that, for example, calling on a friend or acquaintance at any time of the day and without warning was no longer welcome. Others, i.e. servants, clients and friends, were excluded from the nuclear family, which was now reduced to parents and children. The house of the bourgeois family became the place of intimacy, of intimate relations between parents and children. This model, which was initially limited to the nobility, the middle classes, the richer artisans and the richer labourers, was eventually extended to the rest of society.

As the nuclear family advanced, the old sociability retreated. Writing in 1904,

Hermann Muthesius saw the wide use of corridors in Victorian England as a reflection of the 'diminishing desire for sociability', which was gradually replaced by the 'desire to live quietly, in self-sufficiency, secluded from the hubbub of the city' (quoted in Olsen, 1986: 103). Private family life was reinforced at the expense of neighbourly relations, friendships and traditional contracts. The public character of the house was lost and some of its functions were taken up by the club, the café (in France) and the public house (in Britain). The streets and squares of the towns (in France) were used through everyday routines, turning into promenades where people met one another, as is the case now in Italian towns. The modern manners were reformed so as to make it possible to break away from the pressures of society. The house became an exclusive place for the life of a nuclear family cut off from the world and offering protection from it. It was now the social environment in which, together with the school, the future generations were brought up, rather than in the network of relations that connected medieval households together. In this sense, as Ariès argues (1973: 393), 'It is not individualism which has triumphed, but the family.'

The modern family emerged in the eighteenth century, pioneered by the middle class and rooted in the long process of change that started at the end of the Middle Ages. Modern family members kept themselves apart from the others, withdrawing from the polymorphous society so that they could reorganize themselves separately in homogenous environments, where lower classes were kept at a distance. The middle-class neighbourhoods of the modern city are a manifestation of the emergence of the modern family and its desire to live a separate life. Ariès summarizes the way social and spatial change went hand in hand from dense heterogeneity to segmented homogeneity, creating an intolerance towards, and insistence on, uniformity as manifested in the concepts of family, class and race.

> The old society concentrated the maximum number of ways of life into the minimum of space and accepted, if it did not impose, the bizarre juxtaposition of the most widely different classes. The new society, on the contrary, provided each way of life with a confined space in which it was understood that the dominant features should be respected, and that each person had to resemble a conventional model, an ideal type, and never depart from it under pain of excommunication. (Ariès, 1973: 399).

EVOLUTION OF THE HOUSE TYPES

The rise of the modern family has paralleled a process of differentiation and specialization in the organization of space in the house: from a period when most of the activities of large households took place in a few communal spaces to a time when small households use a number of functionally defined spaces for a multiplicity of activities. There has also been a separation of dwellings from each other, creating new house types, from the townhouse to the terraced, semi-detached and detached houses, as well as flats.

In large cities of France, the emergence of the modern family occurred alongside a change from the bourgeois townhouse to the family apartment. This was a process of fragmentation and multiplication of domestic space that accompanied the processes of urbanization, the continued presence of city walls that prevented the horizontal spread of the city, and a cultural adjustment to apartment living, which had to be supplemented by an active public realm of the streets, squares and cafés.

In Britain, this process of multiplication and fragmentation took a different shape. Despite the variety of architectural styles throughout the eighteenth and the nineteenth centuries in Britain, this period is signified by the establishment and continuation of a main house type, the terraced house, with a basic layout. Such was the predominance of this type that by the early twentieth century, at least 87 per cent of dwellings in England and Wales were terraced houses (Muthesius, 1982). Against the background of this framework of unity and continuity, there were clear processes of diversity and differentiation in the social and physical organization of houses and their inhabitants. Both of these processes of unity and diversity continued to affect the practices of the twentieth century.

After the Great Fire of 1666 in London and the introduction of rigid fire laws, along with the penetrating spirit of new ideas from Europe and the emergence of new ways of developing cities, the Georgian house type emerged with a distinctive character. With the increasing demand for housing, especially near London, the rise of speculative builders who developed large numbers of houses for sale, and the involvement of the landowners who could supply large parcels of land for urban development, the new house type became the standard pattern around the country during the eighteenth and early nineteenth centuries. The style, which was distinguished by simple brick façades, was similarly, although with different sizes, used for all classes of people (Cave, 1981).

The formality and simplicity of the Georgian house gave way to the informality of the picturesque, when the overcrowded cities were seen as contrasting with the romanticized countryside. The Victorian period saw the proliferation of ornament and the diversity of styles borrowed from past and distant civilizations. However, this quest for diversity that flourished in the nineteenth century did not fundamentally transform the basic type of terraced house. Within two centuries from the introduction of this type, the vast majority of the British people lived in terraced houses.

This unifying character across space, time and, in the Georgian era, social hierarchies, was partly a result of the detailed legal requirements leading to, and in line with, increasingly standardized production processes and therefore standardized designs, even though the internal layout was not originally standardized. The standardized processes were enhanced by mass production of brick as the main building material in the nineteenth century. A combination of the characteristics of the production process, social status and architectural elements associated with this house type allowed the continued building and use of terraced house to continue for such a long time (Muthesius, 1982).

Georgian terraced houses were basically formed of a room at the front and one at the back. On the ground floor a passage led from the entrance to the stairs at one side of the rear, which allowed the front room on upper floors to use the full width of the plot. In the nineteenth century, many variations of this basic layout were introduced but none of them changed the essential features of the terraced house, whose flexibility to be laid out at different lengths, depths and heights ensured its continuity (Figure 3.5).

3.5 Terraced houses combined a process of differentiation and specialization of interior domestic space with a regard for the public sphere, which required modest appearances (Dublin, Ireland)

By the mid-twentieth century, the terraced house had lost its appeal, to the extent that the Dudley Report (Ministry of Health, 1944: 19) noticed 'that in most parts of the country there is a prejudice against terraced houses and a preference for the semi-detached'. The reasons for these objections included lack of privacy and noise, problems that the Report felt could be solved with cavity walls and the proper placing of halls and staircases.

The suburban, non-basement semi-detached house became the norm after the decline in popularity of terraced houses. In fact, what has been termed sub-urban style has been the style in which the huge majority of houses in the twentieth-century were built. The twentieth-century suburban style has continued with the arrangement of two rooms (or one large room) in connection with a kitchen and an entrance as the core of the public section of the dwelling. The semi-detached house's popularity in Britain started to give way to detached houses, which formed the majority of the houses built in the early 1990s (Gray, 1994). In the United States, the detached house was a centre piece of the suburban life style from early on.

This sequence of house types from terraced to semi-detached to detached houses during the last two centuries shows a process of separation of individual dwellings from each other. This separation was the result of a pragmatic process of responding to, as well as setting the limits of, the market by house builders. It coincided with rising living standards and mobility of the population and a reduction in the size of the households. As against this pragmatic design process, which kept its continuity, there was a, now interrupted, attempt by the rationalist introduction of high rise flats, in which the dwellings were grouped together vertically. Flats never became popular in Britain from the very beginning (Ministry of Health, 1944). The aesthetics of grouping the units together, however, has continued to be powerful as terraced houses are still found to offer greater architectural opportunity than semi-detached houses. The popular house types of the last century, semi-detached and detached houses, shared their general internal arrangement with the terraced house: in the separation of public and private areas and the functional differentiation of space.

SPATIAL DIFFERENTIATION OF DOMESTIC SPACE

It is possible, therefore, to see a continuity and unity in the house types for almost two centuries, only to be challenged by a gradual disintegration of the units in an individualization process. The diversity that was accompanied with, and complementing or causing, this continuity and transformation can be followed in a number of processes of disintegration and differentiation. First, there was a process of disintegration of extended households and the emergence of the nuclear family especially after the eighteenth century. The new type families developed a strong desire to establish an independent arena with a private sphere of their own and a separate identity, as partly manifested in their preference to live apart on separate pieces of land. As Habermas (1989) shows, a clear separation between the public and private spheres has emerged since the seventeenth and the eighteenth centuries. In the eighteenth-century Georgian house the differentiation between the public and the private parts of the house is more stressed than in the medieval period, when most activities took place within the common space of the house. As the typical plans of the Georgian houses show, there was some functional separation of the spaces inside the house: kitchen, parlour, living room and bedrooms being the main ones. This functional specialization was identified by a traveller who described the Georgian houses in 1810 as 'narrow houses, three or four storeys high – one for eating, one for sleeping, a third for company, a fourth underground for kitchen, a fifth perhaps at the top for the servants' (Louis Simond quoted in Cave, 1981: 206).

However, it was in the Victorian era that the strict separation between the public and the private in society was directly reflected in the organization of space inside the house. Along with this process, there was a disintegration of the pre-modern social bonds to be gradually replaced with abstract, commodified social relations, giving rise to a process of individualization partly expressed in the diversification of architectural styles and in the functional differentiation of domestic space. As the disintegration of social bonds and the individualization process threatened the existing social structures, there were attempts to promote new bonds and socialization processes, as best manifested in the strong family ethics of the Victorian period. The building of terraced houses was seen to be one such measure, as it was thought to lead to new forms of social bonds and new arenas for social discourse. An example can be found in 1842, when J.C. Loudon advocated that cottages should be laid out in rows: 'The cottage should be placed alongside a public road as being more cheerful than a solitary situation and in order that the cottager may enjoy the applause of the public when he has his garden in good order and keeping' (quoted in Cave, 1981: 212).

Parallel with this process of transformation of social relationships, there was a process of stratification and differentiation. The establishment and expansion of the Empire and the industrial revolution caused concentrations of wealth and of people. These concentrations brought new forms of social and spatial relationships. Some of these relationships were clearly marked by new forms of stratification, as evident in the social and physical distance between the labourers and the industrialists. However, there were other forms of differentiation that followed more conscious attempts at classification. These conscious attempts could be descriptive, as in the scientific drive to understand the newly explored, far-away lands and their geography, flora and fauna. They could also be normative, such as attempts to create differentiation in domestic architecture.

One of the major processes of differentiation was the separation of home and work, which made possible the suburbanization process, a hallmark of the modern age. This separation coincided with the desire to separate the public and private spheres in general, defining the house as the private sphere, the refuge where men who constituted the public sphere could return to for comfort. It also coincided with the separation of public and private spheres inside the house. Robert Kerr, in a book published in 1864, *The Gentleman's House*, found privacy to be the primary concern of the house.

> It is a first principle with the better classes of English people that the Family Rooms should be essentially private, and as much as possible the Family Thoroughfares. It becomes the foremost of all maxims, therefore, that however small the establishment, that the Servants' Department shall be separated from the Main House, so that what passes on either side of the boundary shall be both invisible and inaudible on the other. (quoted in Boys *et al.*, 1984: 64)

Kerr showed similar concern for the preservation of privacy in his designs for working-class model dwellings, where bedrooms were separated from the living room. Here balconies were introduced for 'the preservation of domestic privacy and independence of each distinct family and the disconnection of their apartments so as to effectively prevent the communication of contagious diseases' (quoted in Boys *et al.*, 1984: 63).

What was promoted was the separation of the servants from the family, the children from the parents, and the different sexes from each other amongst children and servants (Figure 3.6). Inherent in this separation was to institute hierarchies in which obedience was secured of servant to the family, children to parents and women to men. Creation of physical distance mirrored the desire to create social distance and was the vehicle of this new hierarchical order. Space was the key to the establishment of a new set of power relations. This separation that took away the functional mixture of the house and reorganized it on a more functionalist basis was part of an overriding principle in house design in the nineteenth century. According to this principle, which was adhered to across the social strata and preceded the functionalism of modernist design, every function needed to be allocated a separate space, each also associated with a public–private distinction. For Robert Kerr, 'the dining-room, the drawing-room, the library, the billiard-room, and the hall and staircase, are of a public character', while

3.6 The Victorian house reflected the strict separation of the public and the private spheres, separating servants from the family, children from the parents, and different sexes from each other (Manchester, UK)

'the gentleman's room, sometimes the morning-room, and in all cases the boudoir . . . are strictly private', with bedrooms and the nursery having 'a special privacy' (quoted in Olsen, 1986: 103). A mixture of public and private spaces now formed the house, where a number of rooms were connected through corridors and staircases, in a sense following an urban morphology of movement and repose imposed on domestic space to allow for stratification and differentiation.

Through rationalization of living patterns, bedrooms could no longer be used as a living room and their number increased to constitute the heart of the newly emerging private sphere of the house. The number of 'public' rooms, where the strangers were received and members of the family and their servants or visitors could come together, also increased and they were separated from the rest of the house. These were called 'reception rooms' in general but each had a name and a defined function: drawing-room, dining-room, breakfast-room, study, boudoir, library. The proportion of these public rooms in the house could vary from a half in the smaller houses to a third or a fourth in larger ones. In middle-sized houses with two reception rooms at front and back, the terms used for the front room could be sitting room, parlour, living room or best room, leaving the back room for ordinary living. Parlour, which became an indicator for social distinction, was a necessary part of the majority of buildings by the late nineteenth century (Muthesius, 1982: 45–8).

The nineteenth-century Parisian flats were praised in France and envied in Germany and Austria, as the height of luxury and rational deployment of facilities for elegant living. For the British observers, however, they failed in offering domestic comfort and true refinement. Writing in 1857, *Building News* commented that 'A French family may not care at all for privacy' (quoted in Olsen, 1986: 118). The Parisian flats were found to be too overcrowded and small to provide for the segregation and differentiation found in the British middle-class house. In their designs, as well as in patterns of living, however, the distinction between the public and private was clearly made.

DOMESTIC SPACE AND MASS HOUSING

In many ways the trends that had started in the nineteenth century continued in the twentieth. The middle class functional differentiation was extended to the rest of society in the millions of smaller houses that were to be built after the two world wars. This time government intervention ensured such specialization of space that was seen as a mark of relative prosperity of the society, through rationalizing the organization and production of dwelling space. To this aim, a number of standards were set to guide the large-scale housing production that took place. Three main reports in twentieth-century Britain can be seen to have set these trends, influencing the housing development and design.

The 1918 Tudor-Walters Report, which influenced a generation of house building, stressed the need for parlour houses and provision of a large living room to relieve congestion in the kitchen or scullery. Tudor-Walters Committee based many of its recommendations on the early twentieth-century garden city cottages designed by Raymond Unwin and his brother-in-law Barry Parker (Figure 3.7). It asked for the introduction of the parlour, which had become a standard feature of middle-class houses, to working class houses wherever possible, so that in all housing schemes a large proportion of houses should have parlours. Parlour was favoured as a functionally desirable room that could be used as a semi-public space with direct access to the front entrance. However, living room as the public room of the house was considered to be more important, as reflected in its desirable size, minimum 180 sq. feet (16.7 sq. metres), compared to the minimum 120 sq. feet (11.2 sq. metres) for the parlour. This is also evident in the statement that the introduction of the parlours should not be at the expense of the necessary

3.7 The early twentieth-century garden city houses influenced generations of house building (Welwyn Garden City, UK)

accommodation and area of living room and scullery. The living room was to have a south-east aspect and washing-up, cooking etc. were to be eliminated from it (Gale, 1949: 95–7). What had started in the middle-class houses in the earlier periods was now being extended to the rest of society through state intervention.

The next influential document was the Dudley Report (Ministry of Health, 1944), which was produced to take into account the changes in 'national habits and ways of life' (p. 9), and to guide the anticipated postwar growth in house building. It saw the 'rise in the general standard of living and a growing desire for and appreciation of good housing' a main characteristic of the previous quarter of a century and a future trend (p. 9). This was particularly felt for 'convenient domestic arrangements and labour-saving fittings' (Ministry of Health, 1944: 9). In this report, which accompanied the mass public sector house building for working classes, the views of women, stereotyped as housewives, were to some extent taken into account (Boys *et al.*, 1984: 74).

The report offered a rather wide ranging view of design, combining aesthetic and functional considerations. Good design was seen as implying 'good layout, good internal arrangement, good equipment and good appearance'. Its concern for the internal arrangement of the house was, however, mainly functional. This is evident from the stress it put on the cooking arrangement, on which 'the internal planning of small dwellings is very largely dependent' and which therefore 'has an important influence on design' (p. 10). This notion, which gives a centrality to the 'housewife's roles and expectations', is derived from a functionalist principle: 'It is in our view of the greatest importance that in the designing and equipping dwellings, account should be taken of the way in which a house is run and the use that is made of the various rooms' (Ministry of Health, 1944: 10).

The functionalist principles used to analyse the internal arrangement of the house and to propose changes followed the process of functional differentiation of space already in place for larger houses since the nineteenth century. Now the question of setting acceptable standards for size and density of housing was raised to make functional differentiation feasible. The Report's investigations showed a large number of complaints made about inadequate living space. The strongest complaint was about the size of the kitchen or scullery. A need was felt for 'a separate place for laundry work, the drying of clothes, and dirty jobs that should not be done in a room in which meals are eaten' (p. 11). There was no convenient place in the inter-war house for many ordinary family activities, including study and homework by the older children, the reception of visitors; and the transaction of the minor business necessary in every household. The living room was originally intended to be the room in which meals could be cooked and eaten and all other family activities carried on. As against this, there was a growing desire to use it for the social and recreational side of the family life undisturbed by constant interruption for meals. It was proposed, therefore, that 'the municipal house of the future should provide two good rooms on the ground floor, so that meals need not interfere with other activities' (Ministry of Health, 1944: 11–14). The meals should be taken either in a kitchen designed for the purpose, or in a dining recess off the living-room. The report carefully avoided using the term parlour, as it now carried an 'old fashioned and obsolete' implication, while asking for 'a clean cheerful room where meals can be taken with the maximum of convenience to the housewife who does the cooking, but which is free from the dirty work of washing clothes' (p. 14).

Another major improvement in living standards and outlook and anticipation of large-scale housing development gave rise to a new report in 1961 known as the Parker Morris Report (DoE, 1977). This report, like the Dudley Report, acknowledged the work of the previous report and referred to major social and economic changes, the future trends, especially as it was 'promised a doubled standard of living in 25 years', and their impacts on housing production (p. 2). In contrast to the Dudley Report that focused on public housing, this report addressed both public and private housing developments. A substantial change in lifestyle was recognized in that the individual members of the family had a growing 'desire to live their own lives for an increasing part of the time they spend at home' (p. 4). This demand for more individual freedom within a shared space indicated a further process of functional differentiation and spatial specialization. The introduction of the new household appliances and the participation of the husband in the housework provided more free time for the housewife, and the needs of teenagers and others to listen to records and watch television meant a need for major changes in the house. These new functions in the house indicated that the members of the household 'are more and more wanting to be free to move away from the fireside to somewhere else in the home – if only (in winter at any rate) they can keep warm' (p. 4). The report, therefore, was 'not about rooms so much as about the activities that people want to pursue in their homes', so 'rooms grow from the needs and provide for the needs – they evolve as a consequence of thought and not in copying of what has gone before' (p. 4).

These very interesting observations, although expressed in functionalist terms and still assuming a secondary role for women, show how this freedom of choice for the family members potentially affects the social and spatial relationships inside the house. A major impact would be on how and when they would come together and constitute a semi-public, group space. By helping to confront the predetermined spatial bonds within the house, individuals could find more freedom at the expense of the group, a natural continuation of the process that had started several centuries before when the new rooms began to separate from the communal space of the house in a specialization process. The disintegration of the communal space coincided with the rise of privacy. Now a new freedom was being sought from what had remained of this communal space and its functions.

In response to these changes in the lifestyle of households, the report sums up the required changes in two words: space and heating. There should be additional floor space to provide for a wider range of activities than before: 'As well as a place where the family can gather, there must be room in every home for activities demanding privacy and quiet', along with larger kitchens with sufficient room 'in which to take at least some meals' (p. 2). In close connection with more space and a key to design was heating, as it seemed 'entirely wrong to go on building homes in which so much of the available space cannot be used for day-to-day activities throughout the year' (p. 3). The new variety of activities and the freedom to live separate lives by the individual members of a family meant that their homes had 'to accommodate individual and different group interests and activities involving any number, or all, of the family, with or without visitors' (p. 8). The design, therefore, 'must be such as to provide reasonable individual and group privacy as well as facilities for family life as part of a community of friends and relations' (p. 8). This was to be made possible in the living area, which needed enough space for the furniture: two or three easy chairs, a settee, a television set, small tables, and places suitable for a reasonable quantity of other possessions such as a sewing box, toy box, radiogram and bookcase (ibid.: 10). Where four or more people live, there should also be one room in the living area in which activities needing privacy and freedom from disturbance could take place. This living area was to be separated from outside by a filter: the hall, 'a neutral space in which to deal with visitors whom one wishes neither to leave on the step nor to invite to meet the family' (ibid.: 9).

But did this emphasis by the Parker Morris Report on flexibility and freedom of individual result in proposing new spaces? Was this new level of functional differentiation leading to a new organization of space inside the home, altering the way public and private parts of the house relate to each other and to their occupants? After all, what appears to be a strict functional specialization tends to be used in a much more flexible way. Functional differentiation has been a process that has provided a variety of spaces within a dwelling for a variety of purposes. It has been argued that where this differentiation has evolved gradually, as in the development of single family house, it is the nature of the space, rather than its name, that corresponds to the activities taking place within it (Robinson, 1989). Therefore, the place for quieter activities is likely to be the living room, where delicate materials and valuable objects are kept, as distinct from the kitchen with its hard, waterproof surfaces as a place for more lively activities. The dining table can be used for writing or sewing and the bedroom houses not only beds but objects that reflect its occupants' interests and expectations from their private domain.

It appears that, as the Parker Morris Report itself mentions, its stress is on a different pattern of use rather than a new range of spaces. Such flexibility of space in an adaptable house seemed a long way away. The house plans that followed the Report, as for example shown in Essex County Council's Design Guide (1973: 117–19) used the same spaces as previous generations: living rooms, dining rooms, kitchens, bedrooms, bathrooms, garages, toilets. There were new patterns of combination of these rooms, but there were no new levels of functional differentiation. An investigation of the most recent plans also shows the same range of functional variety. Of course, there would be hardly a limit on spatial variety in large houses, especially when today's diversity of lifestyles and activities are considered. But in smaller houses, there seems to be a capacity of differentiation beyond which it is not possible or desirable to go.

The functional differentiation can be seen as resulting in a gradual rationalization of the domestic space. It could also be seen as an instrumental rationality leading the way and forcing the social and aesthetic considerations to adjust accordingly. In this process, individuals and their increasingly complex lifestyles have claimed parts of the common living space for their privacy. This change of balance, which started from the larger houses of the rich was extended to the majority of people through mass public housing and private volume house building. The further separation of private spheres inside the house left the spaces of sociability diminishing in proportions but still important. These processes can also be seen as deriving from a change in the availability of resources and technology. Whereas earlier limited fuel pressed households to use fewer spaces, advanced heating technologies allowed for a more flexible use of space and a freedom from being attached to one common room.

MODERNIST FUNCTIONALISM AND THE OPEN PLAN

After these phases of house design, open plans were introduced, which could offer a large degree of flexibility and could cater for a variety of uses. These appeared to reconstruct the communal space of the medieval house, where many functions could take place in one space. Was this a return, the end of a cycle of differentiation and stratification? Open plan was one of the five points of a new architecture advocated by Le Corbusier (Colquhoun, 1989). The plan and the internal volume were freed from the constraints of the structure, allowing utility and convenience to predominate. In this sense, the functionalism of the modern architecture took on new forms that were breaking away from the traditional patterns of domestic space. As Le Corbusier (quoted in Guiton, 1981: 88) put it:

> We can no longer accept traditional houses, which misuse space. We must . . . conceive a house as a machine for living, as a tool . . . A house was hitherto conceived as an incoherent agglomeration of larger rooms that were always oversized and, at the same time, cramped.

Their large sizes meant that they were expensive. 'As the price of building has quadrupled itself, we must reduce the old architectural pretensions and the cubage of the house by at least one half' (Le Corbusier, 1927: 222–3). These smaller units paved the way for the spirit of building and living in mass produced houses, which was the ultimate aim in housing production (Figure 3.8). Le Corbusier was so concerned with the size and number of dwellings in mass production that he concluded that the internal barriers should be taken away to allow for a more flexible use of the smaller spaces.

The free plan seemed to give priority to the public space of a dwelling. The Parker Morris Report's approach to open planning, therefore, was cautious and somewhat mechanistic: it was not liked by the public housing tenants but was

3.8 Modernist designs hoped to create machines for living, giving priority to the functions of the private interior over the appearance of the public exterior (London, UK)

popular in the private sector. It 'provides little privacy from view, from noise, or from distraction', but 'gives a sense of place' and is attractive (DoE, 1977: 9). The verdict on open planning was that 'With a suitable hall, good heating, and suitable arrangements for activities needing privacy, open planning can offer advantages, especially for homes for smaller families' (DoE, 1977: 9).

It appears, however, that the postmodern reaction to modernist design caused a growth of private domain, in line with the increased owner occupation of the dwellings. It led housing production to return to some form of vernacular aesthetics and organization of space, as evolved and practised during the last two centuries. Its reaction to rationalism, however, could not persuade the house builders and users to abandon the level of functional differentiation achieved during the modern era. The new housing stock is now being built by the volume builders along the same lines. What a generation of postmodernism was able to reject was, therefore, the reductionist notion of house as a machine, rather than the rationalism of the functional differentiation.

TWO CRITIQUES OF PRIVATE SPACE

Privacy and domesticity may have been praised throughout the modern period. There are also powerful criticisms against the construction of privacy and its distinction from the public realm. Dividing the social world into public and private spheres, it is argued, is presented as a natural division. The distinction, however, is,

> a powerful ideological tool, reinforcing as natural and inevitable a set of structured inequalities between groups of people – men and women, adults and children – and favouring the interests of some groups at the expense of others, as well as legitimating the dominance of some individuals over others at a more personal level. (Sapsford, 1995: 317)

Two strands of criticism, a Marxian and a feminist, stand out as attempts to show how this distinction is socially constructed and how the private sphere is a bourgeois invention to oppress the working class and to limit women.

The Marxian perspective sees the private realm as illegitimate and unjustified, as it is the realm in which private gain is consolidated and privileges maintained. This perspective gives full supremacy to the public, ruling out the private realm, at least in the contemporary form, which is closely associated with private property and unequal relations between men and women. Marx and Engels, in their *Communist Manifesto*, took the abolition of private property as its core. They also asked for the abolition of the family. The bourgeoisie, they argued, had torn away the sentimental veil of the family and had reduced it to a mere money relation. Due to its close association with private property, the family, therefore, was condemned to be abolished in the search for the liberation of the working classes. They wrote: 'On what foundation is the present family, the bourgeois family, based? On capital, on private gain.' (1985: 100). The contemporary family in its developed form only existed among the middle classes, and with the abolition of the private property and the vanishing of capital, it will also disappear.

In the communistic household of a distant past, Engels wrote (1986: 79ff), women had the upper hand. In the development of the patriarchal family, it was the concern for property and a social organization to look after the land and the care of the livestock that men found supremacy. The word family originates from the Latin word *familia*, which in ancient Rome referred to the total number of slaves belonging to one man. By being related from the beginning to agricultural services, the family therefore contains not only slavery but also serfdom. 'It contains', Marx wrote, '*in miniature* all the contradictions which later extend throughout society and its state' (quoted in Engels, 1986: 88).

The appearance of the monogamous family was based on the supremacy of man, to ensure the undisputed paternal link to children who inherited the father's property. This was not an arrangement that came about as the reconciliation between men and women, but as the subjugation of one sex by the other, unknown in previous history. This was the first division of labour, coinciding with the first opposition between social classes. It brought about the possibility of development as well as misery. As Engels put it:

> Monogamous marriage was a great historical step forward; nevertheless, together with slavery and private wealth, it opens the period that has lasted until today in which every step forward is also relatively a step backward, in which prosperity and develop-ment for some is won through the misery and frustration of others. (1986: 96)

Among the proletariat, the absence of property and the fact that women had to go out to work meant that the proletarian family was different. Ties were looser and women, who could be the family breadwinners, were not always economically infe-rior. In the bourgeois household, however, where the husband is the main income earner, 'he is the bourgeois, and the wife represents the proletariat' (Engels, 1986: 105). The first condition for women's liberation, Engels argued in this influential book, was to bring them back into employment, which in turn demands that the monogamous family be no longer the economic unit of society. This would bring with it a gradual growth of sexual freedom and with it a more tolerant attitude towards 'a maiden's honour and a woman's shame' (p. 107). From our vantage point in time, we can see how some of these prescriptions of a nineteenth-century revolutionary started to materialize in the twentieth century, even though not through the abolition of private property as he and Marx had envisaged.

The rise of the intimate space, in which the modern family of parents and children were the core inhabitants, was only made possible through a new form of relationship between men and women. This relationship, feminists argue, locked women in an inferior position and as such was unfair.

As Zaretsky (1976) argues, the family is where almost all personal needs are expected to be met. Here is where personal freedom can be protected from the impersonal and anonymous world of capitalism. But the price for this personal freedom is a heavy burden on family members, particularly women, who are forced into isolation. Feminist writers have elaborated on this theme by discussing the way the family restricts women: it regulates their labour through the role of the house-wife; it gives men more power over women's sexuality and fertility; and it structures and reinforces gender identities that are separate and inequitable (Muncie and Sapsford, 1995: 25–6).

Both processes of public–private separation, inside and outside the house, redefined the role of gender as another arena for differentiation and specialization. The house was associated with the women's realm, as distinct from the male public sphere outside (Figure 3.9). But even inside the house, there was a gender differentiation associated with the new functional specialization of space. In larger houses, the drawing room was the women's space, where they 'withdrew' after dinner. The men's domain was the study or the library. In the smaller houses, the women's realm was functionally associated with the kitchen (Roberts, 1991).

The processes that helped separate the home from work and established the new distinction between the public and private realms have been criticized by femin-ist writers. Thinkers such as Habermas (1989), who blame mass society for a loss of distinction between the public and private spheres and the negative effects of this process on public sphere, are criticized for idealizing the gender differentiation (Fraser, 1989).

Women were located within the private sphere and were associated with domesticity, maternity and dependence. Without restricting them to a narrow range of roles and spaces, the creation of a private sphere as a safe haven from the impersonal world of outside was impossible. Men, on the other hand, were associated with the public realm, the world of work, politics, breadwinning, auto-nomy and responsibility. The creation of private realm of the family may have been a necessity for its members to cope with the complexity of urban life. This, however, placed on women the major burden of maintaining the safe haven. The feminist writers, not unlike the Marxist writers, criticized the family for the power relations

3.9 The suburban house was seen as isolating women and excluding them from the public sphere dominated by men (Newcastle, UK)

that it embodied and reproduced. The family and the distinction between the public and private were seen as the source of women's oppression, which structured and institutionalized unequal roles and opportunities for men and women.

The design of the house reflected this oppression of women, as it provided a material framework for the condition of women inside domestic space (Boys *et al.*, 1984). Therefore, the design of the non-sexist home was to change. The experience of Swedish collaborative housing was praised, where multi-unit houses were built with extended shared facilities and collaboration among residents (Sangregorio, 1995). As Hayden suggested in the 1980s, 'attacking the conventional division between public and private space should become a socialist and feminist priority' (Hayden, 1996: 153). The single family suburban house, where women were isolated and trapped, could be rehabilitated to introduce community services and common areas. Larger houses could be converted to a number of smaller units. Groups of suburban houses could be altered in new ways:

To replace empty front lawns without sidewalks, neighbours can create blocks where single units are converted to multiple units; interior land is pooled to create a parklike setting at the centre of the block; front and side lawns are fenced to make private outdoor spaces; pedestrian paths and sidewalks are created to link all units with the central open space; and some private porches, garages, pool sheds, utility rooms, and family rooms are converted to community facilities such as children's play areas, dial-a-ride garages, and laundries. (Hayden, 1996: 151)

TENSIONS OF THE HOME

The house continues to be praised as the best form of accommodation for the future. The British forecast for millions of new homes needed in the next two decades are not to cater for an increase in population but for a rise in the number of smaller households. The traditional family home of the nuclear family continues to be built and used by millions. The shape of the family, however, has changed (Figure 3.10). The typical family of a married couple with a working father and a housewife mother with two children now represents only one in twenty of all households. The major changes that the family has gone through include lower birth rates, fewer children and longer life expectancy.

The home has been fragmented alongside the transformation of the traditional nuclear family. Different forms of living arrangements have also arisen, as the economic necessity of the family unit has changed both through new patterns of working and through the intervention by the state in education, childcare and other areas of family activity. Alongside nuclear families, other forms of households have emerged as a result of cohabitation, same-sex pairings, adoption, fostering, separation and divorce. Between 1961 and 1991 in the United Kingdom, the number of families with dependent children headed by lone parents (in nine out of ten cases the mother) rose from 6 per cent to 19 per cent (Muncie and Sapsford, 1995: 11–13). Despite these changes, striking continuity can also be found in family life, as nine out of ten people marry at some time in their lives; nine out of ten married couples have children; and eight out of ten people live in a household headed by a married couple (Muncie and Sapsford, 1995: 22). What is often at stake is the discrepancy between the reality of most people's lives and an idealized pattern of family, a pattern that is used as a basis for moral discussions and policy decisions.

There is, therefore, a tension at work between the home as seen from outside and what is indeed taking place inside this space. The home is seen as the sphere of the family, a concept that appears to be commonly held. Yet family is a notion that refers to a diverse range of family forms and living arrangements that have emerged in addition to the traditional patterns of family living characterized by

3.10 Can the future housing design, as presented in this futuristic exhibition, cater for the changing form of the household? (Malmö, Sweden)

parents and children. The intimate relationship, that was established as the modern nuclear family mainly from the eighteenth century onwards, has now been transformed to a multiplicity of new forms of intimate living. A tension has arisen between the continued image of the traditional family as the inhabitants of the private realm and the measure of government policy (as well as collective myths and expectations), on the one hand, and the reality of the smaller households with their plural forms of living arrangements, on the other hand.

The modern nuclear family, at its peak in the nineteenth century, was able to provide a protected sphere from the fast changing social world. While industrialization and urbanization were transforming all aspects of life, it was thought that the nuclear family could create and protect a safe haven from an alien and ever more impersonal social environment. As individualism grew, however, the nuclear family was no longer able to protect itself let alone provide the protection it was expected to, as individual members of the family each began to follow their independent routes (Kumar, 1997).

There is, therefore, another tension at work, a tension between the two aspects of the home, i.e. between a haven for the individual and an intimate place for the household. It is a tension that lies at the heart of the contemporary private realm, addressing the way the self and the intimate other relate to each other within the context of the continuous rise of individualism. In this way the home, where self and the intimate other live, may face some of the challenges that the city faces, i.e. where the self and the strangers live side by side. Both are social worlds in which interpersonal relations are nurtured and developed, where power imbalances are present and limits to individual freedom instituted. Home, therefore, is where personal and interpersonal meet, where private and semi-private spheres are juxtaposed. The changing shape of the family and the changing configuration of the house are the outcome of the historically changing relationship between personal and interpersonal spheres inside the domestic space.

The constant change of the family means that understanding the private realm of the home would only be possible through understanding these two tensions. The tension between the individual and the household, and the tension between the external image of the household and its internal reality are two areas that need to be acknowledged and understood.

INTERPENETRATION OF SPHERES

The private sphere is an area of ambiguity between an individual's sphere of personal freedom and a household's intimate realm of interpersonal relations. The constant demand for individual freedom is well reflected by Saint-Exupéry in his book, *The Little Prince*:

> He was free, infinitely free, so free that he was no longer conscious of pressing on the ground. He was free of that weight of human relationships which impedes movement, those tears, those farewells, those reproaches, those joys, all that a man caresses or tears every time he sketches out a gesture, those countless bonds which tie him to others and make him heavy. (Saint-Exupéry, quoted in Ariés, 1973: 396)

This search for freedom is a long historical process that is reflected in many social institutions, especially very clearly in the family and the home. The process that changed the house after the end of the Middle Ages has been interpreted in different ways. According to Olsen (1986: 101):

> The course from the promiscuity of the multipurpose great hall to Virginia Woolf's room of one's own has been presented either as the progressive triumph of refinement and recognition of the worth of the individual, or as the victory of the egoism over the demands of human fellowship.

The difference in interpretation, of course, is largely based on the paradigm that informs it. Much that has been written on cities draws on a social, collective paradigm. As cities are concentrations of large numbers of people, methods of social sciences are used to study them. Urban sociology and urban geography, for example, use these frameworks in studying large-scale, society-level approaches to the city. In contrast, when action in the city is discussed, for example in psychology and economics, an individual, concrete paradigm is used. Here the actions of individuals and organizations are studied, rather than the contexts in which they take place. In the same way the study of the public and private leans towards one or other of these poles. Those who focus on the public tend to use the social collective paradigm, tending to undermine the individual as a potential threat to the community. On the other hand, those who emphasize the private rely on the individual paradigm, looking with suspicion at the intentions of the collective as intrusive and even potentially dangerous. The household is often associated with one or the other of these: a private group distinct from society, or a collective distinct from the individual. And yet cities and societies are places and processes of interdependence, negotiation and adjustment between these poles of individual and society, between private and public realms. The two poles may provide analytical and ideological positions; in reality they are no more than two points on the same spectrum.

Ariés spoke of the family winning over individualism (1973), while many seem to believe that individualism has been the ultimate winner (Kumar, 1997). It is equally possible to say that now it is society that has prevailed over the family and the individual. The nuclear family was set up as a separate sphere for protection against society. But as the forms of communication have multiplied and individual members of the household have established direct links to the outside world, the interior space of the home is no longer protected to the same extent as before. As television screens, telephones, computer networks and the print media connect individuals directly to the world outside the private domestic sphere, it may be the individual that has won the day against the family. It may equally be the society that has triumphed, as individualism is a form of socialization and not an ability or desire to remain in absolute isolation. Through advocating particular forms of individual freedoms, the society may have pushed the interpersonal realm of the family and the household to retreat. It may not be necessarily a Dionysian individual who abandons household in search of pleasure, but a commercial society that promotes self-indulgent consumption, as Dionysian images sell. What may be taken to be extreme individualism may also be seen as a replay, an individual variation on themes that are manufactured by the society in ever more colourful ways. This interpretation, of course, depends on understanding society as a recognizable entity, rather than a multitude of individuals.

When individuals are taken as the measure of social relations, the intimate space revolves around them, rather than the family in its traditional sense. There is a gap that Nagel (1998b: 20) identifies between what is open to public view and what people keep to themselves. 'The veil', he writes (p. 20), 'can be partly lifted to admit certain others, without the inhibiting effect of general exposure.' This is the interpersonal sphere of privacy that is essential for human emotional and biological life.

The private realm of the family, the domestic sphere, is often contrasted with the public realm of the state, the political sphere (Muncie et al., 1995). The public–private relations in the city, therefore, becomes a binary relation between the home and the city. A close scrutiny of each sphere, however, casts a shadow on the clarity of this distinction. The household and the home that accommodates it, is itself an interpersonal world, where individual members have their own private spheres. When they come together as a household, they create a range of semi-private and semi-public as well as private arenas inside the home. The state and the city/country that reflect its space, are on the other hand a mixture of many layers of private, semi-private, semi-public and public spheres.

From our mind to our personal spaces, private territories, properties and homes, we think we are in control of a number of enclosed spaces, a number of boxes where we control their concealment or exposure. However, all the boxes that we think are completely sealed, or that we have full control over, are indeed open to influences and forces from the outside. As human beings, we may need to feel in control, to feel that we are in control of these boxes and can open them whenever we decide. In reality, however, this control is a desire, a normative aspiration, rather than an empirical reality. What is private is indeed a potentially fragile configuration, a half-closed box full of objects, each of which may be half-inside and half-outside, or half-visible and half-hidden.

When we go outside these boxes, which constitute the private realm, and want to establish a public realm, where everything is visible, we find the same problem. Much of what we think as visible is only a surface, hiding behind it a potentially dark and turbulent interior. The sunny exterior of a nicely decorated public space will always be a façade, a door to a world of shadows that lies behind (Figure 3.11). We will not be aware of the psychological torments of this person who strolls the public square, or the grinding poverty of that person who appears to

3.11 The sunny, picturesque public façades of a place always hides a world of shadows behind (Rotterdam, The Netherlands)

be happily sitting on the edge of the fountain. In the public realm, we may at best have half-open boxes on display, rather than a transparent landscape of people and places. What we conceal is made of material that is ultimately exposed elsewhere. What we conceal is ultimately an imposition of will, where the act of shaping and controlling is as important as the contents of the outcome. The act of boundary setting is as significant as what is concealed behind the boundaries.

It seems then that this ability to present and to hide, or in Nagel's words to conceal and expose, is what we strive for. Through it, we can feel in control of our lives. Even though the public may be full of private and the private immersed in public, we constantly need to draw boundaries as part of our need for wellbeing. In the same way that we constantly aspire to understand the world around us and so invent interpretations to explain it, we constantly create boundaries and categories to feel in control. This control is a form of power, which some have or feel they have, and some have not. Therefore, even though it seems a necessity to draw boundaries and identify categories to be able to understand the world and live in it socially, it does not mean that these interpretations and categorizations are welcome by all. There is constant need to revisit these boundaries, to check them against the wishes and interests of those affected by them.

The distinction between public and private, therefore, is not and should not be rigid. It is often a shade rather than a clear-cut boundary. But the need to make distinctions should be acknowledged. Those who believe in the abolition of the distinction are leaning either to one side or to the other, either not believing in the merits of the private realm or of the public realm and wishing to extend one so far as to encompass the other. The experience of cities throughout history, however, has shown that a form of balance between the two is inevitably needed for social life, made more stable through providing mechanisms for its change.

CONCLUSION

As an institution that mediates between the individual and society, family has come under ever rising pressure, from these two sides. On the one hand, the individual members of the family have increasingly claimed their freedom and have asked for a reshaping of family relations; on the other hand, the intervention by the state and society, in areas such as housing, education and welfare, has weakened its role. The private sphere that was established as the domain of the family, to protect its members from the impersonal urban world, has therefore been in danger of being torn apart by tensions from within and without. The shape of the family, and the form of the private sphere associated with it, has shown the dream of establishing a safe haven for a particular form of social organization cannot continue unchallenged. With the reduction in the number of household members, and the transformation of relationships between them, the orders, hierarchies and divisions devised for large nuclear families have constantly come under pressure to transform.

The process of social and physical change in the house after the Middle Ages has been a move from large households living in shared spaces towards smaller households living in smaller, separate dwellings. This has coincided with the rise of individual to claim a set of rights unprecedented in the past. One of the most important of these rights is privacy, whereby each individual aspires to have a private realm. In households, this has been a rise of single-person households, or establishing a private space inside the house, as compared to the period when all indoor, household activities would take place in one large space. This process of the rise of privacy and individualism, which can be seen as accompanied by instrumental rationality, has forced the social and spatial relationships inside the house to change radically. The overall form of the dwelling has changed accordingly, by moving from townhouses to flats, terraces to semi-detached and detached houses, reflecting the weakening of old forms of sociability, the independence of households, and the freedom of the individual.

The historical evolution of the private sphere shows a trend in which the nuclear family emerged by detaching itself from the outside world, replacing sociability with concern for privacy. Separation of home from work, servants from the family, parents from children, and men from women created a new private sphere with new hierarchies for the middle classes. Alongside this was a process of differentiation and specialization of space inside the home. These subdivisions coincided with creating new layers of public and private spaces inside the domestic space. As these arrangements were extended to the rest of society through state intervention, the reality of the nuclear family has changed: the domestic servant left the middle-class family, women found paid work outside home, children found new levels of independence and the state intervened in housing, education and welfare. The space of the home and the policies towards the household, however, continue to be based on the traditional image of the family rather than on its current reality.

Furthermore, even in the traditional image, what was taken for granted as the protected private sphere was in reality an interdependent, interpersonal sphere in which shades of privacy and publicness existed. Rather than entirely private, the family and the home are institutions that mediate between the public and the private, between impersonal and personal. This is an interpersonal realm that has been under constant historical pressure to become a mere personal realm.

Chapter 4
Interpersonal space of sociability

So far, we have explored the dynamics of private sphere through the internal world of mind, the personal space of body, the exclusive space of property and the intimate space of home: the spaces of concealment. In this chapter and the rest of this book, we step outside to explore what lies beyond the private realm, in the public domain, in the spaces of exposure. We will explore the interpersonal space of sociability, the communal space of the neighbourhood, the metaspatial public sphere and the impersonal space of the city.

As in private space, a number of dimensions and layers of public space can be identified. To identify these dimensions and layers, in this chapter we first explore some of the meanings of public sphere. Then we move on to explore one of the key layers of public sphere, which is that of interpersonal space. This is the realm of sociability, where face-to-face communication takes place between people who are not part of the intimate circle of household and friends. Here the relations of exchange between strangers, the management of this relationship as a performance, and the stage on which this performance takes place are crucial elements of the public sphere.

DEFINING THE PUBLIC

The word 'public', which is derived from the Latin *populus* 'people', has a wide range of meanings. The Oxford Dictionary definitions of the term, as an adjective, include: 'of or pertaining to the people as a whole; belonging to, affecting, or concerning the community or nation; carried out or made by or on behalf of the community as a whole; authorized by or representing the community; open or available to, used or shared by, all members of a community; not restricted to private use; also (of a service, fund, amenity, etc.) provided by local or central government for the community and supported by rates or taxes; at the service of the public in a professional capacity; working in local or central government; open to general observation, sight, or knowledge; existing or done openly; accountable to the general public; of or pertaining to a person in the capacity in which he or she comes in contact with the community, as opposed to his or her private capacity etc; of or engaged in the affairs of the community; *esp.* (of a person) occupying an official position, holding a position of influence or authority; devoted or directed to the promotion of the general welfare; patriotic'. ⌋

As a noun, the meanings of the word include: 'in public, in a place or state open to public view or access; openly; organized society, the body politic; a nation, a State; the interest or welfare of the community; people collectively; the members of the community; a section of the community having a particular interest in or special connection with the person or thing specified; a collective group regarded as sharing a common cultural, social, or political interest but who as individuals do not necessarily come into contact with one another'. The word is used in a variety of combinations and phrases, such as general public, going public, in the public domain, public act, public address system, public bar, public company, public education, public figure, public good, public health, public holiday, public interest, public life, public office, public opinion, public ownership, public relations, public sector, public service, public transport, etc.

These meanings of the word 'public' all refer to a large number of people, who are either conceptualized as society or as state, and what is associated with them. As the society, the term may refer to various demographic or territorial scales, including a group, a local community, a nation, or in a capacity that is now rarely used, the entire human race. As the state, it may refer to the various institutional scales of nation state, local government, and even individuals who are part of the state apparatus.

At one level, the society as a whole and the state that governs it are interpreted to be one and the same, especially in the liberal democratic nation states. Here the term public is used with ease to refer to the society and the state, as if they were one single entity. But the complexity of both society and the state appears to make this formula problematic. The society is no longer held to be a homogenous entity, and the state is an ever larger and more professionalized organization. Not only is the society formed of different levels of local and national communities. The society is also the realm of privacy, the realm of individuals and small groups, as well as the realm of the market, which can include large corporations, small firms and individuals. It is in this double interpretation of the society as both public and private that ambiguity arises. It is also in the redrawing of the already fuzzy boundary between the state and the society that ambiguity in the distinction is identified.

In addition to the ambiguity of how to define the society, there is an ambiguity around descriptive and normative interpretations of the public: while for some it describes a condition, for others it offers a recipe for action. At least two major approaches to public sphere can be found in twentieth-century literature. The first is a descriptive approach, which attempts to offer an account of human conduct in presence of, and in interaction with, others. Public sphere is here understood as the co-presence of humans and the impacts they have on each other, whether through interpersonal relations or the interaction between person and society in general. This approach is pursued in social anthropology, social psychology and sociology, amongst others. The key term here is the construction and communication of meaning in public sphere through conduct and performance. The second is a normative approach to public sphere, which attempts to offer a way forward in human interaction, i.e. how this interaction should be conducted. This is pursued in politics, political theory, and critical approaches to social sciences. The key word here is power, which is exerted in the public sphere, through detailed or structural interrelations.

Another source of ambiguity is whether private and public refer to personal and impersonal relations. As Allan Silver reminds us (1997: 43), personal is private and impersonal is public. In our investigations into the private sphere, the public appears to be, broadly defined, the realm of the non-intimate others, i.e. what lies beyond the personal realm of individuals and their intimate circle of friends and family. This realm, however, is further divided into the impersonal and the interpersonal realms. The impersonal realm of the market exchange, legal contract, bureaucracy and the state appears to be one form of the public realm, as distinct from the private sphere of the household and personal relations of trust and friendship. The interpersonal realm, however, which is often the realm of meaningful (as well as instrumental) face-to-face social encounters, stands in the middle ground. At times, it is interpreted as private (when in opposition to impersonal) and at times it is seen as public (in opposition to the personal). This causes ambiguity and overlap in understanding the public and private realms and their relationships (Figure 4.1).

Trying to confront the ambiguity of the divide between public and private, Weintraub (1997) identifies four broad fields in which the discussions of public and private take place:

1   a liberal-economistic model, which focuses on the distinction between the state administration and the market economy;
2   a civic perspective, which sees the public as the arena of political community and citizenship, as distinct from both the state and the market;
3   a public life perspective, which focuses on the fluid and polymorphous sphere of sociability, as distinct from the household; and
4   a feminist perspective, which focuses on the distinction between family and the larger economic and political order, especially as reflected in the market economy.

4.1 Interpersonal, face-to-face social encounters are interpreted sometimes as private and other times as public, causing ambiguity in meaning (Naples, Italy)

This offers a useful mapping of some of the literature. But this map does not yet provide us with a theoretical model of the public–private distinction. Nor does it clarify the relationship between these four pairs of binary relations.

Benn and Gaus (1983) notice the potentially puzzling diversity of activities and practices which are categorized as public or private, ranging, for example, from the public availability of books in a library to the public authority possessed by a government. To clarify this, they identify three broad types which constitute the dimensions of publicness and privateness. These are three dimensions of social organization: access, agency and interest. Most definitions of public space emphasize the necessity of access, which can include access to a place as well as to the activities within it. Even when a place is owned by private agencies, public access may be secured by law (Moudon, 1991). Benn and Gaus divide access further into four sub-dimensions: physical access to *spaces*, access to *activities*, access to *information* and access to *resources*. Public places and spaces, therefore, are public because anyone is entitled to be physically present in them. Access to places, however, is often aimed at access to activities within them. But it is pos-sible to have access to a place but not to the activities going on there, such as access to the meeting of a group of friends in the middle of a public space. Access to information lies often at the heart of debates about privacy, which involves controlling information about ourselves or managing our public appearances. Access to resources allows a degree of influence over the public affairs, which is why the issue of agency is a significant one. Where the agents stand, whether acting privately or on behalf of a community, makes a difference to the nature and consequences of their actions. A public agency dealing with a part of urban space has a completely different mode of operation and aims than a private one. In the same way the dimension of interest plays a major role in determining the public–private distinction. Who are the beneficiaries of a particular action: private individuals or parts of the public as a whole? There are, however, overlaps and ambiguities in these three dimensions, which can be exemplified in the analysis of property with its potentially diverse and complex range of ownership and control. Nevertheless, the three dimensions of access, agency and interest can be usefully employed in empirical analyses of public spaces, where it becomes possible to identify the shades of publicness and privateness of a place or activity. The dimen-sions of agency and interest clearly direct us towards an appreciation of the multi-plicity of perspectives into urban space. The notions of interest, agency and access, however, treat space through an instrumental approach, seeing it as an asset in exchange, using it as a resource, treating it as a commodity. It is drawing on an analysis of social relations as exchange among strangers, rather than a set of emotional and meaningful ties.

Within the broad frameworks of state and society, a public space is therefore often provided and managed by the state and is used by the society as a whole. Using the criteria of access, agency and interest, a space can be considered public if it is controlled by the public authorities, concerns the people as a whole, is open or available to them, and is used or shared by all the members of a commun-ity. As with any other definition, however, this is a generalized statement, each section of which can represent a wide range of possible conditions. Public authori-ties may or may not legitimately represent or serve a community; availability of space may be based on a diverse and complex set of rules and conditions; all members of a community may or may not be willing or able to use a particular space for functional, symbolic, or any other reasons. In this sense, a generalized definition of this kind becomes an ideal type, with a normative value, rather than necessarily describing the public spaces everywhere. A more accurate defini-tion of public space, however, may be based on the observation that public spaces of cities, almost anywhere and at any time, have been places outside the boundaries of individual or small group control, mediating between private spaces and used for a variety of often overlapping functional and symbolic purposes. Urban, open public spaces, therefore, have usually been multi-purpose spaces distinguishable from, and mediating between, the demarcated territories of households and individuals.

One way to confront the range of ambiguities and overlaps is to see that the definition of the 'public' may depend on its context and on the other half of the formula, i.e. on the way the private sphere is understood. As we have seen so far, it seems that depending on what we define as private sphere, the public sphere is defined in relation to it. Put another way, when the private is personal, the public can be interpersonal or impersonal. When the private is interpersonal, the public can be impersonal. Depending on the descriptive or normative orientation of the definition, each of these layers in the shades of meaning can find a different interpretation. Depending on the way the private realm is defined (mind, body, property, home), the public sphere finds a related but opposite meaning. If mind is the private realm, the outside world is the public. If the body is the private realm, the other bodies constitute the public. If private property is the private realm, what lies outside private possession and control is the public. If the household is the private realm, the larger organizations and the rest of society is the public. The private realm can be one or a number of these layers and as such the public realm can be formed of a number of such layers. We shall explore some other such layers in the following chapters.

We will try to address these ambiguities as we develop our understanding of the public realm in these chapters. Understanding the interpersonal realm of social encounters and its different meanings is our first task. Therefore, we start analysing the public sphere as it occurs within the society, rather than the state. Here, it is a realm of interpersonal relations, rather than impersonal relations often associated with the state.

STRANGERS IN EXCHANGE

As the culmination of a long process of change since the Middle Ages, the rise of industrial capitalism and the growth of cities changed the nature and foundation of social relations, from those based on kinship and clan to those based on contracts and exchange. Some of the major figures of the eighteenth-century thought, such as David Hume and Adam Smith, saw this change as a positive development in human relationships (Hill and McCarthy, 1999). This optimism was, for example, reflected in the possibility of new forms of friendship, where people were now considered able to choose their friends, to make a distinction between utilitarian and genuine friendships, and thus to form genuine relationships free from the involuntary ties of clan and kin (Silver, 1997). The new commercial society, where exchange was the primary mode of association, was 'a society of strangers' (Hill and McCarthy, 1999: 38). A society of strangers engaged in exchange, however, needed a strong cultural framework to support exchange relations. Indeed, the development and functioning of civil society became the central area of inquiry in the Scottish Enlightenment. This was reflected, for example, in Hume's 'overarching interest in 'manners', patterns of polite good conduct which would provide a framework for civilized encounters (Copley and Edgar, 1998: xi).

For Smith and Hume, this was leading to a more tranquil, predictable, just, orderly and sociable life, as sympathy and politeness took charge of social inter-action. The faceless mass of strangers became thus internalized in the form of an 'impartial spectator', monitoring and controlling the 'impulses of self-love' (Hill and McCarthy, 1999: 39). This was not, however, easy for all to accept. A contemporary of Hume and Smith, Adam Ferguson was worried about the rise of the individu-ated society, with its alienating, soul-destroying and isolating effects. Instead, he idealized village life, where strong passions and close ties ruled (Hill and McCarthy, 1999: 44–5).

Throughout the nineteenth century, the theme of strangers in the city was a subject of constant attention. For Engels, the crowds in the streets of London 'had nothing in common, nothing to do with one another'. They had only one tacit agree-ment: 'that each keep to his own side of the pavement, so as not to delay the opposing streams of the crowd', without honouring the others 'with so much as a glance'. (Engels, 1993: 37). To the inhabitants of the city, then as now, this may have been a normal, everyday urban experience. But for Engels this was 'brutal indifference', which he thought was 'something repulsive, something against which human nature rebels' (pp. 36–7). This reflected 'the fundamental principle of our society everywhere', which was 'this isolation of the individual, this narrow self-seeking' (Engels, 1993: 37) (Figure 4.2).

The same phenomenon of crowds in the streets, however, was interpreted by a later observer as a sign of order. The tacit agreement of not colliding with other strangers appeared to follow a certain order. As Edward Alsworth Ross put it in 1908:

> A condition of order at the junction of crowded city thoroughfares implies primarily an absence of collision between men or vehicles that interfere one with another. Order cannot be said to prevail among people going in the same direction at the same pace, because there is no interference. It does not exist when persons are

4.2 For the early observers of cities, the behaviour of crowds of strangers in urban public spaces was a sign of 'brutal indifference' to one another. However, as city living matured and its conditions improved in general, interpretations of urban crowds have changed (London, UK)

constantly colliding one with another. But when all who meet or overtake one another in crowded ways take the time and pains needed to avoid collision, the throng is *orderly*. Now, at the bottom of the notion of social order lies the same idea. The members of an orderly community do not go out of their way to aggress upon one another. Moreover, whenever their pursuits interfere, they make the adjustments necessary to escape collision and make them according to some conventional rule. (*Social Control*, The Macmillan Company, New York, p. 1, Quoted in Goffman, 1972, p. 6)

Later still, this was celebrated as an art form (Jacobs, 1961). More than a simple order, it was seen as a performance, in which all passers-by play a role, performing an intricate ballet. With their distinctive parts, individual dancers and ensembles were miraculously reinforcing each other to compose 'an orderly whole' (Jacobs, 1961: 50). The ballet of the good city sidewalks, therefore, expressed a complex, never repeating order, which was played out with new improvisations in each place.

The interplay between the eighteenth-century concern for rationality and the nineteenth-century concern for expressiveness has shaped the modern sense of identity (Taylor, 1989). Both the eighteenth-century proponents of liberal individualism and their nineteenth-century romantic and revolutionary critics agreed that the city was a place of strangers. The twentieth century witnessed a continuation of this view and the tensions around these lines of thought: a city of rational, impersonal strangers linked through exchange within clearly set rules of conduct, or a city of strangers engaged in expression of emotions and individuality. The patterns of thought that emerged were reflections of these tensions around these idealized models. A cultural reflection of this tension, for example, was the opposition between rationalist modernism and expressive postmodernism. In practice, the two models became intertwined through cycles of emphasis on one or the other, and the ever complex patterns of life and combinations of thought that have emerged subsequently. In the twentieth century, the drive to use exchange as a basis for social relations deepened and expanded to larger part of the world. At the same time, the search for expressive freedom of individuals, which was advocated by the nineteenth-century romantics, deepened, opening up new areas of search for expressive individuality and subjectivity.

The paradigm of exchange as a basis for understanding and action has been subject to powerful critiques. Habermas (1989), for example, argues that the exchange paradigm was developed in the context of small-scale market operations and is now superseded by complex, impersonal contacts. With the complexity of the social fabric and the growth of large organizations and impersonal exchange across electronic space, the paradigm of exchange has been replaced by an impersonal, abstract exchange mediated and facilitated through the abstract notion of money. Individuals are still engaged in the exchange of ideas, goods and services, but largely mediated, especially in metropolitan living, through impersonal media, from telecommunication to stock markets and media.

Sociability as performative exchange among strangers is perhaps a main feature of the modern urban society. This, however, differs from pre-modern societies, with their interdependent notion of the self, ties of blood and kin, and strong rootedness of individuals in communities. Here the relations are longer term, based on people's understanding of each other as it has developed in various stages of life. Rules of sociability are therefore different, as they resemble those among family members rather than among strangers. In societies that have moved out of this more stable, cohesive relations, as in many large cities of the non-western world today, the relations among strangers is a fact of life, one that is not so clearly managed through the existing traditions, which had been developed for the smaller communities of the past. Sociability in these circumstances may lead to serious tensions, as under-regulated market processes and under-institutionalized political processes cannot support a stable set of relations among strangers (Madanipour, 1998b).

Despite these criticisms and despite the rise of impersonal exchange, personal, face-to-face exchange still remains the most potent form of communication. This is evident at all levels, from the political leaders who feel the need to establish personal contact in face-to-face meetings; to the educational establishments, where personal presence is essential not only for education but also for socialization of the young; and to the circle of friends, which develops through their wish to meet one another, in spite of what some want us to believe – that the advent of telecommunications has made physical co-presence irrelevant. Indeed, as the cities around the world have grown to house the majority of world's population and globalization finds a faster speed, personal exchange, whether rational and instrumental or expressive and meaningful, becomes ever more important.

FROM SELF TO MASK

We have seen in Chapter 1 that the self is influenced and shaped by bodily impulses and social forces. This creates continuous pressures from all sides that inevitably lead to tensions and imbalances of changing moods, energies and circumstances. Here to acquire a level of balance and stability, and to be able to manage this potentially turbulent and continuous change, individuals rely on masks, which are made of socially mediated suppression of impulses to stage a stable, relatively consistent performance (Figure 4.3).

These tensions may have always existed in human societies, where living within a group demanded from the individual to strike a balance between self and others. The cities, after all, have been the meeting points of strangers ever since their appearance ten millennia ago (Southall, 1998). The maintenance of this balance, however, has become particularly crucial in the cities of the modern period, where large urban populations are no longer tied by traditional rules of conduct and rigid social hierarchies, but are strangers engaged in contractual, even though unequal, relationships. Georg Simmel at the beginning of the twentieth century noticed a particular tension in metropolitan life, where the swift and continuously shifting external and internal stimuli intensified emotional experience. To cope with this intensity of stimuli, as prompted by every crossing of the street or the fast tempo of life in the city, the metropolitan inhabitant takes refuge in an impersonal, rationalistic envelope. To be protected from the threat of profound

4.3 To stage a stable, relatively consistent performance, we wear masks, which are made of socially mediated suppression of impulses (Venice, Italy)

disruption, the metropolitan person is de-sensitized. The reaction of the metropolitan person is thus 'moved to a sphere of mental activity which is least sensitive and which is furthest removed from the depths of personality' (Simmel, 1997: 70). Simmel found a striking parallel between the intellectualist approach of the metropolitan life and the mode of operation of the money economy. Both money and intellect can only develop where two factors coexist: neutrality and lack of character, by which he means both are detached and without any specific direction. Intellect is 'the indifferent mirror of reality' and money 'the mechanical reflex of the relative value of things' (Simmel, 1978: 432).

The necessity of coping with the continuous emotional stimuli of living in the modern society means the need to develop a detachable mask that can be used in exchange relations. According to Robert Park,

> It is probably no more historical accident that the word person, in its first meaning, is a mask. It is rather a recognition of the fact that everyone is always and everywhere, more or less consciously, playing a role. . . . It is in these roles that we know each other; it is in these roles that we know ourselves. (Park, 1950: 249)

The masks we wear to face others are usually made of normal routines. When moving from the private sphere to the public space, these routines change, from changing clothes to shaving or putting make up, to changing the vocabulary, accent and forms of expression, and adopting a more polite, careful manner. The change of mask is done with care and often with the assistance of the mirror, so as to see with the eyes of the others how we might appear to them. This is not preparation for a special occasion. It is just a routine social habit of human beings in their daily social life.

Person and self, as Goffman put it, are 'portraits of the same individual'; whereas person is 'encoded in the actions of others', self is encoded 'in the actions of the subject himself' (1972: 341). But there is an obvious gap between the actual self, which is pulled in all directions, and the mask, which is a remedy for this volatility, expected to be a more stable, elaborate social construct. The mask, then, acquires a normative dimension, one with which the actual self aspires to be associated. According to Santayana,

> Under our published principles and plighted language we must assiduously hide all the inequalities of our moods and conduct, and this without hypocrisy, since our deliberate character is more truly ourself than is the flux of our involuntary dreams.... Our animal habits are transmuted by conscience into loyalties and duties, and we become 'persons' or masks. (Quoted in Goffman, 1969: 49–50)

The notion of mask as the true person is also asserted by Robert Ezra Park,

> In a sense, and in so far as this mask represents the conception we have formed of ourselves – the role we are striving to live up to – this mask is our truer self, the self we would like to be. (Park, 1950: 250)

This picture of an idealized self, however, is by no means unproblematic. The socialized self that thus emerges has major discrepancies with our more actual, 'all-too-human' self. The outcome is to expect a 'certain bureaucratization of the spirit' so that a perfectly homogenous performance can be given at each social encounter. 'Through social discipline', Goffman maintains, 'a mask of manner can be held in place from within' (1969: 49–50). The structure of the self, therefore, can be analysed as having two basic parts: individual as *character* and as *performer*. The performer is 'a harried fabricator of impressions involved in the all-too-human task of staging a performance' (Goffman, 1969: 222). Character, on the other hand, is a normative notion, a set of fine qualities that the performer wishes to evoke. The gap between the actual and ideal individual seems to be covered by staging a performance.

The mask is the boundary between the public and the private in an individual. The treatment of this boundary is what makes the public realm and what also limits and characterizes the private realm of the individual. The notion of mask shows how the divided and multi-layered interior of a subjective space can be hidden by an apparently coherent exterior. This elaboration of the boundary between inner realm and the outer realm shows the ability of the agent to manipulate the image of the self and how this manipulation is a response to the social world around the agent. It also shows how a public exterior is an integral part of trying to maintain internal peace and continuity, of attempting internal structural integrity.

Working with pressure from two sides, social and biological, therefore, the human subject develops a mask over time, as a means of mediation between, and managing, these pressures. In a way the mask may correspond to Freud's ego, which mediates between id and superego. Or it could correspond to Bourdieu's *habitus*, where upbringing and manners can reflect an individual's social environment, inscribing it on the body (Bourdieu, 2000). Rather than a mask that can be dropped at will, as a separable set of appearances, manners and settings, Bourdieu speaks of *habitus*, a mask that is inscribed on a person's body, as it is an embodiment of his/her social environment. For Bourdieu, it appears, the structures of society are far stronger than the individual freedom of action. It may also relate to something much more flexible, which changes according to different circumstances. To the extent that we understand various situations and engage with people and places, we try to adjust to, or reject, them. This means the social masks of a person are varied, not only in number but also in their shape and makeup. Individuals make constant adjustments to their attitudes and behaviour.

The mask, therefore, can be full of inconsistencies and under constant attention and repair. Furthermore, different masks are needed for different audiences. As William James put it,

> ... we may practically say that he has as many different social selves as there are distinct *groups* of persons about whose opinion he cares. He generally shows a different side of himself to each of these different groups. Many a youth who is demure enough before his parents and teachers, swears and swaggers like a pirate among his 'tough' young friends. We do not show ourselves to our children as to our club companions, to our customers as to the labourers we employ, to our own masters and employers as to our intimate friends. (quoted in Goffman, 1969: 42)

These groups do not often come together and the individual can try to keep the masks and their presentation separate. The boundary between the public and the private in individuals, therefore, is constantly changing, adjusting to the public scenes and the private moods.

SOCIAL ENCOUNTER AS PERFORMANCE

The notion of mask inevitably takes us to performance, and to a dramaturgical model, the perspective of theatrical performance, which has been widely used to analyse social life. Erving Goffman (1969) identifies two forms of communication in face-to-face interactions. The first is what he calls 'expressions given', i.e. the process of transfer of information through verbal symbols or their substitutes, which is a narrow sense of communication. The second he terms 'expressions given off', i.e. a wide range of actions performed for reasons other than direct transfer of information, so that others can think of it as symptomatic of the actor. In social interactions people will want to know the facts of the situation. But as these facts are rarely available in daily social interactions, they will rely on some 'predictive devices', such as cues, tests, hints, expressive gestures, status symbols, etc (p. 220). This is where Goffman concentrates: on the more theatrical and contextual, non-verbal and presumably unintentional (pp. 2–4). Goffman assumes that when an individual appears before others, s/he will try to control the definition of the situation by controlling the impression they receive from her/him, which is her/his claim as to what reality is (p. 74). To this end, s/he will use dramaturgical techniques of stage management to sustain such impressions (p. 13), wearing an expressive mask in face-to-face interactions (p. 105). The performer may be 'sincere' or 'cynical', depending whether or not s/he believes in her/his performance (p. 17), but s/he will incorporate in her/his performance the idealized, officially accredited values of the society (p. 31).

According to Goffman, 'if the individual's activity is to become significant to others, he must mobilize his activity, so that it will express *during the interaction* what he wishes to convey' (p. 27). The individual will rely on a 'social front', which is composed of setting, appearance and manner. A social front can be used for different routines (such as business clothes that can also be worn for going to a restaurant). It is only in highly ceremonial occasions that setting, manner and appearance may all be unique and specific, used only for a particular type of routine (p. 26). To maintain the definition of a situation, the individual performer may have to rely on, and work with, others, i.e. a team of co-performers, such as the way members of a family or a group of office co-workers portray themselves in social situations (Figure 4.4). The members of the team have to co-operate to maintain a

4.4 On their own or as a team, individuals use performance to maintain the definition of a situation in social encounters (Bergen, Norway)

given impression, and as such may be considered the basic unit of performance (p. 74). The performances are often played in a front region, and performers are relaxed in backstage, where they can drop their masks (p. 92 ff). A disciplined performer is 'someone with sufficient poise to move from private places of informality to public places of varying degrees of formality, without allowing such changes to confuse him' (p. 191). He can manage his face and voice, so as to conceal actual affective responses and to display an appropriate affective response, e.g. be able to stop himself laughing about matters that are defined as serious. But even for less competent performers, there is usually a significant contribution by the audience, who exercise tact or protective practices on behalf of the performers, so as to maintain the show (p. 206).

When accidents cause a rupture in performance, the audience can see behind the scenes and take pleasure in learning an important lesson, that behind the mask, there is 'a solitary player involved in a harried concern for his production' (p. 207). What is revealed is that behind characters and masks, 'each performer tends to wear a single look, a naked unsocialized look, a look of concentration, a look of one who is privately engaged in a difficult, treacherous task' (p. 207). Disruption in performance can have consequences at three levels of social reality: personality, interaction and social structure. These consequences can discredit the self-conceptions that build an individual's personality, can bring a social interaction to an embarrassed and confused halt, and can have far-reaching consequences for others (pp. 213–14).

Richard Sennett (1976) used the dramaturgical model to investigate the historical changes in the public roles of individuals and the shifting relationship between public and private life. He argued that the modern period has witnessed a decline of public life, which is rooted in the formation of a new capitalist, secular urban culture. Rather than taking pleasure in the cosmopolitan city, which is the world of strangers, people today see public life as a matter of dry formal obligations. Rather than seeing this as a worthwhile part of our life, the emphasis in modern life is on intimate relations, on private life of individuals and their relationships with family and intimate friends. This however, he argued, was not leading to a richer life, as 'the more privatized the psyche, the less it is stimulated, and the more difficult it is for us to feel or to express feeling' (p. 4). Individuals are increasingly concerned with their 'single life-histories and emotions as never before; this concern has proved to be a trap rather than a liberation' (p. 5).

In his later writing, Sennett (2000) distances himself from viewing public life as impersonal encounters. But in his seminal writing, *The Fall of Public Man*, he praises impersonality: 'The obsession with persons at the expense of more impersonal social relations is like a filter which discolours our rational understanding of society' (1976: 4). Public life can only be understood through 'codes of impersonal meaning', rather than trying to work it out in terms of personal feelings and emotions (p. 5). Indeed, the private life is in need of being restrained by a public world in which individuals make 'alternative and countervailing investments of themselves' (p. 6).

Like other theorists of public sphere, Sennett seems to idealize a golden age of public life. In his case, it is the early bourgeois attempts to establish a civilized society out of a rapidly changing environment. In the eighteenth-century capital cities, he maintains, a balance was struck between the public and private life. The line between them was drawn to balance the 'claims of civility – epitomized by cosmopolitan, public behaviour' against the 'claims of nature – epitomized by the family' (p. 18). A quality of the nineteenth-century bourgeois life was 'its essential *dignity*' and the family's 'attempt to preserve some distinction between the sense of private reality and the very different terms of the public world outside home' (p. 11). During the nineteenth century, however, the rise of capitalism and secularism and of the notion of family as a refuge led to a decline of public life.

> As the family became a refuge from the terrors of society, it gradually became also a moral yardstick with which to measure the public realm of the capital city. Using family relations as standard, people perceived the public domain not as a limited set of social relations, as in the Enlightenment, but instead saw public life as morally inferior. Privacy and stability appeared to be united in the family; against this ideal order the legitimacy of the public order was thrown into question.
> (Sennett, 1976: 20)

This decline in public life has been expressed in the urban space of our time. The streets and squares as social centres have been replaced by suburban living rooms (p. 28) and the public spaces of the city are abandoned, to become only places 'to move through, not to be in' (p. 14). Everyone is under each other's surveillance, leading to a decrease of sociability and withdrawing into silence as the only form of protection (p. 15).

By drawing on the tradition of *theatrum mundi*, an old Western tradition of seeing society as a theatre, Sennett related social theory and history to develop a theory of expression in public, using changes in public behaviour, speech, dress and belief as evidence. Sennett identifies three moral purposes in this tradition, which otherwise has no single meaning due to its longstanding use by a variety of people. It introduces illusion and delusion as fundamental questions of social life; it detaches human nature from social action; and, most importantly, it recognizes that people are engaged in acting, playing roles in ordinary life (p. 35). Public life is made of play-acting, as expressed in manners, conventions and ritual gestures. By the erosion of the conditions in which play-acting becomes possible, people become members of an intimate society, where they are 'artists deprived of an art' (p. 29). His hypothesis is that theatricality has 'a special, hostile relation to intimacy' while it has 'an equally special, friendly relation to a strong public life' (p. 37). Where a strong public life exists, 'there should be affinities between the domains of stage and street' (p. 37). Particular emphasis is put on convention, as 'the single most expressive tool of public life', which is undermined in a society that prefers intimacy to public life (p. 37). As play-acting declines, self-disclosure becomes the measure of truth. But people obsessed with themselves cannot be expressive, as they are deprived of the skills only developed in the public domain. As de Tocqueville had argued, '*any* emotional relationship can be meaningful only when it is perceived as part of a web of social relations' (Sennett, 1976: 31).

Performance, and the presentation and exchange of symbols, therefore, lies at the heart of social life. We find this even in societies where industrial capitalism and its associated realm of strangers have not developed. In a celebrated essay, the anthropologist Clifford Geertz (1993) develops a multi-layered, 'thick' description of cockfight as an expressive form, a social ritual and its significance for the Balinese society. The fight, which until being banned was performed in public places, was 'at once a convulsive surge of animal hatred, a mock war of symbolical selves, and a formal simulation of status tensions' (p. 444). The aesthetic power of the fight resulted from its capacity of forcing together diverse realities of its immediate dramatic shape, its metaphorical content and its social context. For Geertz, culture is the webs of significance that human beings have spun around themselves (p. 5). By seeing behaviour as symbolic action, and that the meaning of these symbols can only be understood in public, in interaction with others, he develops an interpretive theory of culture. Following Wittgenstein, he thus insists that 'Culture is public because meaning is' (p. 12). The role of anthropologist, and the student of culture in general, is then to construct a reading, an interpretation of this public set of symbolic actions (Geertz, 1993; 1988). Using drama as a mode of interpretation of culture, it was thus possible for Geertz to conclude, in his analysis of the state ceremonies in Bali, that, 'the pageants were not mere embellishments, celebrations of domination independently existing: they were the thing itself'. In other words, the driving force of Balinese life was 'an intricate and unending rivalry of prestige' (quoted in Inglis, 2000: 166).

For the philosopher Thomas Nagel (1998b), the social space, in which multifarious individuals who are enormous and complex worlds in themselves have to fit, is severely limited. The more this public space becomes crowded, the more pressure there is on trying to control it. Managing the appearances and of public space, therefore, becomes a crucial task, as it is here that all interpersonal contact takes place. Even if it goes fairly deep, the management of the surface is 'the constant work of human life' (Nagel, 1998b: 5–6).

The development of a public self, a mask, through the use of conventions, is a tool that allows individuals 'a sense of freedom to lead one's inner life as if it were invisible, even though it is not' (Nagel, 1998b: 8). Creating a balance between the public and the private would be then possible, where public is managed through conventions and private is the sphere of freedom.

> The idea that everything should be out in the open is childish, and represents a misunderstanding of the mutually protective function of conventions of restraint, which avoid provoking unnecessary conflict. Still more pernicious is the idea that socialization should penetrate to the innermost reaches of the soul, so that one should feel guilty or ashamed of any thoughts or feelings that one

would be unwilling to express publicly. When a culture includes both of these elements to a significant degree, the results are very unharmonious ... (Nagel, 1998b: 9)

In this way, Nagel intends to show the limits to the public and the private spheres. Displaying everything in the public sphere, through excessive frankness and increased exposure, is a serious mistake and inevitably the decline of privacy would coincide with the rise of hypocrisy (Nagel, 1998b: 14). The balance between concealment and exposure is thus the key to a civilized social space.

FROM DRAMA STAGE TO THE CITY

The investigations into the realm of face-to-face social encounters seem to adopt a non-spatial direction. The social encounter, it is true, takes place within physical space. But often in these analyses, this appears to be a formless, universal space that has little impact on the encounter, as it is mainly regulated through masks and performances. The difference in location is often a social and institutional difference; space is no more than a stage set and a backdrop. Yet we know that space plays a crucial role in these encounters. We have already seen (in Chapter 1) how interpersonal distance, or personal space, is an index of, as well as a mode of regulating, social communication. The same is true, even more crucially so, of the way space is being subdivided. Through these subdivisions, of which the most important is perhaps that between the public and the private, do societies express individual differences and preferences, power and identity, social institutions and organizations.

The public sphere is the place where individual masks are displayed, compared and reshaped. In the same way that public space is articulated through the display of the building fronts, public sphere is the place of social fronts of individuals. Indeed, the façade of the buildings plays the same role as the masks of individual (albeit as a fixed rather than an easily changeable one): a boundary between the private and the public realms, a medium of representation and communication, a tool of hiding and suppressing what needs hiding.

If social life is interpreted as an ongoing drama on public and semi-public stages, what can be learnt from the design of theatre stage and its parallel with the theatre of social life? In buildings for performing arts (Appleton, 1996), design focuses on the relationship between auditorium and the platform/stage, which is the main function of the building. The platform/stage may be designed for a particular performance, such as music, dance, drama, or designed to be flexibly used with the help of mechanical devices. The stage becomes a neutral container that can be adapted to a wide variety of performances. Although the interior of a performance hall may have a certain character and a large number of other considerations to take into account, the stage will have to be as flexible and as neutral as possible. Is there any parallel here with the design of cities, where flexibility of public open space used for countless forms of social encounters would require the neutrality and universality of the space design (Figure 4.5)?

We know that in theatre design, when different forms of performance use the same stage, some performers can be undermined. Dancers, for example, may suffer from sharing the same stage with others. Their bodies can be damaged by dancing on stage floors that may be appropriate for other performers (Foley, 1994: 26). These floors may be fitted with floor traps or cable ducts, considerably abused when heavy objects are dropped and dragged, leaving the surfaces badly damaged, or have an inconsistent structure, all inappropriate for dancers. Is there a parallel with city design, in the sense that public open spaces that are presumed to be used by all may be inaccessible to some performers, e.g. young skateboarders,

4.5 There are many parallels between city design and theatre design. Flexible public spaces can easily be used as a theatre stage for festivals and performances (Aarhus, Denmark)

or those with some physical disadvantage, such as the disabled? Are neutrality and flexibility enough to make the place ideal for social performance?

Through its focus on articulation of the relations between the audience and the performers, the theatre design has evolved to separate the two from each other. This has established a one-way visual relationship, in which the audience is a passive recipient of performance from a distance. But the root of all theatrical experience, as Molinari (1975) shows, is participation, as exemplified by the theatre of tribal communities, the early Greek drama, medieval religious drama and secular Elizabethan drama. In contrast, the theatre of imperial Rome and the aristocratic and bourgeois theatre of the modern age have inserted a distance between the audience and the performers. We can see how this separation of audience from the performance developed in the modern period at the same time as the separation of the family from the public realm. They both were signs of new divisions of labour in society and, subsequently, new divisions in society and space.

In the revolutionary Soviet Union of the 1920s, before Stalin's purges, many artists were searching for new forms of expression and the state was promoting arts to support agitation and propaganda. According to the Soviet Commissar on Enlightenment at the time, 'Art is a powerful means of infecting those around us with ideas, feelings, and moods' (quoted in Baer, 1991a: 35). The Commissariat's Head of Theatre was asking designers to come up with ideas for an environment of participatory involvement, a structure for acting that would also unite the stage and the auditorium. One result was a system of staircases, bridges and scaffolding surrounding a partial globe that extended into the first rows of the theatre. According to a critic at the time,

> There is no stage ... There is a monumental platform half moved out into the auditorium. One senses that it is cramped within these walls. It requires a city square, a street. (quoted in Baer, 1991a: 46)

The idea of uniting stage and auditorium was also advocated by Tairov in 1921, who encouraged designers to abandon their fascination with the backdrop and concentrate on the stage floor, to break it up to different levels and angles, so as to help the artistic expression and ease of movement by the artists' bodies (Baer, 1991b: 182).

In France in the 1920s, Antonin Artaud, and later his followers in Europe, advocated involvement by the audience to become once again a part of the theatrical experience. It was thought crucial for theatre to create direct communication between members of audience and between spectators and actors (Molinari, 1975: 312). This ideal of audience participation in performance was of course well known for centuries by religious leaders and was one way of encouraging the audience to share religious beliefs. Its secular version was articulated by Rousseau:

> In the middle of a square erect a pole decorated with flowers, gather the people round it and you have a feast. Better still: present the spectators as the show, make them actors themselves, make each one see himself and love himself in all the rest, so that their oneness grows' (Lettre à d'Alembert, quoted in Molinari, 1975, title page)

We can identify, therefore, two ways of treating space for performance, focusing on the relationship between auditorium and the stage: one that keeps them separate and reduces their relation to mainly visual; and another that brings the two together and creates participation and two-way communication. Both these trends can be found in the design of public spaces: one that treats public spaces as a backdrop, at best articulated to have a monumental effect, where display is the primary function; and another that treats space as a place for communication and social encounters, where the space is understood to have an active part in the performance. Public space, therefore, is treated as a backdrop and a setting; as part of a social front to perform various tasks by individuals and institutions as well as the container in which these acts take place.

In both cases, in theatre and in city, the space is required to offer a degree of flexibility and neutrality. Whatever the nature of relations with the audience, the space is needed for a variety of performances by different actors in different conditions and for different reasons. Public space may have been designed and organized for a particular social ritual, such as an annual festival or religious and state parades. But it becomes the setting for a whole range of other, less specified activities throughout its life. Similarly, a place may have been shaped as the setting for a particular routine during the day, such as a marketplace, but left to be used in a less restricted way at night, when it can be taken over by different routines and activities. It is this possibility of flexible use that differentiates a public place from those that have strict controls.

It is important to remember that social encounters with strangers are not constrained to formal settings. The theatre of social life is not limited to the public streets and squares, as so often the design literature emphasizes. The public places in which masks are displayed are everywhere, in shops, restaurants, buses, airports, libraries, beaches, museums, theatres, etc. In other words, anywhere that social life is going on, where social encounters with strangers take place.

DRAMATURGICAL MODEL OF PUBLIC SPHERE

The dramaturgical model offers distinctive and far-reaching tools for understanding public sphere. There are, however, a number of problems associated with this model.

The dramaturgical model of public sphere has its roots in philosophy of pragmatism and behaviourism, with their emphasis on outward appearances and actions. The viewpoint adopted is a third-person perspective and the emphasis in the model is on the observation of the roles people play in the public. The analysis of these roles tends to emphasize the dramatic and expressive aspects of public behaviour and compares public behaviour to artistic expression, therefore taking an explicit aesthetic direction. While these provide some strengths, they can also be limitations.

The view of society as stage and the separation of the self from mask has a strong affinity with Cartesian dualism, in which mind and body are separate. The mind is the driving force behind the scenes and the body is presented in public for particular purposes of social relations. However, in the same way that mind and body are integrated, the self and the mask are in many ways intertwined. Rather than seeing the person as a whole, the dramaturgical model splits the person essentially into two layers of private and public, where two completely different perspectives are opened onto human beings. This separation helps analyse public behaviour in new ways. But when taken as a normative model, to promote play-acting as the basis of civility, it creates the possibility of hypocrisy and widening the gap between reality and appearances. Only by denying the possibility of a reality independent of the public masks can it establish a foundation for such a normative model.

The differences between the performer and the character may be very vague and it is very difficult to establish whether an action comes from the self or the person. The analysis relies heavily on the assumption that all social behaviour is potentially performing. It does not allow for the real self behind the performer to appear. The model does not say there is no-one there. It says that there is often someone hidden behind a mask. The emphasis on the outward appearances and actions implies the belief in the existence of a player behind the play-acting, who can change masks to adapt to different circumstances. Yet we do not hear about who these players really are. The dramaturgical model is satisfied to compare public behaviour with play-acting, but does not go behind the stage, to explore the dark and complicated world of the backstage. We also do not know how far they are free to change their masks, or whether the masks have been welded onto their bodies permanently.

It is obvious that most people at some stage of their public encounters are play-acting, performing a role for a particular situation. Individuals are aware of the presence of others and take this into account in the way they behave. But it is not possible to extend this principle to all social relations in public and use it as the sole basis of analysing public sphere. The perspective cannot account for the phenomenological perspective of individuals, who may believe they are engaged in truthful behaviour and not in play-acting (Figure 4.6). The actor on stage and the audience know that they are engaged in a fictional, temporary display and that masks will be dropped after the show. In real life, however, individuals may believe they or others are engaged in truthful exchange and while they may use acting as part of their behaviour, they are also aware that much is done through impulses, reactions and accidents, none possibly counted as acting. The dramaturgical model appears to suggest that individuals are always in control of their performance, not addressing the problem that they may be pressed to perform in certain ways. Social roles, in other words, are expected of individuals, with most elements ready made, as in language, placed on shelves to be used by an intelligent operator.

As Goffman himself admits, there are major differences between the stage and real life. Whereas the one is performed with the knowledge that it is make-believe, the other is often not rehearsed and is real. On stage, the performers interact in front of and for an audience. In real life, there is no audience involved and the two sides of the interaction adapt their roles to each other, as they are both players and the audience. Using the theatrical understanding to analyse social life can be interesting but somewhat inadequate. In practice, it is theatre that imitates real life, rather than the other way round. It may emphasize and aggrandize some aspects of life, but ultimately it mimics life, rather than having an a priori existence.

Sennett (2000) is aware of the effect of overwhelming stimulation associated with city life, as discussed by Simmel. But he chooses to see this as a challenge, not as a condition of the modern city life, where the information overload and the intensity of social contact has an inevitable impact on the individual. Individual human beings all need to be, at least to some extent, in control of their contacts with the world to feel secure. When this is jeopardized by the complexity of environment, they may withdraw or limit their contacts. It may thus be moving away from reality by not paying attention to modern society's anxiety and the need for psychological security in a fast changing, overwhelming environment. This is a condition of urban life in which human beings, whose impulses and environmental responses have developed through many millennia of living as hunter gatherers, have to cope with far more complex circumstances.

The dramaturgical model can be seen as a cultural companion to the notion

4.6 The play-acting model cannot account for the phenomenological perspective of individuals, who may believe they are engaged in truthful behaviour and not in play-acting, as exemplified in the religious experience (Milan, Italy)

of economic exchange. As society is more and more structured around the relations of exchange, it is essential, as Hume suggested, to engage in polite encounters. The tradition of emphasizing theatricality finds a comfortable place here, as the decorum with which the relations of exchange are civilized.

This explicit aesthetic direction of the dramaturgical model may make it a powerful, though limited, analytical tool, which can interpret the social world according to a particular angle of vision. It does not, however, account for the relationship between expressive action and the player behind the mask, or between expression and the broader context in which it takes place. An important limitation to be acknowledged is the separation of representation from the material conditions in which representation is produced and exchanged. By separating the actors from their contexts, the understanding of the representation becomes limited. This is a limitation that Henri Lefebvre (1991) had stressed in his analysis of semiotics. It also fails, as Sennett (2000) admits, to have a normative content or a political energy. Therefore, seeing public sphere as a scene of public drama has its shortcomings. Geertz is aware of the dangers of searching for deep meanings in cultural analysis: losing touch with political, economic and 'stratificatory realities' and biological and physical necessities, which can turn cultural analysis into 'a kind of sociological aestheticism' (1993: 30).

Goffman's model of interpreting social life as a drama has been very influential. One of its main shortcomings, however, has been its lack of interest in the historical contexts in which the drama of social life is played out. Goffman's dramaturgical model is ultimately located in here and now, and as such is ahistorical. The fact that, for example, he seems surprised that in China elaborate meals can be served in plain restaurants or delicate bolts of silk wrapped in old brown paper sold in hovel-like shops is an indicator of this lack of historical understanding. Goffman's was then 'a picture of society in which there are scenes but no plots' (Sennett, 1976: 36).

What can be said about the commentators who show an almost nostalgic appreciation of the late medieval and early bourgeois sociability (e.g. Ariés, Sennett, and as we shall see in Chapter 6, Arendt and Habermas), and the apparent balance between the public and private which was manifest then? First, that the attempts to strike a balance were limited to a relatively small section of the population in large cities, gradually but cautiously expanding and, second, that in general achieving this balance was an aspiration, rather than an empirical reality. Looking through the haze of centuries, it is possible to lose sight of the reality, whereby most sections of population were not socialized in this way and that a civilized balance between play-acting and intimate life was a goal to move towards rather than the actual conditions in which the vast majority of people lived.

Emphasis on conventions brings with it the problem of the origins of conventions: who develops the conventions and who benefits from particular forms of conventions? As the size of public life has expanded from small elites to large parts of the population, what are the conventions that apply to all and what are the ways in which these conventions are negotiated upon? Many conventions were formed on the basis of the beliefs of the elite in what constituted civilized behaviour. How far are these conventions acceptable today? In a less hierarchical, more egalitarian society, what are the modes of expression that are understood and appreciated by many rather than few? If masks are to be worn in public so as to enhance public life, what should the masks look like for effective communication? If public spaces are to provide settings for public behaviour and social relations, what shape should they take to accommodate many forms of interaction? Should we bemoan the decline of the elite sophistication of public appearances or should we welcome the rise of popular intimacy, which enables a wider range of relationships free of potentially rigid conventions? Should we be nostalgic about the pomp and ceremony with which the eighteenth-century public behaviour was conducted (which was so effectively ridiculed in the caricatures of the time) or should we welcome the more egalitarian codes of dress and behaviour? Could it be the case that crying for the fall of public man and the decline of public sphere would be a nostalgic cry for the decline of a particular aesthetic form, a particular set of appearances without appreciating the actual changes that have occurred in social life?

CONCLUSION

Public sphere is the realm of society as a whole and of the state. A public space is provided by the state and used by the society. In other words, it is controlled by the public authorities, concerns people as a whole, is open or available to them, and is used or shared by all members of a community. There are, however, ambiguities associated with the notion of public sphere. It refers both to the state and the society, both to their entirety and their subsections, both to universal and particular categories, both to impersonal and interpersonal relations, both to concrete and abstract concepts, both to normative and descriptive notions, and to many shades of publicness, where degrees of access, interest and agency can vary widely.

Interpersonal exchange relations among strangers came to be the dominant form of social relations in emerging cities of post-medieval Europe. The cultural framework that enabled this exchange, good manners and social performance, found a new significance. This meant developing and maintaining a social front, a mask that mediates between the biological and the social forces, as a stabilizing social infrastructure for exchange relations. With a shift from interpersonal to impersonal relations, the significance of the early conventions, of which the masks were made, has changed but the necessity of social masks and performance in the public has remained strong. The mask operates as a boundary between the public and private roles of individuals. The public realm, therefore, becomes a display of masks, which can include the social front of the individuals as well as the façades of the buildings and other objects, hiding private interiors from external gaze and constructing a public performance free from internal shadows. The public realm therefore becomes a display of masks, and the public space the theatre stage in which the performance takes place. There are, however, several shortcomings with the dramaturgical model of public realm, such as its Cartesian separation of the self, its emphasis on the mask at the cost of the agent behind it, its social ahistorical emphasis, its trust of conventions, its lack of interest in normative questions, and its tendency to aestheticize social relations. Yet it remains a powerful tool in the analysis of interpersonal social encounters and the environment in which they take place.

Chapter 5
Communal space of the neighbourhood

Our investigation of the public sphere has taken us outside the private realm of personal space, personal property and the intimate realm of household, to the realm of strangers and their social encounters. But this realm of strangers, we soon realize, is not a homogenous space.[1] The urban space is not only split along a public–private distinction. It is also subdivided into socio-economic and cultural patterns. One of the main manifestations of these patterns of differentiation is the urban neighbourhood, where social groups, ethnic and cultural groups and other subsections of the society tend to find a particular place of their own while the political, economic and aesthetic processes find an outlet to be expressed (Madanipour, 2001). In this chapter, we look at the patterns of urban neighbourhoods and see how they subdivide the urban space and the impact of this subdivision on the public–private division of space. Indeed, it is at the intersection of these two systems of differentiation and stratification that we can find a number of major characteristics of urban space. On the one hand, neighbourhoods show how identity and difference find a spatial shape, while on the other hand public–private distinction works within and across the neighbourhoods to frame patterns of social life. It is here that the universality that is associated with public–private distinction finds a particular flavour, as it falls within the distinctive framework of the neighbourhood. At the intersection of the public–private and neighbourhood systems of differentiation, publicness of public spaces and privacy of the private sphere are both challenged. This chapter, therefore, steps outside the home, but stops at the neighbourhood level, where there is some degree of familiarity with the environment through various forms of attachment.

NEIGHBOURHOOD AS A UNIT OF CITY BUILDING

At Greenwich Peninsula, next to the troubled dome which signified the turn of the millennium in London, English Partnerships, an urban regeneration agency, is developing a new residential area called Millennium Village. The project's overall aim is 'to create a secure, high quality modern community with the traditional values of village life'. The masterplan is designed by the architect Ralph Erskine and 'aims to establish a sense of community through the balanced design of buildings and public spaces, the integration of public transport and pedestrian movement and the creation of a varied urban texture that accommodates different uses and activities over a long period of time' (English Partnerships, 1998: 2). This is a significant project and will transform an important site at the heart of a major world city. There is little doubt that it would develop some high-quality residential space. But, we may wonder, how is it possible and why is it desirable to *create a community*? We may be sceptical of this choice of words as simply some sort of publicity, drawing upon a nostalgic and cosy image of village life for selling the development. But even if it is just advertising, why is it employing the notion of community and not something else, for example the quality of individual units in the scheme, as is the case with many developers? What is the significance of public space, which is specifically mentioned here? What is its role in the creation of community, as envisaged by the scheme? Why can a sense of community be created partly through the balance between buildings and public spaces?

Many generations before us have been involved in planning, developing and criticizing urban neighbourhoods. Creating urban neighbourhoods was once the focal point of urban design and planning, but it faded into the background as severe criticisms were waged against its social claims, which included creating communities. Despite these criticisms, the quest for promoting communities is with us once again, from social and political debates around communitarianism to a variety of design proposals for sustainable urban neighbourhoods. This trend, which could be called micro-urbanism (Madanipour, 1996), promotes the design and development of small-scale, distinctive neighbourhoods and settlements, recreating a small version of a city. Public space, it appears, plays a major role in the vision of micro-urbanists, as it is imagined to have done so in the small settlements and urban neighbourhoods of the past (Figure 5.1). Simultaneously, the establishment of an identifiable part of urban fabric as a neighbourhood appears to be a desire to extend the private intimate space beyond the home.

The question of how to deal with the emotive and controversial notion of community is very complex. Nevertheless, as urban planners and designers are engaged in the shaping of cities, they cannot avoid coming to a clear view about the social significance of urban neighbourhoods and communities. The social scientists who are interested in the re-emergence of the notion of community building may also benefit from an examination of the way urban design approaches the subject. This chapter discusses the notion of design and planning of neighbourhoods through examining the current trend, its historic predecessors, some of the broad contexts in which it is embedded, and the role of public space design and provision in neighbourhood planning. The main questions here are: Why is planning by neighbourhoods promoted? Why does the notion of promoting communities,

5.1 Small towns and their public spaces representing (and helping to create) a coherent social and physical structure have been idealized by micro-urbanists (Coimbra, Portugal)

through social change and spatial transformation, keep coming back to the agenda of those who are engaged in understanding, shaping, and managing cities and urban societies? What are the political, economic, social and environmental parameters that lie at the foundation of such return? What is the role of public space in this agenda? What are the characteristics of public spaces that are so centrally embedded in these neighbourhoods? Does the creation of neighbourhoods help in extending the private realm or enhancing the public sphere? What is the role of neighbourhood in the relationship between the home and the city, between the private and the public?

The Millennium Village is not the only example of its kind. The term urban village is now widely used in many contexts. Even some existing parts of cities, such as Fitzrovia in London, tend to reinvent themselves as urban villages. We see this promotion of urban neighbourhoods in Britain by the Urban Villages Forum, which brings together many housebuilders, developers, funders, planners and designers, and works on around 35 projects with the English Partnerships. In response to the 'bland and monotonous developments of recent years' and rather than 'single use and single tenure estates', their aim is 'to create mixed use urban developments on a sustainable scale'. The qualities of the urban villages are spelled out as offering: 'A variety of uses, such as shopping, leisure and community facilities alongside housing; a choice of tenures, both residential and commercial; a density of development which can help encourage the use of non-housing activities; a strong sense of place, with basic amenities within easy walking distance of all residents; a high level of involvement by local residents in the planning and onward management of the new development' (Urban Villages Forum, 1998). Almost all these principles can be traced in the Urban Task Force report (1999), which is a landmark document in the debates about the future shape of British cities. It recommends the creation of 'a hierarchy of public spaces that relate to buildings and their entrances, to encourage a sense of safety and community' (Urban Task Force, 1999: 71).

A parallel trend in the United States, called New Urbanism, has emerged in response to the suburban sprawl which characterizes the main form of American urban development and whose costs are no longer sustainable: 'the creeping deterioration of once proud neighbourhoods, the increasing alienation of large segments of society, a constantly rising crime rate and widespread environmental degradation' (Katz, 1994: ix). Suburbs have failed for they have lacked the 'fundamental qualities of real towns: pedestrian scale, an identifiable centre and edge, integrated diversity of use and population and defined public space'. To confront the problems of cities today, these 'town-like principles' should be applied to cities and regions alike (Calthorpe, 1994: xv). While suburbia is formed by 'pods, highways and interstitial space', cities and towns are composed of 'neighbourhoods and districts, organized by corridors of transportation or open space'. An ideal neighbourhood is therefore so designed as to have a centre and an edge, an optimal size of a quarter mile from centre to edge, a mixture of activities, a network of streets, and a careful attention to the public space and the location of civic buildings (Duany and Plater-Zyberk, 1994: xvii). If the urban villages are villages in the middle of large cities, New Urbanist developments, whether called Traditional Neighbourhood Development or Transit Oriented Development (Katz, 1994) are small, new towns in the middle of sprawling suburbs. Both ideas favour the creation of distinctive, small-scale developments in the middle of a sea of apparently undifferentiated urban space. A similar development in Australia introduces Liveable Neighbourhoods that are sustainable and foster a sense of community (State of Western Australia, 1997).

Another, closely related trend in Britain is the development of new settlements, which draws upon the garden city and new towns experience. In the 1980s, there were nearly 200 proposals for new settlements in England. These were small, free-standing settlements of between 300 and 4,500 houses for development by the private sector. The government appears to have generally discouraged these developments as they are not self-contained or well-served by public transport (DoE, 1996). They are, however, favoured by some as an alternative form of development, which can be used for accommodating the large number of new dwellings needed in the next two decades. What is asked for in the new settlements is the development of a sense of community through a mixture of house types and tenures, a distinct physical boundary, a minimum viable size to support a primary school, and some employment opportunities (Breheny *et al.*, 1993: 25–6).

Finding measures to promote communities is not confined to the urban planning and design circles. It can be found in social and political debates. For example, Amitai Etzioni (1995), who promotes a communitarian agenda, discusses the need for making the physical environment more community friendly. Therefore, what he asks for is the need to design the places we use, from our homes to the entire cities, so as to enhance the communitarian nexus. At small scales, his suggestion is to 'provide people shared space to mingle', as exemplified in seats, sandboxes, playgrounds, laundries and sport facilities. The public spaces at the neighbourhood level, therefore, are expected to provide the opportunity for social interaction and hence the creation of a sense of community. This should be supplemented with measures at larger scales where he asks to 'plan developments in ways that enhance rather than hinder the sociological mix that sustains a community' (pp. 127–8).

These different formulations, among others, appear to amount to a trend, one that promotes micro-urbanism: small-scale urban environments that can generate a sense of togetherness in the midst of threats of ecological degradation, social fragmentation and spatial segregation. But, we may wonder, have we not heard about the need for creating neighbourhoods and communities before? Is it a new initiative or has it been tested before?

A NEW TREND OR A RECURRING THEME?

Half a century ago, Lewis Mumford (1954) wrote in defence of the notion of 'planning by neighbourhoods', which had been widely accepted in the previous two decades but not yet widely used in practice. He argued that neighbourhoods are a social fact and 'exist whenever human beings congregate' (p. 258). This was sufficient for him to argue further that neighbourhoods should be promoted by conscious design and provision, so that they can become 'an essential organ of an integrated city' (p. 269). This was to be done through the Neighbourhood Unit, an identifiable subsection of a city which was 'the only practical answer to the giantism and inefficiency of the over-centralized metropolis' (p. 266). The neighbourhood unit was to be defined by its limits and by its focal point. It was essential to keep an upper limit of growth and extension, suggested to be around 5,000 inhabitants. It was also important to provide 'a civic nucleus to draw people together and an outer boundary to give them the sense of belonging together' (p. 263). Whether a public school, a square or a park, this civic nucleus defined the heart of the neighbourhood and established a centre of social communication and civic engagement.

Both before and after this mid-century survey, we can see how the urban neighbourhood as a unit of social and spatial organization played an important role both in understanding cities, as was the case for the Chicago School of Ecology, and for transforming them, as exemplified in the notion of neighbourhood unit. A generation earlier, Raymond Unwin had written about the need for a clear definition of the various areas of the city and how it was necessary 'to foster the feeling of local unity' in these areas (quoted in Mumford, 1954: 262). Clarence Perry, who had developed the notion of the neighbourhood unit in the 1920s, was one of the leaders of Community Centre Movement, which aimed at providing a local meeting place to serve as a forum for discussion and collective activities. We can see how the notions of community, neighbourhood and public meeting place were intertwined in these developments.

There were many more who used the notion of communities and neighbourhoods in new developments. From the nineteenth century, utopian model towns to industrial villages, and from artists colonies to planned garden suburbs, there were many attempts in the past two centuries to create new communities. The most systematic attempt perhaps came from the British New Towns, which used the notion of neighbourhood unit extensively. Notable among them was the design of Harlow by Frederick Gibberd, which used a hierarchical organization of space. Two or three housing groups of 200–250 houses, with a primary school and a few shops created a neighbourhood. Clusters of neighbourhoods with a population of around 7,000 were associated with a district shopping centre. The town of 80,000 population was to have a focal point: a town centre with a market square (Gibberd, 1962; Taylor, 1973).

The physical arrangement of elements in the new towns can be analysed as creating groups of clusters and centres (Madanipour, 1993). Different forms and scales of clusters, shaped by groups of houses, green spaces, roads and neighbourhoods, were served by different centres of varying form and size. A cluster, often shaped around a public space, is attributed with the meaning of enclosure, privacy, security, intimacy, identity and communication. This was a well known historical precedent, as the rooms and buildings were placed around a courtyard, a village was formed around a common green, a town around a central square. It is to become an embodied social value: the desired friendly relations between human beings as translated into built form. Centres are provided to serve clusters. In the same way, they are focal points located in the middle of clusters. They are used to enrich the clusters by offering a service such as access or pleasure. From cul-de-sacs and green courts to neighbourhood centres and the town centre, all are different kinds of active centres serving the surrounding clusters. In the new towns, a cluster of houses is usually formed of rows of houses on three or four sides of a square. A number of residential clusters form a neighbourhood unit and a cluster of neighbourhood units form the whole town, all served by a hierarchy of access and circular roads. The criterion of walking distance determines the size and relations of urban elements. It is assumed that every inhabitant of the town can reach work or shopping and community centres on foot in a short time. The neighbourhood centre consists of a series of shops often with a church and a community hall on either side. The three-sided square is enhanced by arcades, protecting shoppers from bad weather. The cluster is completed by a road passing on the fourth side, leaving the square as a pedestrian precinct. On the top of shops and arcades there is a series of flats, mixing the residential function with the neighbourhood centre.

Later new towns, and other residential developments, continued to use the notion of clustering around a public space (Figure 5.2). In Irvine, 30 houses are grouped around a square, as it is intended to 'increase neighbourliness and avoid the anonymity of the traditional street frontage layout' (Irvine New Town Corporation, 1971: 123), nearly the same size and motivation that can be found 50 years earlier in the design of Welwyn Garden City.

The idea of planning by neighbourhoods came under severe criticism for its emphasis on the physical rather than social environment. The belief that it was possible to create communities through a new organization of space was discredited as physical determinism. As learnt through many decades of, at times painful, experience, it is possible to create physical proximity between people but impossible to create the social bonds which are the hallmark of a community. We know very well how it is easier to destroy communities, as many postwar urban redevelopment schemes did, than to create new ones. It was argued that it amounts to social engineering and physical determinism to house people next to each other and expect them to develop a community. As these urban neighbourhoods were being created to be a response to the sprawling metropolis, it is no wonder that some of their main criticisms came from a defence of the metropolis. It was argued that the relationship between the neighbourhood and the larger city was unclear and that it was too restrictive for those who preferred an urban ethos, wishing to

5.2 Many new residential developments are designed as clusters of houses around neighbourhood public spaces (Whitley Bay, UK)

travel across the city for work and for establishing social networks (Keller, 1968). It was further argued that mobility of the motor car and flexibility of telecommunication have demolished the need for physical proximity as a basis for community building, as people are related to their communities of interest wherever they are.

If the bounded notion of community was apparently so shattered by Melvin Webber's non-place urban realm, why do we see it emerging again? What should we therefore make of the new attempts at creating communities? What can we say about the continuous efforts of urban planners and designers (as well as politicians and social scientists) at idealizing and promoting communities? If the idea of planning by neighbourhood has been tested and refuted before, why do we see its return? Why is it that when the postwar, public sector schemes with a claim to create communities were halted and criticized, we see an emergence of various forms of neighbourhoods? Is this another similarity among many apparent similarities between the two periods of the 1990s and the 1960s? Is it merely forgetting, or disregarding, the lessons of the previous generations or is there a fundamental theme which keeps recurring? What are the possible reasons for such recurrence of so many variations on a theme?

AN ENVIRONMENTALLY FRIENDLY URBAN FORM

It may be said that the re-emergence of emphasis on neighbourhoods runs parallel to the rise of environmental awareness and search for sustainable urban forms. The 'green city' planners see the reduction of dependence on car as the most important urban design consideration (Roelofs, 1999: 235). Other appropriate planning measures to promote sustainable settlements include discouragement of low-density housing, some degree of concentration of activities, and integration of development with public transport facilities (Selman, 1996: 39). Small settlements, where it is possible to walk to different destinations and where the need to use motor vehicles is thus reduced, are seen as an environmentally friendly form of development. This is set against the suburbs and exurbs, where any activity outside home, even going to the nearest shop, may have to rely on the use of a motor car. As evident from the historical towns, the central locations are the most accessible places in a neighbourhood, reducing the distances and the need for travel. The significance of central public spaces, especially when enhanced by services, becomes evident for reducing the use of the car.

Caring for the environment in urban development, therefore, appears to be promoting urban neighbourhoods and villages. A well-known proposal by Peter Calthorpe (1996: 470–1) promotes 'pedestrian pockets' as the 'post-industrial suburbs', with up to 2,000 units of housing and defined as 'a balanced, mixed-use area within a quarter-mile or a five minute walking radius of a transit station'. This pattern, which closely resembles some second generation British New Towns such as Redditch, Runcorn and Irvine, is meant to offer a choice of using different modes of transport. But against this apparently pragmatic step towards rationalizing suburbs, there are powerful forces at work: the land and property markets prefer the clarity of single use areas, and the advocates of pedestrian pockets have no mechanism to ensure such mixture of use that the need for travel is seriously reduced. Public transport often does not find the necessary investment and drivers prefer to use their cars. The small populations of these neighbourhoods cannot support a wide range of activities. People's patterns of movement are increasingly complex as living, shopping and leisure activities are located in a large number of places across an urban region and follow widely different time routines. Is there a danger that the built version of pedestrian pockets becomes completely devoid of the original ideals, to be merely well designed housing estates?

New settlements of 10,000 dwellings (25–30,000 population) which can support employment and other services are considered to be one of the most environmentally sound forms of development (Breheny et al., 1993). An historic example of this form of development is the British New Towns, which aimed at creating self-sufficient towns and neighbourhoods, where almost all that was needed for a 'healthy' life could be found in the locality: homes, jobs, shops, parks, etc. After all, it was Ebenezer Howard who had advocated a marriage of town and country in small garden cities of around 30,000 population (Howard, 1960). After the development of the early new towns, however, it became evident that a mobile population with complex social networks and lifestyles could not entirely live within the limits of small neighbourhoods and towns.

To find an environmentally sustainable way of providing housing for the increasing number of households in Britain (initially estimated as 4.4 million by the year 2016), the Department of the Environment promoted two possible scenarios: new settlements, which was a rising trend in the 1980s but discouraged by the government, and the use of existing built-up areas. The latter could take place through the development of vacant or derelict sites, redevelopment and intensification of urban development in the older, low-density suburbs. Here we see also the idea of urban villages is enlisted as one in which private developers get together to create mixed-use developments of 3–5,000 populations in the existing urban areas (DoE, 1996: 22–3). Both scenarios for sustainable development, therefore, refer to the creation of distinct, small-scale development, whether as urban villages or as new settlements.

At best, a spatial organization which offers some local facilities within easy reach can reduce some of the trips that a household has to make. Compared with the sprawling suburb or the single-use housing estate with no facility, planning by neighbourhoods offers some obvious advantages. This is one of the main lines of promoting planning by neighbourhoods in the literature. It is, however, by no means the only way of securing an environmentally sound urban form.

An alternative pattern is linear development alongside transport corridors (Barton, 1996; White, 1994), an idea which has been around for a long time. In the search for a sustainable pattern of settlement, however, many seem to agree on the need for containing cities. Agenda 21 asked for encouraging intermediate city development to counterbalance the large urban agglomerations (Quarrie, 1992: 78). It has been argued, for example, that a good spread of facilities in a compact, overlapping urban area would have a similar effect. Despite criticisms (Breheny, 1992), there is strong support for the intensification of urban areas and the notion of compact cities which can confront suburban dispersal and specialization of land use (CEC, 1990) (Figure 5.3). The Urban Task Force promotes the idea of compact city, but as it works within the micro-urbanist paradigm, it envisages the compact city as a collection of neighbourhoods linked together through public transport. The idea may seem logical as a diagram (Urban Task Force, 1999: 53, 55), but it only works if these neighbourhoods have the necessary density to

5.3 Compact cities are examples of overlapping neighbourhoods as well as energy efficient environments (Porto, Portugal)

sustain the services that would turn them into semi-autonomous functional units of the urban renaissance planners. For example, to have a group of local shops, 5,000 to 10,000 population is needed (p. 61). The question is: in the current conditions in which many post-industrial cities are losing population, through suburbanization or the erosion of their economic base, how realistic is it to expect such densities in this orderly manner? A proposal to develop an urban village along these lines in the West End of Newcastle paradoxically intended to increase the population and density of an area that has suffered from multiple deprivation, population loss and collapse of property market. Can supply guarantee demand? Can the provision of housing turn the misfortunes of a city into prosperity? Planning by neighbourhoods may be a useful tool for growth management. Can it equally be useful in reversing decline? Can the provision of a well designed public space encourage a lively community?

It is clear that urban infill development performs better on social and environmental grounds than new settlements (Breheny et al., 1993). The main difficulty is that the new developments have traditionally been developed on cheaper land on urban fringes rather than on recycled land in the cities. Furthermore, in Britain the prospects of urban intensification suffer from the government's reluctance to provide necessary incentives and people's cultural preference for houses with gardens, rather than flats.

Therefore, planning by neighbourhoods has some contribution to make in searching for sustainable urban form when introduced to manage the growth in the suburbs. The introduction of an active public space, where the residents can go to on foot and have access to a range of services, can potentially contribute to the quality of local provision as well as reducing some car use. But it is hard to see how the introduction of new urban villages in the middle of cities can have the same claim. Neighbourhoods are not the only sustainable urban form and can only be effective if accompanied by substantial investment in public transport and by structural changes in urban development process, property markets and popular lifestyles. Can it be guaranteed that the public spaces and public services are supported by sufficient population numbers and densities with enough resources available to maintain them? Are there any reasons other than environmental sustainability that make planning by neighbourhood a popular choice?

A MEANS OF URBAN MANAGEMENT

It may be said that the new attention to the neighbourhoods is in line with the new interest in focusing on space by policy makers and the rise of new forms of urban governance. The Conservative government in Britain had emphasized a spatial focus for urban policy, as a means of targeting resources and relaxation of regulation in particular locations. The New Labour government has continued and intensified the spatial focus by arguing that for too long departmental and sectoral separation has prevented effective attention to be paid to the mounting social problems. What is asked for is 'joined up' working, crossing the barriers between various government agencies and between the public and private sectors. A renegotiation of the division of labour is needed to pull down some of the functional boundaries between the departments and agencies, boundaries which could have a negative impact on the delivery of services. Bringing these forces together, therefore, requires a new focus, which has increasingly been the 'place' (Madanipour, Hull and Healey, 2000). To create this spatial, rather than functional, focus, a number of area-based initiatives have been introduced, such as The New Deal for Communities, which deals with regeneration of small neighbourhoods, or Single Regeneration Budget, which targets larger areas with average 25,000 people, or Health Zones, Education Zones and Employment Zones (Social Exclusion Unit,

2001). Furthermore, the idea of neighbourhood management, as a way of involving citizens in decision making and promoting good governance is advocated, asking for securing 'real trusteeship', 'super-caretakers' and 'neighbourhood wardens' (Urban Task Force, 1999: 113, 119).

The idea of subdividing the city into manageable and identifiable sections has been a long-standing concern of urban planning and design: from the Hippodamian system of dividing citizens by class and land by type (Gorman, 1995) to the early twentieth-century, German notion of dividing the city into specialized zones (which was used by Perry to develop his concept of neighbourhood unit) (Mumford, 1954). The trend developed in Britain and the United States and was adopted in a variety of countries. Even the Nazis in Germany, who saw cities as 'the seat of Judaism' and the 'place of Marxism' accepted the city as a necessary evil and adopted neighbourhood planning as the way forward (Schubert, 2000: 127). To ensure the control of the conquered lands to the east, the Nazis promoted the idea of the local group as a settlement cell. The urban form that local groups would take, Heinrich Himmler, the commander of the SS announced, consisted of 'small cells and ultimately in small streets, as well as the clear arrangement of the squares, residential courtyards and neighbourhood groups' (quoted in Schubert, 2000: 129). The terminology and the ideological framework may have been significantly different; but the idea of managing citizens through creating some form of distinction and order in the apparently disordered city remained largely the same in different places and times.

The distinctions that are imposed on the city may be merely administrative and unrelated to those on the ground. For example, in 1973 a councillor for Lewisham borough in London tells us about how out of 265,000 population of his constituency, only 2,000 can be clearly identified with the urban village of Lewisham (Taylor, 1973). The distinctions may be functional, as developed by the planning system to separate zones for industrial, commercial and residential activities. It is this system of official distinction that led to an artificial fragmentation of cities and which has been confronted by a generation of protest (famously by Jacobs, 1961) and now by policies promoting mixed use developments (DoE, 1997). The distinctions may also be attempts at controlling the overall shape of the city's growth.

More severe forms of imposing some order onto cities have been the redevelopment schemes, where it was possible to dislocate real, working communities with a physical notion of community expressed in a physical delineation of the neighbourhood and its centre. In these cases, the city was being reshaped in the name of community building without paying much attention to the reality of life in the city. Strangely, social engineering could take contradicting social and spatial shapes. On the one hand, it could lead to attempts at abolishing difference and diversity in the city, as spatially expressed in the imposition of long and wide avenues on existing urban fabrics, as in Paris, or by planting an undifferentiated gridiron onto the natural landscape, as in New York (Figure 5.4). Social engineering could also take a reverse trend and try to promote small-scale neighbourhoods to confront the anonymity of the metropolis, which was thought to threaten the moral and social order. Stranger still, when these ideas were transplanted into the cities outside the industrial world, both these systems could end in the erosion of local social systems of signification, in dismantling real communities in the name of creating them.

Legislation, therefore, has imposed some form of order on an otherwise frenetic urban development process, favouring a process of 'containment' (Hall, 1973), as exemplified by the attempt to curb the sprawl of new ribbon developments into the countryside in the 1930s. New suburban developments in Britain stretched along the existing roads, causing cries of anger for blocking the views

5.4 Imposition of geometry onto the urban space has been a longstanding means of ordering and managing cities (Paris, France)

into the countryside and making the provision of services difficult. The Restriction of Ribbon Developments Act in 1935 was a response to these problems (Greed, 1993). What followed was that new residential areas, both municipal housing and private suburbs, took the form of more compact developments with their own internal roads. The new urban neighbourhoods and villages are a continuation of this tradition of containment, as a form of rationalization of urban development to promote a more effective urban management.

While place-based initiatives can establish horizontal links, they can lead to imbalance and differential treatment. Some areas are favoured at the expense of others, as some areas may be perceived to be more significant for the local economy, which could cause turf wars between their political representatives. Some areas may be stigmatized and suffer from particular forms of attention, or from a blanket treatment of a diverse population within a neighbourhood. Attention to the urban region as a whole and developing a strategic point of view may thus be undermined. Is this not a rather crude form of management? In the information age, where management can be supported by a variety of subtle and sophisticated tools, is physical separation not an inadequate means of managing an entity as complex as a city? The pressure to protect and maximize return on investment has led to total management of environment and privatization of space (Madanipour, 1999). Are distinctive neighbourhoods not creating semi-private places by reducing access and openness? If this is the case, what is the status of 'public' spaces in the middle of these controlled and managed sub-sections of urban space? Are they places of open communication and sociability or the places of conformism and control? History is full of examples of public places that signified authority and control, filled with symbols of power, from the statues of kings to the corporate logos.

A VEHICLE OF MARKET OPERATION

As urban space is treated as a commodity, the conflict between exchange value and use value has a major impact on the shape of cities and the life of citizens (Logan and Molotch, 1987; Lefebvre, 1991). This commodity lies at the heart of land and property markets, which institutionalize the differentiation of urban space (and stratification of urban society) on the basis of perceived qualities of each place. For doing so, the markets partly rely on social and spatial clues which represent a place. The result may not be a clear-cut picture, but it outlines a framework of differentiation, which changes often slowly and has a deep impact on the nature of social relations and physical configurations of a city. Land and property markets are, therefore, a clear indicator of (and a contributor to) the social divide that so characterizes the modern city.

When this framework of differentiation is combined with (and evolves around) the policies of containment, the outcome can be the creation of a mosaic of socio-spatial difference, in which social groups and their associated environments are separated from each other. At their extremes, this separation is manifest in walled neighbourhoods of the rich and the pockets of deprivation. It is with this adherence to social and spatial differentiation that the land and property markets favour a separation of land uses.

The New Urbanist ideas can be seen as the residential equivalent of business parks, industrial parks and shopping malls, which for long have agglomerated similar activities in functional nodes in the sprawling suburbs. Now there is a call for the residential areas to be organized in a similar way. Together they form a trend of re-organizing the space of the city region in new agglomerations of homogenous functional zones, accessible by car and as such potentially socially exclusive. The circle becomes complete. Residential areas were among the first to leave the city, followed by shops and workplaces and other activities. Now they are the last to be regrouped and rationalized along new lines, to make a more effective use of an infrastructure that is the backbone of a more dispersed and disjointed urban region. This is in line with the intentions and capacities of the large players in the development industry.

The nature of the development industry has changed dramatically since the beginning of the twentieth century (Whitehand, 1987; 1992; Logan, 1993). Locally based, small-scale developers have given way to large-scale, national and international developers. Large development companies have access to more resources and more advanced production capacities (Figure 5.5). For these reasons, they prefer large-scale development schemes, where the costs of production are lower and a flow of return on their investment seems more secure. Large-scale production is an essential feature of housing production in Britain and the United States. The industrial and commercial property markets are also dominated by the large financial institutions (Pratt and Ball, 1994; Guy, 1994).

In addition to this structural change, there is a large surplus of capital available from a decade of economic growth in Britain and the USA, which finds its way into the built environment. Accumulation of surplus capital reaches such levels that the creation of large-scale, new developments and the re-organization of urban space can once again come back onto the economic agenda. The urban renaissance agenda is partly drawing on this prosperity and, more fundamentally, responds to the demands of the post-industrial, service economy, which now claims the city as a site of its operations. In Britain, this also draws on the process of Europeanization, which means more attention to city living.

Therefore, changing urban economic base, availability of finance, changing

5.5 Large development companies have access to large resources and advanced production capacities, enabling them to transform cities at high speed. This leads to a preference for large-scale developments and highly managed public spaces (Boston, USA)

scale of the development industry and the preference of the land and property markets for segregation of land uses and stratification of urban space all lead to the development of large-scale, segregated areas, as mostly expressed in the shape of urban neighbourhoods. The economies of scale and the nature of space production require large-scale operations, hence the development industry prefers grouping of buildings, rather than individual buildings. As urban regeneration takes place through public–private partnerships, the development industry is well placed to promote its preference for larger-scale operations. As the built up areas of cities rarely offer this opportunity, the cheaper land on the margins or in the decayed inner areas is used to build new, large-scale developments. Urban development takes place within a market framework and a regulating regime. The combined effect of the market and the regulation appears to create enclaves, preferring concentrated, large-scale rather than scattered, small-scale development around the city.

But if the building of neighbourhoods makes economic sense for its producers, does it do the same for the economy as a whole? If community building is successful and people are deeply integrated into communities, would they be economically performing better? It appears that people with weaker, rather than stronger, ties are better able to take advantage of or cope with change. Some even see economic development as directly engaged with individual freedoms (Sen, 1999), which may not be found in very tightly organized communities.

The question that comes to the fore is, What is the character of public spaces that are developed within such a market framework? Do they address the needs of the consumers of these products or their producers, or both? Are public spaces showcases, selling points in the development of large-scale new settlements; or are they being provided as a necessary part of living in a neighbourhood in response to essential needs?

A FRAMEWORK FOR SOCIAL INTEGRATION

The entry into the industrial era was characterized by a disruption of centuries old agrarian communities, uprooting individuals from their towns and villages and amassing them in large, anonymous cities. Victorians saw their age as that of great cities, but while some were proud of the progress that these large cities represented, others were frightened of the unknown dimensions of the city (Briggs, 1968). This caused a fear of social disintegration and of uncontrollable masses, which drew the middle classes away from the cities, causing further social fragmentation. The response of the Victorians was attempts at social integration, through promoting various kinds of either religious morality or secular solidarity.

The influences of religious and political leaders in the small towns and villages were quite clear. Not in the large city, as this was a place where people could be anonymous or be constantly on the move. The result of such anonymity and mobility was a concern for the breakdown of social order and the loss of social control. Richard Vaughan, a Victorian Unitarian minister wrote:

> In a neighbourhood where every man is known, where all his movements are liable to observation, and the slightest irregularity becomes a matter of local notoriety, a strong check is constantly laid upon the tendencies of the ill-disposed. In such connexions it is felt that should the law fail to punish, society will not. The crowded capital is to such men as some large and intricate forest, into which they plunge, and find, for a season at least, the places of darkness and concealment convenient for them. (quoted in Briggs, 1968: 61)

In other words, while the public spaces of the neighbourhood were places of exposure, where individuals were under the scrutiny of others, the crowded streets and public spaces of the big city were the places of concealment, where they could hide and live the life in the way they wished. But this extension of freedom to masses was frightening the elite. The privacy that the large city offered to the individual was not available in the small town or in the neighbourhood. The scrutiny of the others was needed to limit this privacy in the name of social order.

As early as the first decade of the nineteenth century, the City of London lost population for the first time. Other cities, such as Liverpool, Birmingham and Bradford, followed later in the century (Briggs, 1968: 26). Life in the city was identified with industrial activities and with overcrowding, disease, poverty and crime. Those who could afford it fled to the countryside, where for centuries the aristocrats had resided. Living in the countryside was seen as the sign of success, and therefore was idealized by the urban middle class. This social and spatial segregation intensified the concern for social fragmentation and loss of control, as the city represented crowds of anonymous, atomized, individuals living in potentially explosive conditions. Political and religious leaders saw social polarization as very dangerous. There are two nations living in the same island, said Disraeli. Before him, Dr William Channing of Boston, another Unitarian minister, wrote: 'In most large cities, there may be said to be two nations, understanding little of one another, having as little intercourse as in different lands' (quoted in Briggs, 1968: 62).

The Victorians shared this mistrust of large cities with their ancient predecessors. For Aristotle, as well as for Plato, the size of a city was important. Whereas Plato had a more definite prescription for the size of a city, Aristotle accepts that there must be a limit but does not determine the number of inhabitants. What matters for him is that a good city is based on good laws and order, and in a large city it becomes impossible to keep the order. In his words, the ideal city must 'not be so large that it cannot be easily surveyed' (Aristotle, 1992: 405).

Fear of the unknown, of the uncontrollable masses, drew the middle classes away from the cities. This was 'a collective effort to live a private life' (Mumford, quoted in Fishman, 1987: x), resulting in what now houses the majority of population in Britain and the United States. Suburbia, as Fishman (1987: x) puts it, was 'the collective creation of the Anglo-American middle class: the bourgeois utopia'. But this trend, even from the early nineteenth century, led to social segregation. Engels reported on how Manchester was built in such a way that 'a person may live in it for years, and go in and out daily without coming into contact with a working-people's quarter or even with workers' (1993: 57).

With the spread of industrial capitalism across the world, cities everywhere were concentrating crowds, which caused anxiety for those concerned with social control. Cities were also a concentration of wealth and power, which caused anxiety for the revolutionaries who wanted to change the established order. The early years of the Soviet Union shows a mistrust of large cities and a desire to curb their size and relocate their population to small towns (Bater, 1980). This was reaching an extreme later in Vietnam and Cambodia, where cities were forcefully depopulated. A similar trend, as we saw, can be detected in Nazi Germany of the mistrust of cities (Schubert, 2000). Even the western democracies continued their suspicion of the large city and promoted decentralization policies, complaining about the association between overcrowding and crime and with unhealthy living conditions.

Cities were everywhere full of anonymous crowds, segregated and explosive. These caused fear and anxiety, but also generated enormous energies, new forms of associations and institutions, which have been the hallmark of the modern industrial city. The new public spaces of parks, museums, libraries etc. were the great achievements of the age. The old social ties of kinship and history in the small towns and villages were broken free in the large city, at once freeing individuals to explore the world and build new relationships and at the same time filling them with nervousness and unease about an unknown future and the lack of support from the old certainties. In the city, it was access to resources, more than anything else, which gave the key to establishing new relations and identities. These trends, therefore, carved out the main contours of the modern city, which have remained in place up to this day. Although the general conditions of the urban populations have considerably improved, the same features of anonymity and mobility of individuals, social polarization and segregation, and suburbanization can still be identified with the cities now. What Engels reported about socio-spatial segregation in Manchester of the 1840s is valid for many cities today. While racial and social segregation in American cities are well known, the European city also suffers from increased threats of social fragmentation and polarization (European Commission, 1994). As the industrial era draws to a close in many cities, a new age of anxiety and loss of old certainties has begun.

As expressed in the work of many sociologists, among them Tönnies, Durkheim, Simmel and Wirth, city life was not conducive to community life, a view known as the 'community lost' argument. Later, however, others such as Jacobs and Gans showed the existence of some cohesive groups in cities who lived in urban villages and had close social ties with a sense of community among people who shared a common territory, a perspective known as 'community saved' argument (Knox, 1995). A way out of this traditional dichotomy is to concentrate on the sequence of historical events in the cities, to observe the formation and disintegration of communities in urban neighbourhoods.

Generations of working and living together developed new urban communities, which emerged as ethnic enclaves protecting each other in an unknown environment or as working-class groups establishing close social networks through common work and living space. What was once displacement and uprootedness turned into cohesion. But the rationale for these communal groupings started to disappear. As a result of technological change and globalization of economy, many traditional industries have disappeared, relocated to less regulated, lower-wage economies, leading to mass unemployment for those engaged in such activities as ship building, coal mining, and heavy engineering. As opportunities for industrial work for men have dwindled, a host of social problems have emerged. The security of long-term employment supported by a strong welfare state has given way to a casualization of work and a constant discussion of radical reform for social insurance. As women increasingly join the workforce, there is a difficult path for jobless men to learn new skills and to find a new social role in the household and in the community. As stable, working neighbourhoods have turned into pockets of deprivation, the communities of the industrial era have also come under heavy pressures for disintegration (Madanipour, Cars and Allen, 1998; Madanipour and Bevan, 1999). As the industrial era draws to a close in some cities, communities are once again torn apart, as evident in the disintegration of many social networks, rising crime, physical decay and loss of population.

The shifts into and out of the industrial era, therefore, have caused major social changes, which have generated new energies but also much anxiety and fear. It is in the context of the need to overcome these anxieties that a constant theme can be identified in the last two centuries: the need to redefine and rebuild the fractured social relations. As society was becoming increasingly individualized, there was a need for new modes of social integration. As social fragmentation found clear spatial manifestations, in the growth of suburbia and in social segregation of social groups, it was thought that a spatial solution should also be found. By bringing people together in distinctive neighbourhoods clustering around focal public spaces and institutions, it was thought a foundation was being laid for the creation of new communities out of displaced individuals. The origins of modern urban design and most of its activities should be studied in this context, to be partly an attempt against social fragmentation and its spatial manifestations.

But how can modern anxieties be treated with these old remedies? Are cohesive relations welcome by all? There are some who welcome new tribalism as a way of revitalization of society (Maffesoli, 1996). But the establishment of a new community means establishing a system of power relations, which many will not welcome. It means intrusion into the private sphere of individuals by community groups and hierarchies. As for the inhabitants of the city, the urban neighbourhood offered a refuge if they felt a need for material and emotional support in an unknown urban world. For those who felt strong enough, however, the communal bonds of a neighbourhood appeared stifling, a context from which it was essential to break free. The cohesive communities formed by displaced groups of working class had hierarchical, male-dominated, close social ties developed as a result of working and living together under intense pressure, coupled with lack of mobility. Although these ties were valuable coping mechanisms, are the conditions of developing them existing or desirable? What social ties can be developed in highly privatized and differentiated lifestyles of the modern city? What form of social integration develops out of increasingly temporary social ties? The displaced and the disadvantaged have no access to employment, to decision making, or even to shared experiences. Under these conditions, can the community building agenda be mistaken for an exercise in social control, and the pressure to develop social capital for an exercise in abandoning social responsibility?

There are some clear contradictions in the intrinsic features of distinctive urban neighbourhoods. They promote differentiation, which may be a useful framework to counter anonymity and atomization. But they may enhance social disintegration through the creation of visible spatial and social barriers. The extreme cases are fortified neighbourhoods of the middle class where walls and gates separate parts of the city identified as secure neighbourhoods, as exemplified by thousands of neighbourhoods in the USA and many other countries around the world (Figure 5.6). Here, as in the medieval neighbourhood, where gates and walls separated groups and institutionalized factional strife, the public space is completely limited to the use by neighbourhood members. Others are considered outsiders, watched and controlled in these areas. Only the familiar, the resident, the approved can be present in the public spaces of these gated neighbourhoods. A neighbourhood that sets out clearly defined and highly guarded limits from the outside world is more an extension of the private sphere, rather than an attempt to create a community. Its negative side of emphasizing differences from others and creating segregation from the outside world is much stronger than its drive for integration among its residents. As the example of South Africa's gated neighbourhoods shows (Landman, 2000), in addition to 'security villages', many public streets are sealed and gated to create segregated enclaves that are painful reminders of the apartheid past. Rather than being a community of communities (Etzioni, 1995), the society may become the site of exaggerated differentiation, which leaves it with more fractures than before. This might lead to a neo-medievalism of factional strife among localities and communities, rather than the development of abilities to negotiate for a set of common platforms and shared experiences.

5.6 Gated neighbourhoods are extreme forms of differentiation and stratification of urban space, extending private space beyond home to the neighbourhood level (Los Angeles, USA)

A MEANS OF DIFFERENTIATION

Most examples of designing urban neighbourhoods try to delineate clearly the neighbourhood so as to create a sense of distinction and identity. Creation of distinctive areas as a means of urban management and a vehicle of market operation are both attempts from *above*, from the viewpoint of those who have the power of transforming the city through their professional activities detached from personal engagement. In addition to these political and economic dimensions, however, there is a cultural dimension, as seen from a viewpoint from *below*. This is the viewpoint of the people who use and inhabit urban space and hence contribute to its transformation through their living patterns and demand. Together and when in operation, these processes lead to a *collectivization of difference* in the city, which is partly expressed in urban neighbourhood.

In the atomized world of the city, where the stability of coherent communities appears to be either nonexistent or under serious threat, new social ties have to be forged. These new social ties are, however, dependent on (and a constituent of) how individuals develop their identities. Social identity is a process, which systematically establishes and signifies the relationship of similarity and difference between individuals, between collectivities, and between individuals and collectivities (Jenkins, 1996). One of the important components of social identity is its spatial dimension, i.e. where we live, how we move about in the world around us, where we can or cannot go, etc. Through their consumption of space, among other commodities, individuals establish a relationship of similarity and difference with others, i.e. identifying themselves with some people and areas of the city and distinguishing themselves from others (Figure 5.7). As clearly signified neighbourhoods offer easier frameworks to establish similarity and difference, the urban neighbourhood is reproduced and promoted successfully. For some, an exclusive neighbourhood is the means with which they feel they can rise above the mass society. They are at the same time establishing their similarities with others in that neighbourhood and difference from others outside it.

The neighbourhood can be a small world where meaning is created, where

5.7 Displaying particular systems of symbols in public space develops a visible framework to establish patterns of similarity and difference and a distinctive identity for an urban area (Chinatown, San Francisco, USA)

children are socialized and go through the process of self-identification. As Philip Roth puts it:

> Perhaps by definition a neighbourhood is a place to which a child spontaneously gives undivided attention; that's the unfiltered way meaning comes to children, just flowing off the surface of things. (1998: 43)

The problem of authenticity may not present itself to all those who have an interest in this process of signification. When we design and develop an urban village, we are likely to reproduce an appearance of a village: a small settlement with a few shops, a village green and the possibility of leaving the car aside and just walk everywhere. This may have aesthetic and indeed environmental significance, but what about its social meaning? In what way is it different from any housing develop-ment anywhere? Even many 'country' villages, as distinct from 'urban' villages, are no longer coherent entities. They house urban populations who commute to cities and who partly see villages as a dormitory and at best a retreat, rather than a place in which they have to be actively engaged. On the surface, these may seem to be villages. In reality what appears rural is urban in many senses of the word. Urban villages reject the single use, single tenure qualities of the postwar public housing schemes and aspire to some of the qualities of a 'real', unplanned village. The only difference appears to be that these urban villages are instantly created rather than gradually evolved and that they are urban, planted in the middle of an urban context, as for example the Forum's projects show: Crown Street in Glasgow and Hulme in Manchester, among others. If the traditional village was developed over a long period of time in the middle of countryside, now the urban village is to be instantly developed in the middle of an urban world. Both urban and rural villages, however, are thought to remain entities which are physically identifiable from their surroundings.

The desire to establish a sense of distinction for the neighbourhood has been a major part of urban design practice. Kevin Lynch, for example, paid much atten-tion to the identification of districts within cities (1960), a practice which has con-tinued ever since in enhancing character zones and the promotion of distinctive sub-areas in cities (e.g. the design guide for Birmingham: Tibbalds *et al.*, 1990). The public spaces of the local neighbourhoods, therefore, become one of their means of identification and distinctiveness.

We can draw an interesting parallel between this desire for local differenti-ation in the face of undifferentiated urban space and a much larger phenomenon: the desire to assert local distinctions in the face of the global flows of resources and what some see as the drive for cultural homogenization across the world. Both are attempts to assert local distinctions in opposition to an external threat of domination and alienation. As such, both these trends can be seen as means of differentiation, asserting, as Lefebvre (1991) would say, the right to be different. Both are seeking psychological security through taking refuge in the small-scale environment of a locality (in the case of globalization) or a neighbourhood (in the case of urbanization), hoping to be safe in the middle of a potentially hostile world. At its smallest scale, urban design has sought to establish spatial enclosures in urban areas, i.e. streets and squares, which are partly expressing this need for psychological security and a refuge from the unknown large city.

The reasons for seeking such systems of local distinction, however, are not confined to psychological and cultural needs. Many cities now promote their distinctiveness in a global, competitive marketplace as a vehicle of economic development and regeneration. In doing so, they hope to attract investment, both from employers whose white-collar workers prefer to live in well designed and well managed localities and from tourists who can potentially revive the urban economy. But this process is by no means unproblematic, as high stakes are involved in what signifies the locality and how. Furthermore, as the experience of post-Socialist countries, among others, shows, the politics of identity have serious shortcomings. Even at the neighbourhood level, violent forms of differentiation can appear, such as the gang territories and the walled and gated neighbourhoods of Los Angeles (Davis, 1992), the gang wars of the Parisian suburbs (*The Guardian*, 12 May 1998), which remind us of the factional strife of the medieval city neighbourhoods (Vance, 1977).

The distinctive neighbourhoods, therefore, are a vehicle of differentiation: for individuals, to establish identity and social status, for developers, to distinguish their products from the rest, and for cities in their competition for resources in the global marketplace. The role of public space appears to be helping to establish the distinctive identity of the place and create the conditions in which the neighbourhood population can develop their relationships. This can be a process of identification for individuals, branding for commercial organizations, and image making for political authorities. Neighbourhoods can also exacerbate social fragmentation by subdividing urban space into separate units, which have real divisive roles going beyond the questions of superficial differentiation.

CONCLUSION

In an impersonal world, the social encounter is reduced to an abstraction, where instrumental action is the main aim of the encounter. This lies at the heart of the paradigm of society as the realm of individual strangers. To confront this alienation, communities are seen as frameworks that protect the individual and the household from the impersonal world. A community, it is hoped, would establish an interpersonal level of encounter, hence preventing alienation.

Neighbourhoods, therefore, are intermediary levels of organizing space, reducing the effects of a dichotomous divide between the public and private spheres. On the one hand, they seem to semi-privatize parts of urban space, i.e. create a clearly defined area for the residents to feel in control and for the non-residents to feel outsiders. In other words, the neighbourhoods are created to extend the private sphere of individual property and intimate home to a larger part of the city. On the other hand, the neighbourhood appears to be a mechanism with which groups find supremacy over individuals, so they can intrude into the private sphere of individuals and households. By defining a separate part of the city, in which social encounters are potentially intensified among limited participants, the possibility of privacy and concealment is reduced under the gaze of the group.

We have seen that splitting the city into distinctive, small-scale neighbourhoods inside or on the periphery has been advocated as an environmentally friendly urban form. We know that it is popular as a means of urban management and as a vehicle of market operation, in line with the organization of the development industry. People have identified with urban neighbourhoods as these have been a means of differentiation, where the collectivization of difference has taken place. Social and political theorists, in their mistrust of the emergent individualism of the Enlightenment era, have promoted holism, development of communities, which have been partly expressed in the physical shape of urban neighbourhoods and small settlements. These are substantial foundations for the notion of development by neighbourhood, or micro-urbanism. In this delineation of small parts of cities and towns, public space has played a crucial role by being the focal point, the centre of attraction, where sociability and community building can be exercised. Without the focus on a clear centre and the demarcation of its outer boundary, the idea of neighbourhood planning loses two of its key defining characteristics.

These foundations suggest that the idea of micro-urbanism will stay with us. Each new generation seems to discover for itself the dangers and pleasures of the city, the freedoms it offers and the threat of anonymity. Each new generation throughout the last two centuries has 'rediscovered' the need for community building and the physical shape that this takes. The rise of the city has created a continuous fear of anonymity and atomization of individuals. The elusive theme of building bridges and forging socio-spatially identifiable communities comes back to the agenda of those concerned with understanding cities and with transforming them. There would be a return to the theme of neighbourhood building as long as some find themselves lost in the crowd and need to belong to an identifiable corner, and some need to separate themselves for establishing a status or avoid what and whom they feel should be avoided, and some are pushed to one corner to live apart from the rest, and some are fearful of the loss of control over the affairs of the city and the state; in other words, as long as there is social difference, stratification and control.

We know, however, that micro-urbanism cannot provide the only possible, or the best, answer to the questions it raises. In urban management, the more sophisticated forms of information and management mean that the need for a crude dissection of a city is no longer needed. Sustainable urban forms include small neighbourhoods but also compact and linear cities. Neighbourhoods seem to be more useful in growth management than in arresting decline. Substantial production capacity of the development industry can produce a variety of physical forms. The high rate of population mobility and social pluralism makes the process of signification and identification far more complex than ever before. The refuge from anonymity can at best be temporary and tangential, as it is no longer possible to create strong social bonds that only develop through long-term stability and common experience. Subdivision of the city into distinctive neighbourhoods may create further social fragmentation, rather than the planned social cohesion. These make the work of building communities difficult, if not impossible.

The implications of this for urban planning and design must be to become aware of all these various aspects of planning by neighbourhood and to avoid a blind faith in the impact of spatial organization. Whether promoting a communitarian agenda or democratic individualism, the relationship between individuals is only possible when a series of social frameworks are in place. Space is one of these frameworks and design of urban space provides a platform for social relationships. In societies where radical individualism has continuously been a fundamental principle, there is no doubt that social relations will be increasingly fluid. Permanence may be an unaffordable, or even unwanted, luxury. The best that a social action such as urban planning and design can do is not to pretend that it can create cohesive units, but that it can positively contribute, albeit in a limited way, to the development of social relationships rather than merely accepting the alienation of the crowds.

The role of public space in the creation of this sense of cohesion is what most forms of neighbourhood design hope to achieve. By creating lively public spaces in their centres, designers hope to put in place the necessary framework for sociability. At the same time, we have seen that public space can also be used as an image, a selling point for the commercial firms and the political authorities, a vehicle of differentiation contributing to further social fragmentation rather than social integration.

Chapter 6
Material and institutional spaces of the common world

We have studied the significance of the public space for interpersonal realms of sociability and community. This chapter focuses on the significance of the broader notion of public sphere for the development of a democratic society, where different individuals and groups can participate in collective self rule. This investigation is done mainly through engagement with the work of some of the major writers on the subject of public sphere, including Hannah Arendt, Jürgen Habermas, Charles Taylor and Seyla Benhabib. The chapter deals with the question of understanding public sphere at the intersection of various perspectives and approaches. It also deals with the notion of public sphere as a vehicle of common action, as discussed and understood in social and political thought. The role of space in the constitution of the public sphere, and how the overall operation of the public sphere takes place in an impersonal, metaspatial level are then examined.

PERSPECTIVES INTO A COMMON WORLD

The spaces around us everywhere, from the spaces in which we take shelter to those which we cut across and travel through, are part of our everyday social reality. Our spatial behaviour, which is defined by and defines the spaces around us, is an integral part of our social existence. As such, we understand space and spatial relations in the same way that we understand the other component parts of our social life. The facts about the world, John Searle (1995) argues, can be divided into two categories. The first category is what he calls 'institutional facts', facts that only exist by human agreement, because we believe them to exist. The second category is that of 'brute facts', those that exist independent of human institutions. Most elements of the social world belong to the first category, from money to marriage, property and government. The fact that a piece of paper has a value of, for example, five pounds is a social fact. Without our institutionalized agreement, it is no more than just a piece of paper. The brute fact about the space of our cities, therefore, is that it is a collection of objects and people on the surface of the earth. The social fact about the cities, however, is that these objects and their relationships have been created by human agreement and bear particular significance and meaning for people. The sheer physical presence of roads, schools, and houses does not render them meaningful. It is the collective intentionality, the capacity of humans to assign functions, to symbolize these objects beyond their basic presence that makes them part of the social reality.

The significance of symbolism in the construction of social reality, however, shows how there can be more than one interpretation for the social facts. As one of the most important dimensions of our social world, space finds different interpretations and meanings. As different groups give different meanings to space, it becomes a multi-layered place, reflecting the way places are socially constructed (Knox, 1995).

The various perspectives on space can be classified as those looking from inside, i.e. the subjective views from the first person's point of view, and those looking from outside, i.e. the third person's external view. What is a home for one person, becomes a mere object for another. What is for one person a refreshing experience of feeling in touch with nature becomes for another party just a person walking past in the park. What is a rich web of emotions and attachments to places of a town for one person becomes a set of statistics on pedestrian behaviour for another. The diversity of views that can be found in the everyday experiences is also traceable in the academic studies of, and professional approaches to, space. The question always is how to approach this multiplicity. Is there a single correct interpretation of space and place? Or does this multiplicity of views mean that we should give in to a kind of relativism, where all interpretations are correct as they each represent a particular, equally valid perspective?

The perspective of phenomenology concentrates on the world as seen and narrated from the viewpoint of individuals. The problem it has to deal with is how human beings, who are therefore limited to their own experience of the world, can relate to each other. Here the question of public sphere finds a central place, as it is where interpersonal relations are played out. How these individuals make sense of each other and how they can relate to one another is at the heart of social life. The meeting of different subjectivities results in a social world in which meaning is constructed through intersubjective relationships.

Public space allows us to experience other people's presence and get to know their viewpoint, which is an essential ingredient of living in human societies. It is impossible for me to see the world entirely from the viewpoint of another person and I am not able to enter the private realm of strangers and experience life from their perspective. I can, however, albeit in a narrow sense, have the same perspective as they might have in public space. I can stand where they stood and experience common space from the same perspective, even though my experience may be completely different. I may not be allowed to look out to the city from inside the walls of a gated neighbourhood, from the exclusive balcony of a luxury private residence, from behind suburban net curtains, or from the broken glass of a run down apartment, as these are private spheres of strangers. But if we are all present in the same space, I will be able to share the same street corner with the residents of these four private realms, looking at the city from the same angle. The space we share, therefore, allows us to share an experience of the world around us (Figure 6.1). This is, however, temporary and limited. For a homeless person who lives in the public space, all experience is inevitably shared with others, as a private space does not exist.

This may appear to be a mere visual experience of looking onto the same physical reality from the same vantage point. It is, in fact, part of a multi-layered experience of the presence of others. According to Alfred Schutz, when we, for example, listen to someone speaking, we catch the Other's thought in its vivid presence. Schutz uses this notion to develop a general theory of alter ego, where he defines alter ego as 'that subjective stream of consciousness whose activities I can seize in their present by my own simultaneous activities' (Schutz, 1962: 174). This means that I can understand how this stream of thought has the same fundamental

6.1 Looking onto the same physical reality and co-presence in public space allow us to share an experience of the world around us with each other and with previous generations (Stockholm, Sweden)

structure as my own consciousness and how far the Other is like me. Sharing a present, which is common to both of us, can construct a 'pure sphere of the "We"' (Schutz, 1962: 175).

Public space is not only a site for intersubjective presence, where space allows simultaneity. It is also a place where we can share experience with past generations, who could have stood on the same street corner and looked onto a physical reality that had some commonality with ours. The same may apply to future generations, who may have a similar experience mediated through spatial and institutional continuity. Presence in a common space, therefore, can cross time and relate to other generations before and after us. Spatial presence can be a clue to an understanding of temporal presence, albeit limited and thoroughly mediated.

This line of analysis clearly draws on Nietzsche's perspectivism, on Husserl's phenomenology, and on Heidegger's analysis of Being. The question that needs addressing is: how is it possible to go beyond the perspectives through which we observe and understand the world? Can presence in a common world be enough to bridge these subjectivities?

PUBLIC SPACES OF CO-PRESENCE

One of the main theorists of public sphere in the twentieth century is Hannah Arendt, whose focus changed from philosophy to politics as she fled Nazi Germany and concentrated on the analysis of totalitarianism (Young-Bruehl, 1982; Benhabib, 1996). Through a phenomenological analysis (Canovan, 1998: ix), Arendt identifies three forms of activity that are fundamental to the human condition: labour, work and action. Labour corresponds to life and the body's biological processes. Work corresponds to making and to the world of objects made by humans. Action corresponds to the plurality of distinctive individuals, which is 'the condition . . . of all political life' (Arendt, 1958: 7). It is 'the only activity that goes on directly between men without the intermediary of things or matter' (ibid.). It may seem naive to us, and even to her (see below), that relations between humans can exist without reference to the material world in which they live, nevertheless, this formulation of 'action' was the activity that she praised most. She rejects the separation of philosophy from politics, of theory from action, and adopting introversion and contemplation (*vita contemplativa*) as a way of life. Instead, she promotes an outward looking, political and public life (*vita activa*), in which the public realm takes centre stage. As against this, a private life remains unfulfilled, as we saw (in Chapter Two) her contempt for an entirely private life, which she sees as to be deprived of essential ingredients of human life (Arendt, 1958: 58).

According to Hannah Arendt, the term public has two closely related meanings. Its first meaning is about appearance in front of others, which is the foundation of objective reality. The term public then means,

> everything that appears in public can be seen and heard by everybody and has the widest possible publicity. For us, appearance – something that is being seen and heard by others as well as by ourselves – constitutes reality. (Arendt, 1958: 50)

The public and private realms are therefore different in that in the public realm things are shown and in the private they are hidden (Arendt, 1958: 72) – essentially the same features of concealment and exposure that Nagel writes about a generation later, albeit in support of protecting private life (Nagel, 1998b). Indeed, this is what Arendt had discussed herself.

> The distinction between the private and public realms, seen from the viewpoint of privacy rather than of the body politic, equals the distinction between things that should be shown and things that should be hidden. (Arendt, 1958: 72)

In the common world of the public realm, it is possible for individuals to appear before each other from their own different locations. There are therefore many perspectives into the world existing together and allowing the reality of the world to appear truly. It is only in tyrannies, where the common world has ended, that only one perspective prevails.

> Only where things can be seen by many in a variety of aspects without changing their identity, so that those who are gathered around them know they see sameness in utter diversity, can worldly reality truly and reliably appear. (Arendt, 1958: 57)

The second meaning of the term public refers to the world, 'in so far as it is common to all of us and distinguished from our privately owned places in it' (Arendt, 1958: 52). In her reference to the world, Arendt is drawing on Martin Heidegger's notion of 'Being-in-the-world', where 'the world is always the one I share with Others' (Heidegger, quoted in Benhabib, 1996: 53). This is not, as Arendt stresses, the natural world, but the world of human artefacts and the relationships among people who live there together.

> To live together in the world means essentially that a world of things is between those who sit around it; the world, like every in-between, relates and separates men at the same time ... The public realm, as the common realm, gathers us together

and yet prevents us from falling over each other, so to speak. What makes mass society so difficult to bear is not the number of people involved, or at least not primarily, but the fact that the world between them has lost its power to gather them together, to relate and to separate them. (Arendt, 1958: 52–3) (Figure 6.2)

In both these meanings, space of appearance and the in-between space, Arendt provides a basis for analysing an integrated understanding of the public realm of politics as well as the corporeal public space of the city. In a sense, the two meanings can be integrated by seeing the public space as the in-between space which facilitates co-presence and regulates interpersonal relations.

The artefacts that humans create bring with them a measure of permanence and durability to human life and at the same time condition human existence. '[H]uman existence', Arendt wrote (Arendt, 1958: 9), 'is conditioned existence, it would be impossible without things, and things would be a heap of unrelated articles, a non-world, if they were not the conditioners of human existence.' The

very important...

6.2 According to Hannah Arendt, to live together in the world means essentially that a world of things is between those who sit around it; the world, like every in-between, relates and separates people at the same time (Copenhagen, Denmark)

integration of humans and things in the construction of public space endows the public realm with permanence.

> Only the existence of a public realm and the world's subsequent transformation into a community of things which gathers men together and relates them to each other depends primarily on permanence. If the world is to contain a public space, it cannot be erected for one generation and planned for the living only; it must transcend the life-span of mortal men. (Arendt, 1958: 55)

In this way the world of artefacts not only mediates between the present members of the public, it also links them to other generations through time. This integration of people and objects in the analysis, and the appreciation of how social relations are mediated through objects, is a key point in Arendt's analysis of public space. Although at some points she seems to contradict herself, as reflected in the definition of action quoted above, she uses this notion of the world to embed the social world in a particular context. Later theorists of public realm unfortunately abandoned this integrated analysis and focused on institutional, rather than material public sphere. Notable among these theorists is Jürgen Habermas who, as we shall see, shifted the emphasis away from public space to public sphere, leaving the things-in-between aside. On the other hand, there are other theoreticians who include the material world in their analysis of society. They, however, can unfortunately overemphasize this materiality, giving equal significance to material objects and humans, and even speaking of the Parliament of Things (Latour, 1993).

Arendt draws heavily on the idealization of ancient Greeks, who thought the public realm of politics stood in opposition to the private realm of the household. The public realm of the city-state (*polis*) was that of action and speech and excluded anything that was merely necessary or useful. In this common world of free men, everything was decided through words and persuasion, rather than through force and violence. This public realm was reserved for individuality, as everybody was constantly trying to distinguish himself from the others by unique deeds and achievements. It was to show their individuality that these men were prepared to share in the burden of jurisprudence, defence and administration of public affairs.

In contrast, violence belonged to the private realm, where these men, as heads of households, ruled with despotic powers. Violence also belonged to the outer realms of barbarian foreigners. The private realm of the household was the realm of necessity and natural processes. The household was a natural community formed for the maintenance of life and necessity ruled over all activities performed in it. In short, the public realm of the *polis* was the realm of speech, action and freedom, while the private realm of the household the realm of violence and necessity. According to Arendt (1958: 31),

> What all Greek philosophers, no matter how opposed to *polis* life, took for granted is that freedom is exclusively located in the political realm, that necessity is primarily a prepolitical phenomenon, characteristic of the private household organization, and that force and violence are justified in this sphere because they are the only means to master necessity – for instance by ruling over slaves – and to become free.

The picture that emerges is one of a minority of free men constructing a common political sphere of speech and action among themselves, which is only possible by exerting violence towards the majority of the city's inhabitants, including women, children, slaves and foreigners, who are not allowed to enter. In other words, freedom and violence are two sides of the same coin, a point that many analysts of the Greek public realm have preferred to overlook. The two realms, therefore, are intertwined and interdependent. Only by the suppression of one realm can the establishment of the other be achieved. Only by binding the majority of population to the despotic rule in the private realm of the household could the heads of households participate as free equals in the public sphere. By idealizing the Greek *polis*, Arendt seems to accept and rationalize inequalities that existed there, in the name of the quality of public sphere that a few could enjoy at the cost of suppression of all others. A key feature of the Greek *polis* is considered to be its autonomy. However, by the fourth century BC, the majority of *poleis* were dependencies rather than independent city-states. There are therefore those who see the notion of associating autonomy with the Greek *polis* a modern invention, rather than an empirical reality (Hansen, 1995).

Arendt associated the ancient distinction between the public and private realms with the city-state and the household. In the modern period, the rise of the nation state has been parallel with the rise of a third realm: social realm. Arendt is critical of the rise of the social realm of mass society, adopting an overtly elitist standpoint.

> Within this society, which is egalitarian because this is labour's way of making men live together, there is no class left, no aristocracy of either a political or spiritual nature from which a restoration of the other capacities of man could start anew.... Surely, nothing could be worse. (Arendt, 1958: 5)

The medieval period saw the absorption of all activities into the private sphere, where the public sphere was absent (Arendt, 1958: 34). The modern period, however, is characterized by the 'emergence of society', where economics, i.e. 'housekeeping', and associated activities have risen 'from the shadowy interior of the household into the light of the public sphere' (Arendt, 1958: 38). As a result, the borders between the two realms of political and private and even their meanings have changed considerably. A social realm has emerged which is not clearly distinctive from the political realm. In other words, 'society has conquered the public realm' and the drive for equality and conformism has meant that distinction and difference have become private matters of the individual (Arendt, 1958: 41). With the rise of society, there has been a decline of family and the private realm is identified as a realm of intimacy, as first articulated by Jean-Jacque Rousseau and the Romantics, who thought intimate and social were both subjective modes of human existence. Arendt compares the actions of the ancient Greeks, who she thinks strove to glory and rare deeds, with the behaviour of the masses, which is ruled by conformism and understood through statistics. In this respect, she is showing a romantic appreciation of individuality as performed in public. 'Every activity performed in public can attain an excellence never matched in privacy' (Arendt, 1958: 49). She complains about the rise of the society, which has 'transformed all modern communities into societies of labourers and jobholders' (Arendt, 1958: 46). In doing so, she adopts the nineteenth century, expressive critique of Enlightenment rationalism.

Arendt appears to idealize a face-to-face, public relationship not mediated through things or matter. But any such relationship is also set within a context of social institutions and frameworks. In other words, any such relationship is mediated not only through natural processes and human artefacts, it is also mediated through social institutions and symbols. She sees the appearance in the public realm as the utmost test of reality (Arendt, 1958: 51). But, if we give so much priority to the public realm, we will have to confront the problem of suppression of individuality and privacy, as individuals are judged and condemned if not conforming to the rules of appearance in the public realm.

A key contribution of Arendt to political philosophy has been the emphasis on the public sphere as a central notion for the development of egalitarian and participatory democracy. Her concept of public space may seem, as Benhabib (1996: 198) argues, to be left 'institutionally unanchored, floating as if in a nostalgic chimera in the horizon of politics'. A key strength of this work for the analysis of public sphere, however, lies in its integration of social and physical, of material common world as a key part of the public realm.

PUBLIC SPHERE OF INTERPERSONAL COMMUNICATION

Another major theorist of public sphere is Jürgen Habermas, who set out to provide a historical and sociological account of the emergence, transformation and disintegration of the bourgeois public sphere (Habermas, 1989). Arendt had used the term *der öffentliche Raum,* translated as 'public space' (Benhabib, 1996: 199). Habermas was inspired by Arendt's analysis of public space, but shifted the meaning away from the material and spatial, to use the term *Öffentlichkeit*, which has been translated as 'the public', 'public sphere' and 'publicity'. While Arendt concentrated on material common world and lacked a focus on institutions, Habermas focused on institutional, rather than material, public sphere, trading one imbalance for another. For him the pre-eminent institution of the public sphere is the press. His concern was to analyse how public opinion is developed in modern society through mass media, and how this process is no longer based on face-to-face, rational–critical debate, which was a main feature of the public sphere in its early phases of development in the eighteenth century (Habermas, 1989). This analysis led him later to develop his theory of communicative action, in which he promotes intersubjective communication based on an enlarged notion of rationality (Habermas, 1984; Calhoun, 1992; McCarthy, 1978).

For Habermas (1989), public sphere is rooted in the development of the civil society that originated in late medieval Europe. At the start of the modern period, there was a transformation of public sphere. By then, public sphere was limited to the nobility and monarchy, who presented themselves before the public. The rise of the modern state changed all this, so that the public realm was now equated with the realm of the state. As the monarchy evolved into the modern state, the public sphere changed from the realm of the court to the realm of the state. In this process, the 'town' started to dominate the cultural scene, as against the 'court' that constituted the focus of literature and art. The new institutions of coffee houses, in their golden days of 1680 to 1730 in Britain, and *salons*, in the period between regency and revolution in France, became the cultural heirs to the court. A literary, apolitical public sphere emerged, which provided a training ground for critical public reflection, helping private individuals to undergo a process of self-clarification. In these arenas, bourgeois intellectuals rose to a certain parity with the aristocratic society and conversations turned to criticism, first literary and later also political. In coffee houses and increasingly through print media, exhibitions and performance halls, new forms of cultural production developed, which brought these art forms to a new enlarged public away from the confines of the court and nobility (Habermas, 1989: 29–32).

At the same time, the new intimate sphere of conjugal family facilitated the subjectivity of individuals to be oriented towards an audience, as best exemplified in the rising tradition of letter writing, where individuals unfolded themselves in their subjectivity towards a reader. This enabled the family to attain clarity about itself and to construct a self image as a sphere of intimacy that generated and nurtured humanity. The development of subjectivity in intimate sphere of the household was in parallel with the development of autonomy in the private realm of the market economy. The bourgeois public sphere of the Enlightenment age was ultimately based on this link between the sphere of intimacy, where humanity was the focus, and the sphere of common interest, where property was the key. The private man's status, therefore, 'combined the role of owner of commodities with that of head of family, that of property owner with that of "human being" *per se*' (Habermas, 1989: 28–9).

What emerged was a bourgeois public sphere, as the sphere of private individuals come together as a public and engaged in public and critical use of reason, which was the essence of enlightenment and lay at the heart of the modern constitutional state (Habermas, 1989: 27). Habermas' analysis closely resembles Kant's, who had said, 'The public use of one's reason must always be free, and it alone can bring about enlightenment among men' (quoted in Habermas, 1989: 106). To Kant, therefore, world in all its purity was 'constituted in the communication of rational beings' (Habermas, 1989: 106).

It is this Kantian idea of public use of reason that Habermas finds ultimately appealing, rather than the critique by Hegel, who thought of public opinion as particularistic and representative of special interests creating a powerful bloc against the state, and of Marx, who found public opinion as false consciousness reflecting the character and interests of the bourgeois class. Even liberal thinkers started to deny the usefulness of public sphere, as soon as it spread. Mill, for example, found it unduly to expand the powers of society over the individual and Tocqueville saw it as a compulsion toward conformity rather than a critical force (Habermas, 1989: 117ff). This shift of emphasis in critical thinking marks a turning point in the history of the Frankfurt school of critical theory, of which Habermas was a leading member (Rasmussen, 1996).

Liberalism accompanied an economic model of petty commodity exchange among individual commodity owners. But as capitalism became more organized during the one hundred years that followed the height of liberalism, the bourgeois public sphere eroded. As it expanded to incorporate new sections of the society, it lost its political function, which was to subject public affairs to the control of a critical public. Critical publicity, which was the principle of public sphere, started to lose its strength (Habermas, 1989: 140). As the welfare state developed in the twentieth century, new areas of the private sphere became dominated by the state. At the same time, private organizations such as employers associations and trades unions assumed public character. The equal contractual relationship of liberalism was replaced by inequality between partners and their dependence upon each other. State and societal institutions fused into a single functional complex, where public and private spheres could no longer be differentiated (Habermas, 1989: 148). It is this analysis that leads Habermas to his notions of systems and lifeworld, which later lay at the core of his social philosophy.

As the conjugal family was disengaged from the reproduction of society, only an illusion of an intensified private realm remained. In this process, the culture-debating public turned into a culture-consuming public, that was engaged in individuated reception and consumption of cultural products, rather than public communication and rational–critical debate. Conversation becomes administered and discussion assumes the form of a consumer item (Habermas, 1989: 164). The public sphere becomes the sphere of publicizing private biographies and finds advertising functions as a vehicle for political and economic propaganda, which is exactly the reason why it loses its political function and becomes pseudo-privatized. The publicity in the public sphere 'serves the manipulation *of* the public as much as legitimation *before* it' (Habermas, 1989: 178).

Habermas' public sphere is one that lies between the private sphere of individuals and the public sphere of the state. But he seems to generate a degree of ambiguity that runs through his analysis. His 'blueprint' of the bourgeois public sphere in the eighteenth century explains:

> The line between state and society, fundamental in our context, divided the public sphere from the private realm. The public sphere was coextensive with public authority, and we consider the court part of it. Included in the private realm was the authentic 'public sphere', for it was a public sphere constituted by private people. Within the realm that was the preserve of private people we therefore distinguish again between private and public spheres. The private sphere comprised civil society in the narrower sense, that is to say, the realm of commodity exchange and of social labour; imbedded in it was the family with its interior domain (*Intimsphäre*). The public sphere in the political realm evolved from the public sphere in the world of letters; through the vehicle of public opinion it put the state in touch with the needs of society. (Habermas, 1989: 30–1)

This sketch and his overall analysis show a society formed of different layers of public and private spheres, where some of these evolve into others (e.g. literary public sphere to political public sphere) without necessarily the first one disappearing. Some are entirely located within the other (e.g. public sphere of private people within the private sphere); while others are tangentially connected (e.g. the state public sphere and the private 'authentic' public sphere). The picture which emerges is therefore one of multi-layered, overlapping spheres that have at times a tense relationship with each other and in any case are always changing and evolving. This stands against Habermas' insistence that public and private realms were, and should be, strictly separate realms. He is not, however, willing to accept that public and private spheres have always been parts of a continuum, rather than necessarily occupying pole positions (Figure 6.3).

Habermas sets two conditions for a public sphere to be effective in the political realm. One is 'a relativizing of structural conflicts of interests according to the standard of a universal interest everyone can acknowledge' (Habermas, 1989: 235). The political task of the bourgeois public sphere had been the regulation of the civil society (Habermas, 1989: 52). In the public sphere of the civil society, a political consciousness emerged that articulated the notion of, and the demand for, general and abstract laws. Public opinion that resulted from the public and critical

6.3 Public and private spheres are parts of a continuum and cannot be treated as completely segregated social and physical realms, as exemplified by a private sphere formed by a group of friends in the middle of public space (Edinburgh, UK)

use of reason among private individuals, therefore, came to be the only legitimate source of this law (Habermas, 1989: 54). The public sphere in the political realm was established by the constitutional state to ensure a link between public opinion and law (Habermas, 1989: 80). The general and abstract rules remained external to individuals and secured space for the development of an intimate sphere.

> These rules, because universally valid, secured a space for the individual person; because they were objective, they secured a space for what was most subjective; because they were abstract, for what was most concrete. (Habermas, 1989: 54)

Optimism in universal truths, however, was not shared by all. Rather than arriving at a universal truth after rational critical debate, John Stuart Mill promoted a form of tolerance and possibility of many-sided truths, as 'only through diversity of opinion is there, in the existing state of human intellect, a chance of fair play to all sides of truth' (quoted in Habermas, 1989: 135). It is this pluralist attitude to the public sphere that is one of its main features today, rather than the promotion of a universal standard as Habermas wishes to see. His first condition for an effective public sphere, therefore, is undermined by an inability to reconcile the need for common moral and political agreements with the pluralism of the human condition.

The second condition of an effective public sphere, according to Habermas (1989: 235), is 'the 'objectively possible minimization of bureaucratic decisions'. The problem is the absence of face-to-face communication, which has been replaced by mediated communication between large-scale organizations.

> A repoliticized social sphere originated that could not be subsumed under the categories of public and private from either a sociological or a legal perspective. In this intermediate sphere the sectors of society that had been absorbed by the state and the sectors of the state that had been taken over by society intermeshed without involving any rational-critical political debate on the part of private people. The public was largely relieved from this task by other institutions: on the one hand by associations in which collectively organized private interests directly attempted to take on the form of political agency; on the other hand by parties which, fused with the organs of public authority, established themselves, as it were, *above* the public whose instruments once they were. The process of politically relevant exercise and equilibration of power now takes place directly between the private bureaucracies, special-interest associations, parties, and public administration. The public as such is included only sporadically in this circuit of power, and even then it is brought in only to contribute its acclamation. (Habermas, 1989: 176)

Habermas constantly compares the modern welfare-state society with the liberal bourgeois society in its initial phases of development, finding the former inferior in the quality of the state–society relations and the public sphere that connects them. With this comparison and with his idealization of bourgeois public sphere, Habermas seems, albeit unintentionally, to anticipate, and even pave the way for, the rise of neo-liberal thinking, which has argued for a reduction in state interference in society and for the defence of private sphere.

As these two conditions show, Habermas seems to be concerned with the relationship between particular and general: how the pluralism of particulars can be negotiated to arrive at the general; and how this process of negotiation and communication has been distorted by the increasing organizational complexity of the world of particulars. The public sphere is the vehicle that can facilitate this process of reconciling particular and general. But the main problem in this analysis is the nature of the general and how far it encompasses the particular.

Development of the public sphere, as analysed by Habermas, can, in one reading, be studied as the development of a group consciousness and a voice among an emerging elite, at the intersection with the establishment of the modern state based on its claim to universality. The members of the rising elite were able to project their group consciousness onto the institutions of the state, so as to legitimate their rule as being universal and based on critical rational debate. Like the ancient Greek prototype, universal principles and language provided a normative notion, to aspire towards rather than see in reality, legitimizing a minority's rise to power. Habermas (1989: 87) believes that the universality of the rules and ideas that emerged out of this formative stage sufficiently approximated reality so that the interests of the bourgeoisie could be identified with the general interests.

Arendt and Habermas cannot come to terms with the rise of what was termed mass society, which puts them in a nostalgic rather than critical standpoint. They both seem to assume an elitist point of view when they come across the involvement of large numbers of people and new forms of organization in social relationships. Habermas looks nostalgically to the eighteenth century, when 'The "people" were brought up to the level of culture; culture was not lowered to that of the masses' (p. 166). Arendt's nostalgia is about a golden representation of the ancient Greece.

Writers who look at the eighteenth century public sphere with a nostalgic eye see the phenomenon in its infancy. As the development of technology and the complexity of the city grew, the birthplaces of face-to-face public sphere gave way to the widely available print media in the nineteenth century and the electronic media in the twentieth. While the evolution of these new media has taken the emphasis away from face-to-face interaction, there is no evidence to suggest that the early public spaces were more democratic or more accessible, as the time constraints, spatial distance, the gendered nature of coffee houses and their localized or pro-fessionalized clientele determined their limitations. The fact remains, perhaps even more in the French salons, that these public spheres were elitist.

Arendt and Habermas both rightly appreciate the quality of public sphere in the ancient Greek *polis* and the eighteenth-century Western Europe of the Enlight-enment, and its continued significance for democratic government today. They both complain about the rise of the mass society, which has eroded this quality. What they both overlook is that the public spheres they admire were elitist and could only develop and function by keeping the majority of the population out. When the public sphere was opened to larger numbers of people, the inevitable result was a change in the nature and quality of public sphere. Rather than coming to terms with the reality of modern society, in which large numbers of people engage in complex interrelations, they depict a simpler, more straightforward picture of these past periods as ideals which have been lost. The ideal of face-to-face interaction by the elite will have little chance if applied to the large, complex society of today. The outcome of such a drive for intersubjective communication may be communitarian-ism. Both Habermas and Arendt are nostalgic about a situation in which a small number of well-endowed elite could engage in debate in a narrowly defined place, at the cost of excluding all others. The order and quality of such conversations can of course change if opened up to large numbers of people with varying capacities. This has been a challenge of modern times, one that Habermas and Arendt are rather quick to dismiss.

METATOPICAL PUBLIC SPACE

From a trajectory which draws on both Continental and Anglophone traditions of thought, Charles Taylor (1995) explores the meaning of public sphere in a liberal society. He defines the liberal society as one which tries 'to maximize the goods of freedom and collective self-rule, in conformity with a rule of right founded on equal-ity' (Taylor, 1995: 184). Rather than a negative meaning of freedom, of being free from others' interference, he prefers a positive notion, where freedom involves 'real self-determination, an excellence of moral development' (Taylor, 1995: 184). The liberal society is often characterized through its emphasis on the rule of law, on entrenched rights, recovered by judicial action, and various modes of dividing power. The liberal society also involves the presence of a vibrant civil society, which in its post-Hegelian sense refers to the secular, free associations that lie outside the state. In Western society, two major forms of civil society are the public sphere and the market economy.

By public sphere, Taylor means 'a common space in which the members of society are deemed to meet through a variety of media: print, electronic, and also face-to-face encounters; to discuss matters of common interest; and thus to be able to form a common mind about these' (Taylor, 1995: 185–6). The ability to communicate with each other, even if mediated, and form a common mind about matters allows a society to see itself as free and self-governing, where people can form their opinions and where these opinions matter. The public sphere, therefore, is a central feature of modern society, which is why it is under constant scrutiny, to see whether it is being manipulated by the powerful or whether the nature of the modern media permits open debate. Market economy is another major part of civil society. It is similar to the public sphere in that it takes place outside the political domain of the state as a set of secular interactions, which amount to an overall pattern. It also shares its origins with the public sphere, as both are rooted in the cultural changes of early modern Europe (Taylor, 1995: 199).

Taylor uses the term 'topical common space' to define the common space in which people come together for some purpose, from a more intimate scale of conversation to the larger more public scale of deliberative assemblies, rituals, performances, celebrations, sports events etc. The public sphere, however, encompasses and transcends these topical spaces. It 'knits together a plurality of such spaces into one larger space of nonassembly', a 'nonlocal common space', a 'metatopical common space' which can only be found in the modern liberal society (Taylor, 1995: 190) (Figure 6.4). It enables the society to come to a common mind independent of the government but with the moral authority to influence the decisions of the government. It is, therefore, 'a locus in which rational views are elaborated which should guide government' (Taylor, 1995: 191), or in other words, an 'extrapolitical, secular, metatopical space' (Taylor, 1995: 199).

The secularity of the public sphere, Taylor maintains, is reflected in that as an association it is 'constituted by nothing outside of the common action we carry out in it' (Taylor, 1995: 194). Yet it is clear that the actors involved in the public sphere bring their ideas and motives not only from within the public sphere but also from the variety of private and semi-private spheres in which they are embedded. In this sense, Taylor's insistence on the objectivity, separateness and independence of the public sphere can come to be questioned, unless they are phrased in ways that qualify and limit his definitions of public sphere. This is a limitation that is known by Taylor, as he admits that his representation is of ideal types, which in practice can be very different. Neither the public sphere nor the market economy is free from state intervention or from the influence of powerful players. Despite encroaches on these arenas, however, the fact that they 'operate and are seen to operate by their

6.4 The public sphere encompasses and transcends the public spaces of assemblies, rituals, performances etc (as exemplified by this summer fair), knitting together a plurality of these spaces into one 'larger space of nonassembly', a 'metatopical common space' (Newcastle, UK)

own dynamic' has played a powerful role in the limitation of power and maintenance of freedom in the modern West (Taylor, 1995: 200).

Taylor emphasizes the commonality of discussion and of mind, which can occur among people who never meet but understand themselves to be engaged in a common debate. While this might be true for some individuals, the more accurate picture is often the existence of many parallel debates in many different forums and with many different outcomes and opinions. The same is true of being in the presence of others for what appears to be a common purpose, such as attending a ritual or a performance. The commonality that is created through co-presence is real but limited. Individuals who participate may come from their own entirely different worlds and return there at the end of the event. The effect of the public sphere is therefore not necessarily the creation of singular outcomes, but the possibility of developing different responses; not only seeking consensus but also exploring difference. Public space is then the space of co-presence and simultaneity, where different actors can be present in the same place at the same time, where individuals can develop freely within a plurality of possibilities that are negotiated collectively. The convergence of time and space in a particular node has been under threat in modern cities, where large populations have spread in all directions and where new technologies have made communication from across long distances and different time zones possible.

TENSIONS OF INDIVIDUALS AND COMMUNITIES

The two main goals sought by liberal society are individual freedom and self-rule (Taylor, 1995), which represent the two ingredients of liberal democracies, i.e. liberalism and democracy. The two may seem to be in a harmonious relation in the modern context, but they are indeed in a constant dialectical interplay (Bobbio, 1990). Two camps can be identified in Western democracies as to how these goals can be identified. One camp puts the emphasis on individual freedoms and the limitation of the state power, which is called by some negative freedom. For this camp the realm that lies outside politics, i.e. public sphere and the market, are the main bulwarks of freedom. The other camp is concerned more with self-rule, where collective decisions are made to shape the conditions of our lives. In this camp, public sphere not only limits the power of the state. It also can contribute to the development of common debate and exchange, which informs collective decisions. This is a tension between the primacy of the individual and the primacy of the group, as manifested in many layers of debate.

On the surface, the new debates around community building may be related to the social and political contexts of the past two decades. The 1980s saw a resurgence of individualism, as reflected in the famous remarks of the British Prime Minister Margaret Thatcher – There is no such thing as society: there are only individuals. The results of such extreme individualism, however, have included increased social polarization and fragmentation. In response, the 1990s witnessed an emergence of communitarianism, hence the need to (re)build neighbourhoods and communities. After all, Etzioni (1995) identifies a number of political leaders in the Western countries to be among the supporters of communitarian ideas. The communitarians argue that 'the pendulum has swung too far towards the individualistic pole, and it is time to hurry its return' (Etzioni, 1995: 26). Too much has been said about the rights of individuals. Now it is time to talk about the responsibilities of individuals to the community. The community has been lost and needs to be rebuilt, 'not only because community life is a major source of satisfaction of our deeper personal needs, but because the social pressures community brings to bear are a mainstay of our moral values' (Etzioni, 1995: 40). This tension, however, goes back further in time.

The Enlightenment period promoted a notion of radical autonomy for individuals, which has remained a central feature of the Western civilization ever since. With its emphasis on individuals, it looked at nature and society as merely the potential means to the satisfaction of human desires. Nature and society were to be reorganized through scientific social engineering to bring about happiness to individuals. In this sense, the Enlightenment had a utilitarian ethical outlook and an atomistic social philosophy. The generations that followed the French Revolution, however, found the notion of absolute freedom for individuals to be without content. As against this emphasis on the instrumental significance of society and nature, Hegel stressed the importance of *Sittlichkeit* (some times translated as 'ethical life'), in which individuals have moral obligations to the ongoing community of which they are a part. It is, he argued, in a community rather than in a vacuum that morality finds its completion. The freedom and fulfilment of individuals can be achieved within a community, rather than in an undifferentiated context (Taylor, 1979).

Hegel's notion of *Sittlichkeit* is a major landmark in a long historical line of social and political thought known as organicism (or holism) (Bobbio, 1990). In its development, he drew upon the discussions about the ancient Greek *polis*, where the public life of the city was thought to be the essence and meaning of individuals' lives. According to Aristotle (1992), the *polis* 'exists by nature' (p. 59) and 'has a natural priority over the household and over any individual among us' (p. 60). He thus laid out the foundation of organicism: 'For the whole must be prior to the part. Separate hand or foot from the whole body, and they will no longer be hand or foot except in name' (Aristotle, 1992: 60). Rather than being autonomous, individuals are interdependent, cooperating to further their joint collective life, which is embodied in the corporate structure of the city-state.

In contrast to this ancient organicism, the emerging individualism of the Enlightenment era was a thoroughly modern notion (Bobbio, 1990). An influential articulation of this tension between individualism and holism in society was developed by Ferdinand Tönnies at the end of the nineteenth century, in his two contrasting ideal types of *Gemeinschaft* 'community' and *Gesellschaft* 'society' (Tönnies, 1957). The *Gemeinschaft* described the traditional communities which were rooted in particular places, where individuals were related to each other through natural will and united through ties of blood and history (Figure 6.5). This was distinguishable from the *Gesellschaft*, the modern societies in which trade and science created groups of individuals who are only related to each other through rational will to achieve certain ends. *Gemeinschaft*, therefore, refers to the organic union of individuals, based on the 'assumption of perfect unity of human wills as an original or natural condition' (Tönnies, 1957: 37). *Gesellschaft*, on the other hand,

6.5 Organicism describes close-knit communities, where individuals are related to each other through natural will and united through ties of blood and history (Tainan, Taiwan)

refers to the voluntary association of individuals for particular purposes, or in his words, 'the artificial construction of an aggregate of human beings' (Tönnies, 1957: 64). Although in both *Gemeinschaft* and *Gesellschaft* individuals live together peacefully, the resemblance between these two situations is superficial. Their difference lies in that in the *Gemeinschaft* individuals 'remain essentially united in spite of all separating factors, whereas in the *Gesellschaft* they are essentially separated in spite of all uniting factors' (Tönnies, 1957: 65).

Some elements in the ideas of the *Gemeinschaft* and *Gesellschaft* can be traced back deep into the historical past and as such their various manifestations are seen as variations on an eternal theme (Sorokin, 1957). The formulations of holism in the modern period, as developed for example by Hegel and Tönnies among others, often had some roots in romanticism and drew upon an idealized past (whether the Greek *polis* or the medieval community) in which strong social bonds tied individuals together and social norms and values had primacy over individual gains. Less, however, has been said about how these communities were sites of economic, political and sexual exploitation, marked by high infant mortality, low life expectancy, child labour etc. The extreme manifestations of holism came to the fore in the twentieth century in the shape of fascism and communism, in which millions of individuals died or suffered in the name of collective ideals.

This controversy between individualism and holism has remained a central concern of social philosophy to this day. Although this dualism may be analytically unconvincing for some, it plays a powerful normative role. Its normative dimension in political philosophy has been the controversy between communitarianism and liberalism. While liberals see the society as a collection of individuals, a *Gesellschaft*, communitarians promote the importance of the society, to which the rights of individuals should be subordinated. The extreme opposition to holism can be found in libertarians, who often support free market economics, oppose any state intervention in society, and are sometimes associated with social Darwinism, advocating the survival of the fittest (Narveson, 1995). Bobbio (1990) identifies two distinct forms of individualism: liberal and democratic. Liberal individualism 'amputates the individual from the organic body, makes him live – at least for much of his life – outside the maternal womb, plunges him into the unknown and perilous world of the struggle for survival'. Democratic individualism, on the other hand, joins the individual 'together once more with others like himself, so that society can be built up again from their union, no longer as an organic whole but as an association of free individuals' (p. 43).

Whether interpreted as social fragmentation (Honneth, 1995) or as mobility of individuals (Willetts, 1998), the emergence of individualism lies at the heart of the changes and pathologies of modern societies. What was new in the new individualism was the ability (and the pressure) to evaluate critically and to transform the social ties in which the individuals were embedded. The result was on the one hand a disruption of communities and social ties, on the other the liberation, or uprootedness, of individuals. From the start this was a socio-spatial phenomenon, manifest in the growth of large cities. From early on, individualism found a comfortable home in the cities and was expressed in crowding, anonymity and social segregation. From early on, such anonymity and segregation caused fear and anxiety about how to maintain social order and promote social integration. Creation of communities has been a main form of practising holism, by promoting togetherness and the development of new social ties, which would maintain a potentially explosive or disintegrating social fabric. Utopian thinking of the past two centuries and the practical steps urban planning and design has taken to create local distinction, physical proximity and intersubjective interaction in public spaces can be seen as part of a long line of holism, where the main preoccupation has been with a promotion of social integration in the face of what seemed to be the atomization of the society. This holism, however, has often been prescribed for the lower income groups, while the more affluent have expected to live as free individuals.

This is a point that Bobbio (1990: 89) raises as depending on the position of the judge. Liberty is defined to have negative and positive forms. Liberals prefer as little intervention as possible by the state, while democrats are keen to promote self rule for all citizens. Judgements that are made between these two definitions of liberty, which reflect the tension between liberalism and democracy, depend on the historical circumstances but, more importantly, on the position of the judge in social space. Those who are well placed in social space usually prefer the negative definition and those who are lower in the social scale the positive definition.

PUBLIC SPHERE FOR DIVERSE SOCIETIES

The tension between the two ingredients of liberal democracies, i.e. individual freedoms and collective self-rule, is a deep-seated one. In both cases, however, the role of the public sphere is undisputed. On the one hand, public sphere is needed to protect individuals from the state power; on the other hand, the public sphere is needed for individuals to form common opinions and arrive at common decisions.

One of the questions that needs addressing is how it is possible for collective decisions to be made so as to reflect genuine self-rule, rather than through manipulation of the mass media and political process by interest groups and elites. Public debate seems to be conducted outside the institutionalized public space of Parliament, in the form of a constant tension between politicians and journalists, an intersection that makes 'spin' and media performance the currency of exchange. Apart from some well-known cases of Swiss cantons, how is it possible for the entire population to get together in one place and at the same time? Convergence in time may be possible when almost everyone is expected to participate in the nearly simultaneous ritual of voting. But convergence in space is almost impossible for the large and complex populations. There seems to be no alternative but to have a series of forums for public discussion in which arguments are heard and opinions made.

But in societies and circumstances where this myriad of arenas for public debate is not available or suppressed, convergence in space and time may occur, leading to explosive and revolutionary upheavals. In cities that undergo some form of revolution, from Paris in 1968 to Berlin in 1989, from Moscow in 1917 to Tehran in 1979, a convergence in time and space means large numbers of people coming together in the public spaces and charged with massive amounts of energy that is directed towards the political establishment. Public space becomes the meeting place of very large numbers of people unable (or unwilling) to engage in political debate, which can influence political processes. In these cases, takeover of the public space is the outward expression of the revolution (Madanipour, 1998). In the absence of mechanisms and institutions that can respond to people's frustration, an existing institution, public space, is utilized by them spontaneously to change the conditions of their lives. In these moments of moving towards unanimity, the ambivalence of majority decisions in democratic societies seems pale and ineffective. Yet the supporters of unanimity find it difficult to accommodate diversity, to acknowledge the range of different opinions, aspirations and agendas.

Diversity can be served by those who take individual interests as their starting point and argue that collective decisions should favour the interests of the majority. It is important, Charles Taylor (1995) argues, to notice that these interests are not fixed and can be altered through debate, and that self interest is not the only criterion that people use in their decisions, as they also belong to a community. The Jacobin tradition, that sees the true people's will through class or factional rule, or the objective interest tradition, that sees people's will as the interest of the majority, focus on comparing the outcome with some preexisting standards. For the former this standard is the general will and for the latter the individual's interests.

Leaving these traditions behind requires an emphasis on the process. But where the democratic process does exist, a key concern is about the limited level of participation, which means that not all voices are heard, and about the impartiality and effectiveness of the public sphere to help develop a freely formed public opinion which can inform and influence public policy.

The alienation of citizens in large, centralized and bureaucratic societies is a familiar concern. The public sphere may appear to be dominated by a narrow range of interest groups operating in core regions and close to central administration. One way to confront this alienation is a decentralization of public sphere, where smaller public spheres are nested within larger ones and potentially inform and influence them. Some political parties and social movements, such as environmentalists and feminists, can also play a similar role, providing nested public spheres, especially when their internal discussions are openly made for all to see. Rather than unitary public space of the eighteenth century, then, 'a multiplicity of public spheres nested within each other', whose boundaries with the political system is more porous and relaxed, would now seem to more appropriate (Taylor, 1995: 209). Rather than nostalgia about the past, as it seems to be displayed by many who promote public sphere, the nature of the new public sphere and how it can improve in practice is what is needed. In a fragmented society, where individual and factional interests are pursued and the large size of society and its state is coupled with a sense of powerlessness and exclusion, common projects and successful common actions are needed to bring a sense of empowerment and identification with the political community. A network of nested public spheres can potentially confront the sense of exclusion and alienation, by allowing voices to be heard, issues discussed, and ideas developed, which can feed into the large-scale public spheres and political processes.

This indeed shows how the nature of impersonal relations has changed. In the eighteenth century such impersonal relations may have been a novelty worth pursuing, in the interest of establishing an impartial infrastructure through which individual rights and freedoms could be secured. Small-scale market exchange relations and relatively small-scale public sphere dominated by the elite could make this possible. But the civil society has become increasingly more complex, both in the market exchange where large corporations and huge flows of resources are involved, and public sphere, where national and international players dominate the scene. Under the weight of the complexity of the state, it appears that the public sphere, as part of the larger civil society, has disappeared. The impersonal nature of public sphere appears now alienating rather than inviting, which to some extent explains the rising tide of interest shown in human dimensions of economic and political exchange. But rather than mourning the passage of true public sphere, what needs pursuing now is a new balance between personal and impersonal, between particular and universal.

Rather than emphasizing the personal at the expense of the universal, which at times seems to be the case in some cultural trends, a new balance should be sought between the two. The political theorist Seyla Benhabib agrees with the desirability of the Enlightenment's ideals, but argues that they need to face the challenges of difference. Benhabib defines complex democracies in modern society as 'self-reflecting and self-criticizing institutions of deliberation as well as decision making' (1996: 209). The ideal of self-ruling public that is collectively deliberating about the common good is, she argues, 'a regulative ideal, as well as a constitutive fiction of democracy' (ibid.). It is a regulative ideal in the sense that it is a norm that is used to scrutinize and criticize the fairness of decisions and the processes of making them. It is also a constitutive fiction in the sense that the reality of democracy in modern, complex, multicultural and globalized politics causes anxiety for and appears to limit the possibility of such autonomous, rational deliberations.

The idea of 'public' has always excluded certain groups of individuals from participation or deliberation. The social complexity of modern society has led to the rise of representative democracy and the bureaucratized structures of government, which need to be supplemented by self-organization at the level of a free society. Rational critical deliberation needs appropriate procedures and institutions so as to guarantee equality, freedom and participation rights for those who are potentially marginalized. This needs to be supported and scrutinized by constitutional courts and judicial review. This will require a re-mapping of the boundaries between the public and private spheres that theorists such as Arendt drew, so as to create new energies and encourage innovation. The public sphere today, Benhabib (1996: 210) argues, has 'a crucial role in moulding the elective identities of anonymous citizens in increasingly complex nation-states'. It is a mirror in which the diversity of the human society is reflected. Benhabib adds a liberal twist to Rousseau's assertion of the necessity of a people becoming present to itself through public symbolic observations. 'To recognize its own diversity, and to come to grips with the implications this diversity may have for its own self-understanding, a democratic people needs to reenact its identity in the public sphere' (Benhabib, 1996: 210). If there is equal access for all groups within civil society to re-present themselves in public, the threats of being different can be diffused, rather than turning into resentment. Self-presentation and articulation in public allows the individuals and groups to take the standpoint of the others into account and see the world from their point of view. This is a crucial virtue in a civic polity, especially under the conditions of cultural diversity and social opacity.

Equal access to such representation should ideally be present in democratic societies. In practice, however, there may be gaps between the idea of cultural diversity and the practice of representing it. When representation takes some permanent form, as in public art, it seems to establish long-term connections between people and places. While a permanent claim to a place may fulfil some people's aspirations for self-expression, it may worry others. Marxloh, a working class neighbourhood in Duisburg, Germany, is where a large number of Turkish immigrants live. As part of its regeneration, a competition was set up for public arts in the area, which would represent its international character. The prize-winning scheme used the theme of sculptures of native North Americans, which were installed in public places. The gap between reality and representation, while both pointing to the international dimension of the area, is fairly wide (Figure 6.6).

Representation of difference and promotion of self-understanding may be a useful function of the public sphere. But it should not be seen as its only outcome. We have seen in our discussions so far that the notion of public space as display, as a vehicle of exposure and a site of recognition is only one dimension of a complex phenomenon. Struggle for recognition, which Honneth promotes following Hegel (Honneth, 1995), cannot be seen as the endpoint of social interactions as it must be associated with substantive results. Public sphere must also mean a vehicle for participation in the political processes, in forming common views that can inform and influence collective action.

6.6 Representation of difference in the public space: Native American symbols are used in public art to represent the international character of an urban area with a large population of Turkish residents (Duisburg, Germany)

CONCLUSION

We have seen how the public sphere has both material and institutional dimensions, and how it is important to recognize the interdependence of these two dimensions. Arendt and Habermas share the focus on public sphere as the sphere of politics. While Arendt incorporated the material space into her analysis, Habermas was more interested in the development of the press as the institution of public debate. For Arendt, public space was a test of reality through exposure to others, as well as a common world, a space in between, which people shared with each other and with future generations. Both used historical points of reference, from the ancient Greece to the European Enlightenment, to raise a critique of the contemporary public life, through nostalgic eyes. They shared a belief in the necessity of face-to-face communication as the basis of public life. Both, however, failed to appreciate that the extension of the public sphere from the elite to the larger society was not a merely negative development. Taylor defines public sphere as metatopical and tries to offer an understanding of the nature of public sphere in complex societies. Without sliding into nostalgia, Taylor stresses the centrality of public sphere in the free society. Public sphere acts as a central component part of civil society, providing protection from, and the ability to scrutinize, the state power. It also is the arena in which citizens engage in forming common opinions and shape or influence common action. To do this, Taylor promotes a network of nested public spheres, so that diversity of population and alienation of individuals in large complex societies can be taken into account. Benhabib also criticizes nostalgic approaches and argues for the centrality of public sphere for the diversity of the complex society. It allows diverse individuals and groups to present themselves before each other and so to become aware of themselves and the others. Co-presence in public space is then an essential part of the route to Honneth's struggle for recognition.

While public space of sociability emphasizes interpersonal relations in public places as an essential ingredient and a cohesive gel for social life, it stops short of promoting a normative political agenda. On the contrary, the public sphere of politics is largely focusing on a normative agenda, seeing public sphere as a vehicle of good governance, while often failing to acknowledge the spatiality of public sphere. Here, as Taylor stresses, public sphere may include many public spaces, but it is a 'metatopical' space, or in other words it is metaspatial.

The significance of this assertion for spatial arts and sciences should be acknowledged. Much that constitutes the public sphere of a complex society is beyond the spatial and temporal convergence that the spatial practitioners appear to idealize. While spatiality of public sphere is an essential part of social life, it is only one ingredient of the larger social processes that constitute public sphere, itself a key component of civil society. Hannah Arendt's emphasis on the common world is an important contribution to the understanding of public sphere. The size and complexity of the society, however, has made this common world in complex, bureaucratized, technologically advanced societies ever more an abstraction rather than an empirical reality. In a metaspatial public sphere, co-presence and exposure will be more representational than material, with the obvious danger of creating a large gap between representation and reality. Public sphere, therefore, is the integrated material and institutional common arena that relate individuals to one another, allowing them to regulate their relations partly through controlling exposure and concealment. It allows them to express their differences and identities, test their own reality, experience permanence through relation to other generations, while scrutinizing the state and forming common opinions, thereby integrating the positive and negative meanings of freedom.

Chapter 7
Impersonal space of the city

We have examined the public space within the context of interpersonal relations, as an arena of sociability or community building, as well as integrating material and institutional dimensions as a part of a metaspatial tool for self rule. We now move on to the impersonal public spaces of the city. This chapter traces the transformation of urban public spaces from the integrated core of the small town for interpersonal communication to their current dispersed and impersonal presence in the metropolis. It follows an historical account of this change in the Western city, with a brief visit to some of the cities of Asia and the Middle East. The modern city and its expansion, associated with the problems of spatial segregation, social polarization and privatization of space, are then discussed. The uses of public space in social cohesion and reintegration, as well as in economic regeneration of cities are examined to find out about the contested social, economic and political role of the public realm in the contemporary city.

FROM ANCIENT AGORA TO MEDIEVAL MARKETPLACE

Today, as compared to most historical periods of the past, the importance of public space in the cities seems to have diminished. This has partly been a result of decentralization of cities and despatialization of public sphere. There is a clear transition in many cities from a time when a high degree of socio-spatial concentration gave an overarching significance to some central public spaces to a time when places and activities in cities have found a more dispersed spatial pattern. Public space thus appears to have lost many of the functions it once performed in the social life of cities (Madanipour, 1999). As the circumstances of a city change through history, its social and spatial configuration changes accordingly. When the focus of activity moves from one part of the city to another, its once significant public spaces may lose their importance and be forgotten, while its other public spaces may not find any degree of significance at all, particularly in marginal areas, where fewer people and activities are concentrated. Some spaces, however, have continuously been a distinguishable node in the history of a city and the social life of its citizens.

The best known public space of all time was perhaps the ancient Greek agora, the main public square which was the meeting place of the town. It was first and foremost a marketplace, as Aristotle reminds us: 'For of necessity in almost every city there must be both buyers and sellers to supply each other's mutual wants; and this is what is most productive of the comforts of life; for the sake of which men seemed to have joined together in one community' (quoted in Glotz, 1929: 21–2). But the agora was more than a marketplace: it also served as a place of assembly for the town's people and a setting in which ceremonies and spectacles were performed. The agora, therefore, was a place in which economic, political and cultural activities were performed alongside each other, acting as an integrative platform for the social life of the city. The concentration of civic activities in the centre and leaving the rest to residential uses was a feature that Greek cities shared with the older civilizations of the Near East (Lawrence and Tomlinson, 1996: 191). Originally, the agora was just an open space located somewhere near the centre of the town. With specialization of activities and spaces, various public buildings grew around it, such as the meeting place of the city council, the offices of magistrates, temples and altars, fountain houses, law courts, and covered halls for the use of citizens and merchants. Although with the growth of the city and the need for larger places of assembly some of these activities might eventually be housed elsewhere in the town, the agora remained the heart of the city and its civic activities (Ward-Perkins, 1974). The agora was therefore seen as a necessary condition of city life, both in democracies and in the cities where citizens exercised no political rights at all. Indeed, the Greeks looked down with contempt upon those cultures whose towns did not have such a place of assembly (Glotz, 1929: 23).

The agora was, therefore, a node for the integration of the city life. But we know that the agora and the institutions it housed were not the only vehicles of social integration. The activities which supported the *polis* went beyond the formal democratic institutions of the assembly, the magistrates and the law-courts, which clustered in and around the agora and which have so widely fascinated the scholars. The collective activities of cult associations, groups of friends, age groups, and other types of grouping in the city played an intermediate role in the promotion of social cohesion in the *polis*, providing arenas for socialization, apprenticeship in political life and civic values, and places where the social order could be expressed (Schmitt-Pantel, 1990). In addition to the agora, the communal practices of these groups took place in sanctuaries, gymnasia, and even in the private realm of the house, where a special room catered for the meetings of the head of household (Jameson, 1990). The social cohesion which was being reproduced in these arenas and through these institutions and collective activities was exclusive and hierarchical, where women, slaves and aliens were kept at bay. Nevertheless, the agora was the main node in a network of public places and collective activities which made up the city-state, even after the political significance of the city-state and its democratic institutions declined with the rise of the Macedonian empire.

In the Hellenistic period that followed, the agora was much extended as the largest plan unit in the town. It was supplemented with colonnaded main streets, especially in the eastern colonies, which became a general pattern under the Romans (Lawrence and Tomlinson, 1996: 196). The main agora's unity and relative significance, however, somewhat declined as the second century BC witnessed the rapid rise of different sects and religions (Fyfe, 1936: 157–8). The larger commercial towns could have a number of subordinate agoras and markets, each with its own stoas, colonnades, a few of which might be devoted to particular trades but which were mostly used indiscriminately. In Delos, for example, Italians had their own separate agora (Lawrence and Tomlinson, 1996: 197–204).

According to Vitruvius, the celebrated Roman architectural theorist who lived in the first century BC, the Greeks designed their agora on 'a square plan with exceedingly spacious double porticoes' (Vitruvius, 1999, V, 1, p. 64). However, the Italian cities, with their custom of gladiatorial games in the forum, he thought, required more spacious intercolumnations around the performance space. In inland cities, the forum was to be placed at the centre of the city, while in seaside cities it had to be right next to the port (Vitruvius, 1999, I, 6, p. 31). Temples and other public places were to be adjoined next to the forum and the senate house, in particular, and built so as 'to enhance the dignity of the town or city' (Vitruvius, 1999, V, 2, p. 65). The forum's dimensions depended on the size of the city's population, as 'its area should neither be too cramped for efficiency nor so large that for lack of population it looks deserted' (Vitruvius, 1999, V, 2, p. 64). The proportions of 3 by 2 for its length and width were recommended. The forum's configuration was therefore oblong and 'its design effective for mounting spectacles' (ibid.).

The Greek approach to spatial organization was based on human cognition, in sacred precincts as well as in agoras. Buildings were so spaced around an open space that they could all be seen from a three-quarter view, and were located at distances of 30–70 metres, from a main entrance vantage point (Doxiadis, 1972: 3–5). For the Greeks, even after the Hippodamian orthogonal town plans, each building was an end in itself and they were satisfied if it was beautiful and accessible. This, however, changed with the Romans, who subordinated their streets and marketplaces to dominant buildings and axial planning. The city space was organized along the two main north–south and east–west axes (cardo and decumanus). As the size of the city and the power of the state grew and democratic practices were abandoned, long vistas, mechanical symmetry, centralized effects and sacrificing other considerations to the façade were sought. This difference between the

Greeks and Romans in the approach to urban space seems to have provided a basis for future trends in the West. The Middle Ages unconsciously reverted to the Greek method, while the Renaissance and what has followed since have revived the Roman ideal (Robertson, 1969: 191–4).

The ancient integration of spiritual and temporal had already started to be eroded with the growing size and specialization of urban space. In the Middle Ages, the distinction between the two found new expression in public spaces of cities, where secular and spiritual spaces were separated. In Italian cities, for example, there were two or three principal squares each associated with one set of activities. The cathedral square was separate from the main secular square (*signoria*) and from the market square (*mercato*) (Sitte, 1986). Despite this specialization of space and functional separation, there was an intensive use of public space for public life. The city squares were decorated with fountains, monuments, statues and other works of art and were used for public celebrations, state proceedings and exchange of goods and services. But all this started to change in the modern period, when the public squares of cities started to be used as parking lots and the relationship between them and the public buildings around them almost completely disappeared (Sitte, 1986: 151–4).

In early medieval Britain, the towns were shaped or influenced by the church and the castle. Later, however, it was commerce that was the major influence on shaping the newly growing towns. 'Everywhere the towns grew outwards from their market squares, from a road junction, or from a swelling in the street' (Platt, 1990: 94). At the meeting point of the trading routes, the secular space of commerce gave character to the public space. Most of the trade was conducted along streets flanked by narrow burgage plots, which formed the basic element in medieval towns (Figure 7.1).

The tension between public and private space was perhaps nowhere more evident than in the medieval city. The medieval city was a place of trade. The great majority of English towns, for example, were located at the intersection, or the converging points, of major trackways. This determined not only the location of the town but also the way its streets and markets were organized (Platt, 1976). One or more marketplaces in the medieval city were devoted to trade, as the main public spaces of the city. However, as Saalman reminds us, 'the entire medieval city was a market' (1968: 28). This meant that in all parts of the city, in open and closed spaces, whether public or private, trade and production for trade went on. Within this trading space, however, there was a constant struggle between public and private interests, which largely determined the shape of the medieval city. Individuals and households needed space for production, trade and living. As the availability of space within the walls was limited, there was continuous pressure

7.1 Medieval towns grew at the intersection of trade routes, creating a secular space for commercial exchange. Their space was shaped by competing commercial interests (Richmond, UK)

for claiming space for private use. On the other hand, there was a need for some free movement and interchange of goods and persons and for meeting places, which could also accommodate the trading visitors to the city. All this meant that the city needed public spaces as well. As the public power and its associated public institutions grew, the public spaces and public buildings grew. There was, therefore, 'a fluid balance' between 'Infinitely expanding public space and the eternally encroaching buildings' (Saalman, 1968: 35). The streets of the medieval city, which appeared to some modern commentators as an anarchic maze, reflecting the behaviour of pack donkeys rather than humans (Le Corbusier, 1971), were indeed formed by constant struggle between public and private interests.

As trade was the main function of the town, the street would be as long as it needed to be to give each trader an opening in trade (Platt, 1976: 30). Unlike continental Europe, the English towns did not all have a recognizable central square, while they all had at least one street. While the word street originates from the Latin *strata*, there is no English equivalent for *piazza*, *plaza*, *place* or *platz* to refer to the central focal point of a town. Market *place* or town square, which found a new meaning after the eighteenth century, were not a complete match (Lloyd, 1992: 46). The towns that developed later were usually provided with recognizable marketplaces or streets wide enough to accommodate several rows of market stalls. Trade, however, was not restricted to market stalls. The significant number of craftsmen and traders that made up the town's population were engaged in trade inside private spaces and outside in the public areas. As the ability to extend the private commercial space was limited, especially in the walled cities of Europe, a constant competition for control and use of space was reflected in encroachments into public space and a permanent struggle between the public and private spheres (Saalman, 1968).

THE CITY OF HARMONY AND SYMMETRY

In the Renaissance period, the Roman notions of symmetry and harmony were revived. Beauty was defined as the harmony between all parts (Alberti, 1988, XI, 2. p. 156) and architecture was conceived to be applied mathematics (Wittkower, 1971: 69). For Alberti, a major architectural theoretician who was hugely influenced by Vitruvius, ideal proportions for a town square meant that it had to be in the shape of a double square, and the dimensions of the surrounding buildings and colonnades in strict relation to open space, so that it appeared neither too large due to the lowness of these structures, nor too small due to their excessive height. 'The ideal roof height would be between one third and a minimum of two sevenths the width of the forum' (Alberti, 1988, IIX, 6. p. 256; Borsi, 1975: 327).

Large town squares were desirable, Alberti (1988, IV, 8, p. 116) stressed, 'as marketplaces and exercise areas for the youth during peace, and when at war as places to stockpile timber, grain, and other such commodities, essential for sustaining a siege'. It was possible to have different forums for different purposes, a marketplace for currency, vegetables, cattle, wood, etc., but 'each type of forum should be allocated its own site within the city and have its own distinctive ornament' (Alberti, 1988, IIX, 6, p. 263–4). Despite this specialization, many open spaces were basically a variation on the theme of crossroad (Figure 7.2): 'For a forum is but an enlarged crossroad, and a show ground [which included theatre, circus, and gladiatorium] nothing but a forum surrounded with steps' (Alberti, 1988, IIX, 6, p. 262). While private buildings were expected to be modest in their appearances, the significance of public buildings (civic and sacred) was to be emphasized by ornaments (Alberti, 1988, IX, 1. pp. 292–3). The public space was to be clean and elegant:

7.2 Many public open spaces in the city are variations on the theme of crossroads (Porto, Portugal)

> Apart from being properly paved and thoroughly clean, the roads within a city should be elegantly lined with porticoes of equal lineaments, and houses that are matched by line and level. The parts of the road that need to be particularly distinguished by ornaments are these: bridges, crossroads, fora, and show buildings. (Alberti, 1988, IIX, 6, p. 262)

The Renaissance and Baroque periods were characterized by the principle of central composition, which found its boldest application in town planning (Pevsner, 1968: 330). The first wholly symmetrical town plan in Western history was for Sforzinda by Filarete in the fifteenth century, which was a regular octagon with radial streets and with palace and cathedral on the square in the middle (Pevsner, 1968: 185). Centrally planned towns were to be actually built later, or long and straight roads cut through cities, famously in Rome by Sixtus V and in France under Henri IV, reflecting the rising power of the state. In the eighteenth century, the main examples are Karlsruhe in southern Germany, which was designed as a huge star with the Ducal Palace in the middle, and L'Enfant's plan for Washington D.C. (Pevsner, 1968: 330–2).

The Renaissance and Baroque public space, therefore, was a carefully planned display, symmetrically laid out, restricting the private spaces behind the neat rows of uniform, relatively modest façades (Figure 7.3). The public sphere that it represented was the royal court, the rising power of the secular state and the emerging age of reason. It was a complete reversal of the gradual and flexible way in which the medieval town had grown, allowing the private interests to compete with each other, encroach into and take over the public sphere.

The Renaissance idea of symmetry and harmonic proportions, however, was refuted in the eighteenth century, famously by Hume, when proportion and beauty became a matter of individual sensibility rather than inherent in the object or a priori mathematical ratios (Wittkower, 1971: 153). In Britain, Wren's plan for London was not implemented. Instead, London's contribution to town planning of the seventeenth and eighteenth centuries was the square, 'an isolated, privately owned area

7.3 The Renaissance and Baroque public space followed a symmetrical layout and a carefully planned display which restricted the private spaces behind neat rows of uniform, carefully planned façades (Turin, Italy)

with houses of, as a rule, similar but not identical design, examples of good manners and not of regimentation' (Pevsner, 1968: 332).

THE CITY OF UTILITY AND DISPLAY

Symmetry and harmonic proportions lost their influence on the imagination of the nineteenth century romantics, who promoted medievalism and a revival of Gothic and Classical styles. Below this surface of the primacy of sentiment over reason and nostalgic outlook for the past, however, this was the age of scientific discoveries, technological innovation and dominance of Western industrial capitalism over the rest of the world. In the growing cities, there was a coexistence of extreme segregation and the creation of many new public institutions and a considerable growth of the public sphere. According to Pevsner, the vast majority of the best examples of architecture in the nineteenth century were governmental and municipal buildings. To these were added later private office buildings, museums, galleries, libraries, universities, schools, theatres, concert halls, banks, exchanges, railway stations, department stores, hotels and hospitals. These were 'all buildings erected not for worship nor for luxury, but for the benefit and the daily use of the people, as represented by various groups of citizens' (Pevsner, 1968: 383). Despite the nineteenth century preference for medieval architectural styles, the public space of the city was not reshaped in a medieval fashion. The space of the cities was restructured to create new public spaces embellished by these new public institutions and buildings, so that the public space was treated as a display. The new public spaces were also places of utility, as they allowed for an easier and faster movement of goods and services across the urban space. The British bye-law streets and the French boulevards were examples of different mixtures of utility and display.

A century ago, Camilo Sitte complained about how the plazas (or public squares) of his day could be empty spaces formed by four streets bordering a piece of land. After studying the spatial organization of a number of European cities, he came to some clear ideas about how the public spaces of the city should be organized. For him, the main requirement for a public square, as for a room, was its enclosed character, which offered closed vistas from any point within it. The centre of this space was to be kept free and there was a need for a strong relationship between the public space and the buildings around it (Sitte, 1986).

With the age of the motor car in the twentieth century, the dimension of utility was meant to take over and the display be limited to the absolutely necessary. This, however, meant that the space of the city was no longer to be experienced on foot. There was no need for the street, which had to be abolished, as advocated by Le

Corbusier (1971). Places of assembly were to be inside huge buildings. Now build-ings, seen from a moving car, were the objects of display. There was no need for ornaments. In one sense, this was the abolition of the urban public space as known before.

Modernism essentially incorporated movement into its view of the world (Giedion, 1967). The functionalism of modernists, therefore, gave priority to cars and fast movement across urban space, a notion which undermined the close rela-tionship between open spaces and buildings around them. The existing urban enclosures with closed vistas, such as streets and squares, were to be demolished in favour of vast open spaces which provided a setting for a free and flexible loca-tion of buildings (Le Corbusier, 1971). Despite their emphasis on the primacy of public interests in the city, as promoted in the Charter of Athens (Sert, 1944), the modernists paid little attention to the historically created public spaces of the city. What they sought was a redefinition of the relationship between public and private space, which would reshape the urban space, creating large quantities of open space for hygienic as well as aesthetic reasons. What resulted was vast expanses of space which could have little or no connection with the other spaces of the city and could be left under-used, only to be watched from the top of the high rise buildings or from the car windows.

The modernist break from the city of the past can be studied in the figure-ground relations, which reveal how the relations between public and private spaces have changed. In the pre-industrial city, the public space was the void, surrounded by the mass of the buildings, which housed private functions. There were also public buildings, whose interior space shared public functions with the public open space of the street, as shown by Nolli's famous plan of Rome in the eighteenth century. The modernists changed this relationship between mass and void, as they consciously tried to dismantle 'corridor streets' (Le Corbusier, 1971). This essen-tially changed the way space was conceptualized, from being within a labyrinth to looking from outside at a pyramid (Madanipour, 1996). This might appear to be a domination of public space, as it was drastically expanded, in the form of parks in the middle of which high rise buildings were erected. However, this space was ill-defined and under-used, indeed it was 'lost space' (Trancik, 1986), where none of the functions of the public space could be performed; sociability was becoming impossible.

The subdivision of the city into functional zones eroded the public space further. The effect of these functionally defined zones was to limit the diversity of people in the public spaces of these zones. The logic of the modernist city was indeed following the logic of the buildings' interior, as it gave priority to the living conditions of the private sphere, which could then be mass produced to create machines to live in. The house was designed from inside out and form followed function (Brain, 1997: 252). This meant that the public space followed the logic of private space, the void became subordinate to the mass, the public space was to become a residue of the buildings, a leftover. The balance between the public and the private, between the void and the mass that characterized the pre-modern city was thus lost.

This loss of public–private distinction paralleled the radical ideologies of the time that advocated the abolition of private property. In the new world, old distinctions were thought to make no sense any more. The new public space that was being created was taken over by the fast moving cars, allowing for a new experience of the buildings, combining the speed of movement and monumentality of buildings. After the static, enclosed public spaces of the past, the new public spaces were to be free-floating, fast-moving and all-encompassing.

As in the nineteenth century, the twentieth century had its own return to romanticism, in the shape of postmodernism. Once again, below the surface of this return to the primacy of sentiment over reason, of concrete over abstract, there was an intense process of new scientific discoveries, new technologies and a world-wide process of breathless globalization. The recreation of the public space in the city in the latter part of the century was at once again an attempt at combining utility and display.

For those who remained unconvinced by such an imposition of an abstract notion of space onto the existing urban environment and the everyday life (Lefebvre, 1991), a return to the historic notions of public space seemed inevitable. Once again, creation of spatial enclosure became a main prerequisite in urban design (County Council of Essex, 1973; Cullen, 1971). As nodes and landmarks, public spaces became a means with which to navigate in the city (Lynch, 1960). Streets and squares became the alphabet with which to read, and design, urban space (Krier, 1979). Creating lively and active edges for these spaces was seen as an important condition of their success (Jacobs, 1961). Small, mixed land uses that generate a strong relationship between the public space and the buildings around it were promoted (Bentley et al., 1985). It became absolutely essential for urban design to create 'positive urban space', i.e. space enclosed by buildings, rather than what is a leftover after the construction of buildings (Alexander et al., 1987). A prime example of these changing and often contradictory interpretations of and approaches to public space is the city centre of Birmingham, which had been dominated by a network of motorways. It was first transformed by dismantling half of the fast road network and then by introducing a number of public spaces, pedestrianized and embellished by public art (Tibbalds et al., 1990) (Figure 7.4).

7.4 A city centre that was dominated by a network of motorways was transformed by dismantling half of its fast road network and by introducing a number of public spaces, pedestrianized and embellished by public art (Birmingham, UK)

PUBLIC SPACE IN THE EASTERN CITY

Some similar trends in the relations between technology, politics and society can be found in cities in other parts of the world. The political significance of public space may have been manipulated in cities where the rulers have kept an often violent distance from the ruled. The significance of some form of public space, however, has been essential for sociability and for economic transactions across time and space, as some examples would show.

The ancient Chinese cities were square-shaped and walled, with gates on four sides and the main gate on the southern wall. The city was organized on an axial symmetrical pattern, the roads forming a chequer-board grid, running north–south and east–west, with the palace at the centre, at the main crossroad, and all the major buildings facing south (Liu, 1989: pp. 41ff).

The Chinese traditional organization of space within buildings was based on a number of multi-purpose, mainly south-facing rooms around courtyards and along longitudinal or horizontal axes in orthogonal order, with the most important part located at the northern end and the main entrance at the southern end (Figure 7.5). This arrangement of space could be used for both public and private buildings,

7.5 The Chinese traditional organization of space within buildings was based on a number of multi-purpose, mainly south-facing rooms around courtyards and along longitudinal or horizontal axes in orthogonal order, with the most important part located at the northern end and the main entrance at the southern end (Tainan, Taiwan)

houses as well as temples and palaces, and would be extended to form cities (Liu, 1989: 27ff). Plans were symmetrical and orthogonal, to reflect the Chinese cosmos, and their orientation reflected an acknowledgement of the spirits and of climatic and topographical conditions. The axial planning made the spatial arrangement a sequence of solids and voids. The use of high walls, which enclosed the house and the introverted courtyards as the centre of activity, made the Chinese house a private space protected from the outside world. This was a small world by itself, where Confucian ideas of hierarchy of generations and code of ethics ruled and where philosophical content was expressed in private gardens. Within an orthogonal, axial layout, there was a poetic, picturesque, organic design for the garden, a dialogue between a rigid, rational framework and a drive for expressive freedom.

Political institutions and control dominated the centre of the traditional Chinese city. There was no public square in the classical Chinese city, as the government or emperor discouraged public gatherings. The emperor was the Son of Heaven and the centre of the universe. The central location of his walled palace in the capital and his governors in the provincial cities ensured full control over the movement of people. The halls of large houses and the courtyards between the halls were the only places of gathering. The word for city in China (*cheng*) also meant wall, in the same way that the two words are linked in European languages, as we saw in Chapter 2. In the first Chinese dynasty, Xia, there was a saying, 'To build city to protect the emperor, to build wall to watch the people' (Liu, 1989: 41). Residential neighbourhoods and markets had walls and gates, although these were dismantled later to allow houses and shops to have direct access to the street. When cities grew larger a number of markets could develop, some of them along streets (as in Changan), or outside the city walls for international trade (as in Luonyang). A second centre could develop for business, cultural and recreational facilities (as in Nanjing during the Ming dynasty). Some roads were wider (up to 150 metres wide in Changan), lined with trees (as in Gaozhu), where crowds and chariots mingled (as in Linzi).

The public urban space, however, remained a closely controlled space. Liu suggests that the absence of a town square was the main difference between the Chinese and Western cities (Liu, 1989: 53). This absence of public squares, however, is not reported in a detailed study of China's provincial life more than half a century ago (Yang, 1945). A wider main street in the village, and a public square in the market town, where the roads converged, were multi-purpose spaces of sociability and trade for residents and visitors. In the village,

> The central section of the main street is quite spacious. To the south it opens on the river and affords a view of the open country. On the levees built by some of the wealthier families along the riverbank grow rows of willow trees. This part of the main street is something of a social centre or public square for the village. In the summer, the villagers sit on the stones or on the levees under the trees and talk through the hot afternoons. In winter, the old people relax against the walls in the warm sunshine and watch the children at play in the square. Men weaving baskets or knitting straw rain coats or perhaps working on farm tools work out here rather than in their narrow and smoke-filled homes. (Yang, 1945: 6)

The functional separation between the public and private spheres may become blurred in this public square, or in a farmer's house. Here the hired labourers, guests, the family members, as well as the spirits of ancestors would live together, and the farmer's bedroom could be a place of meeting friends and neighbours (Yang, 1945: 38–40). In the town, all the important streets and avenues met at the centre to form a public square (Yang, 1945: 190). On market days, all available space was 'crowded with booths, counters, and platforms heaped with merchandise' (Yang, 1945: 191). Teahouses and wine shops of the market town were the meeting places of the farmers and traders, where historically officials would visit in disguise to find out about public opinion (Yang, 1945: 194), which was the chief instrument of social control in villages (p. 150).

In the modern cities, the public space has continued to be a place of sociability and of political contest, the latter exemplified famously by Beijing's Tiananmen Square in 1989. The city's growth, as in Taipei, has led to a fragmentation and dispersal of functions across the urban space, as well as new forms of specialization, as exemplified by the takeover of the old centre's public spaces by the young. The public space of the modern city suffers from the impact of motor vehicles, as in most other cities of the world (Figure 7.6).

Further to the west, the ancient Iranian cities were also organized according to axial, geometrical patterns. The walled towns and villages that started to develop in eastern Iran from the middle of the first millennium BC were square-shaped and had an internal axial layout. A main street stretched from a single gateway, flanked by courtyard houses, and led to a central square, which was the communal park of the cattle (de Planhol, 1968: 425–8). The ancient cities of Merv (College, 1977) and Herat (Gaube, 1979; English, 1973) were square-shaped settlements with two main axes intersecting at right angles leading to four gates. This was a pattern which continued in Parthian and Sassanian cities until the Muslim conquest in the seventh century. Despite the Muslims' attempts to break its symbolic, pre-Islamic significance, it can be found in Iranian cities until the nineteenth century, as was the case in Tehran (Madanipour, 1998b). The axiality of urban form, however, did not rule out some form of public square. The squares were the places of festivals (as the festival of fire recounted by Ferdowsi) (Boyce, 1983: 793), as well as open marketplaces for trade, which could also be used by the rural populations of the surrounding areas as a refuge during war (as in Jayy, Isfahan) (Gaube, 1979). The squares could be used as a meeting point between the governor and the townspeople, located between the citadel and the city, as in medieval Bukhara (Frye, 1965: 42, 92, 94), or even in nineteenth-century Tehran, where two squares inside and outside the citadel were used for political and economic activities (Madanipour, 1998b).

The most sophisticated form of central urban square in Iran was the Meydan-e Naqsh-e Jahan in Isfahan (also called Shah Square and later Imam Square), where polo was played and some trade took place (Figure 7.7). It was surrounded by the royal palace, the central mosque, the main bazaar entrance, a music pavilion and religious schools. This was the integrated heart of the capital city in the sixteenth century. Isfahan's Meydan-e Naqsh-e Jahan was renowned in Shakespeare's England and even until the middle of the twentieth century was the largest public square in the world (except for Red Square in Moscow) (Groseclose, 1947: 8). It predated the Place Royale (Faghih, 1984), which was the first great public square

7.6 The public spaces of the modern city (even their pavements as shown here) are taken over by motor cycles and cars (Taipei, Taiwan)

7.7 A large square was located at the heart of the capital in the sixteenth century, integrating the political, economic and cultural life of the city (Isfahan, Iran, Photo by Hamid Imanirad)

in Paris and the model for London squares and other European city squares (Vance, 1977: 237). During the twentieth century, the urban squares of Tehran and the large cities, such as Baharestan Square in front of the parliament, have frequently been the spaces of political contest. Whoever controlled these urban spaces, controlled the city and society. While the kings used them as displays of their power, the revolutionary masses used them as their meeting points and places of challenging authority. The two revolutions that have shaped Iran's modern history were both performed in its public spaces. In this sense, there was a close link between the social movements and the public spaces of the city (Madanipour, 1998b: 42–4).

The interplay between the public and private spaces was clearly known in the medieval cities in Western Asia and North Africa. As Rumi, the great classical Persian poet (whom the current Whirling Dervishes consider as their founder), wrote in the thirteenth century, the mosques were built to promote social integration and solidarity.

> That is the secret of why mosques were erected, so that the inhabitants of the parish might gather there and greater mercy and profit ensue. Houses are separate for the purpose of dispersion and the concealment of private relations: that is their use. Cathedral mosques were erected so that the whole city might be assembled there; the Kaaba was instituted in order that the greater part of mankind might gather there out of all cities and climes. (Jalal al-Din Rumi, quoted in Arberry, 1994: 227)

The public realm that is thus created finds a strong religious and social purpose, with the intention of bringing people together. This was also the case for the Jewish temple, as synagogue is a Greek word to refer to a place of assembly. One aspect of the Middle Eastern city that has been criticized is the lack of public urban squares like those of the medieval European cities. The equivalent of this major urban square, however, should be considered to be the courtyard of the cathedral mosque, a large open space surrounded by arcades, albeit giving the public space a specific religious rather than secular character (Figure 7.8). In addition, many small public squares existed within the neighbourhoods, at the crossroads where they could be roofed and arcaded as shopping streets, or in front of the public buildings, playing an important role in the social life of cities. A major open space, such as Bein al-Qasrein in medieval Cairo, was the main open space of the city in front of the palace, a place of ceremonies as well as trade and a meeting place between the town and the political institutions that dominated it (Nasser, 2000).

The organization of space and the appearance of cities have been traditionally regarded as the most distinctive feature of the Islamic lands from Central Asia to the Middle East and North Africa. After four centuries of transition and evolution, the cities of the Middle East found their general physical characteristics in the eleventh century (Lapidus, 1973), to remain largely unchanged until the nineteenth and twentieth centuries. The space of the city was, at a functional level, clearly divided into public and private realms. The public realm, often in the town centre, contained all the common activities of the town, such as trade and commerce, religion, education, administration and other public facilities. On the other hand, the house, where extended families lived, constituted the private realm. One of the main dividing lines between the two realms of the town was the distinction between spheres, temporal routines, and patterns of activities of men and women.

The public and private relations inside the introverted courtyard houses were organized along the lines of familiar-stranger, family member–guest and, most

7.8 The courtyard of the mosque, a large open space surrounded by arcades, was the religious public square (Blue Mosque, Istanbul, Turkey)

importantly male–female relations. The space of the larger house could therefore be subdivided accordingly, with separate areas designated for the guests, servants and the subsections of the extended family. In these houses, the private and semi-private spaces formed the inner core of the house. There was a semi-public space closely associated with the entrance, the domain of men where the guests were received and the public affairs conducted. Even now, in some of the larger modern houses in the Middle East, although the courtyard plans have been replaced by Western style villas, these subdivisions persist, where separate servant quarters and separate entrances and guest quarters are provided for men and women (e.g. Al-Khobar in Saudi Arabia, as explained by Al-Dossary, 2001).

The internal space of the house, therefore, had a range of public and private areas. The private realm of the house, however, was sharply separated from the public space outside by blank walls and controlled entrances, leading to semi-private cul-de-sacs, which were sometimes gated. Residential areas were formed of neighbourhoods, which could be walled and gated, with their own small local market and, at times, workshops. They were geographical entities as well as homogeneous communities that were closely knit, forming the basic unit of society. The solidarity between the small group of people living in every quarter was based on family, clientage, common village origin, ethnic or sectarian religious identity, in some cases strengthened by common occupation. There was no evidence to show the homogeneity of social classes as a base of solidarity since they were communities of both rich and poor. These village-like communities within the urban whole, with relatively few institutions connecting them to each other, and even at times completely hostile to each other, were administrative units represented on the city-wide political or ceremonial occasions, by a head who was selected by the governor (Lapidus, 1967: 85–95; 1969: 49–51). The small size of the population and their strong social bonds with each other reduced the publicness of urban space inside the quarters. The local mosque and market were often frequented by the local people. These were potentially, and practically, exclusive spaces, which strengthened the quarter's social and spatial cohesion. They were, therefore, another layer in the public–private continuum that constituted the urban space.

The main public activities of the town were located around its geographical centre or along its main axes. The citadel, the Friday mosque and the bazaar, as the centres of political, spiritual and symbolic, and economic power, constituted the focal points of the city. One of these elements, the main (often covered) street or streets of the city, the bazaar, functioned also as a communication channel, connecting these to each other and to the less important activities such as public baths, water storages and educational centres, hence creating a vivid public realm in a spatial continuum. This space was the meeting place of the townspeople with each other, with the political, religious and economic hierarchies, and with the outside world. This was a place in which, in many cities, the factional strife between the living quarters could be relaxed. Yet the public space was always under threat from the privatization of space by individual encroachments or by powerful interests. In medieval Cairo, for example as reported by al-Maqrizi, the amir Gamal al-Din al-Ustadar had over a span of a few years managed to own a great deal of property along the street called Khatt Emir as-Salih in Bein al-Qasrein. In order to protect his properties, he privatized the street, aided by the ruling of a judge, transforming a thoroughfare into a blind alley. He constructed a commercial building over the northern entrance to the street blocking it, and placed several gates at the other end to prohibit access. (Nasser, 2000: 211).

Generations of modernists and modernizers described the traditional Middle Eastern cities to have formed an apparently disorderly layout, a tangle of blocks hardly ventilated by a labyrinth of winding lanes and dark alleys, low houses, stretching into the distance between closed courtyards with high walls, and the vivacity of a narrowly circumscribed bazaar contrasting with the silence of the residential quarters (de Planhol, 1970: 453). The absence of order as they saw it meant a call for redevelopment of the cities to be brought into the modern age. A modern image was to be created out of what was considered to be outdated. In particular the new infrastructure that was needed for the penetration of cars as well as utility networks such as electricity, gas, and telephone made the case for this redevelopment. The new public spaces that emerge, however, were similar to the modern spaces of their Western counterparts: dominated by the cars rather than pedestrians, losing much of their meaning and role in social life (Figure 7.9).

FROM THE INTEGRATED CITY TO FRAGMENTATION AND PRIVATIZATION

In the modern era, the functional integration of the ancient city has almost completely disappeared. The growing size of the city has led to a specialization of space, which has dismantled the symbolic and functional coherence of both public and private spheres. As places of work and living were separated in the industrialization process, life in the private sphere was completely transformed. As new transport technologies have made it possible to live and work outside the city, the central spaces of the city can be avoided by large numbers of citizens. Furthermore, the ability to pass through the urban space at high speeds has undermined the close physical contact between townspeople and their built environment, as had existed throughout history (Sennett, 1994).

The speed of movement has contributed to the despatialization of activities,

7.9 The public spaces of the modern Middle Eastern city have been transformed to adjust to the motor car, losing their historical characteristics (Dubai, UAE)

which is associated with new transport and communication technologies. Following the printed word, networks of communication and transportation have created a despatialized public sphere, severely undermining the political, economic and cultural significance of the public spaces of the city. The public sphere is formed of a large number of arenas which may never overlap in space or time. As political debates, exchange of goods and services, and participation in rituals and ceremonies can take place in different locations through a variety of means other than face-to-face communication, the functional role of public space, which once could house all these activities, is no longer central in a city. Public spaces of the city have become either residual spaces, used for parking cars, or at best associated with particular, limited functions, such as tourism or retail. Many public or semi-public places, from the ancient church to the public libraries and museums of the modern period, have come under pressure from these changes. The modern city has therefore gone through a spatial and temporal dispersion of its functions and a despatialization of some of its activities, which have created multiple, non-converging networks working against the cohesive, nodal role which the urban public space could play in the past. The public sphere is no longer equated with public space, but, as we saw in the last chapter, with being metaspatial: the sum total of many arenas of communication.

Furthermore, many places in cities are open to the public and are seen as public but have particular functional definitions and restrictions. Restaurants, museums, libraries and theatres are among the public places of a city. These places, however, have a particular functional significance. In the same way that a shopping mall is focusing on trade, a restaurant has a definite function and working hour schedule, which poses its own particular set of restrictions. The open public spaces of the city, which are most accessible and have the most functional overlap and flexibility, however, have come under pressure from the specialization and functional disintegration of the modern city.

The technological innovation and the use of new transport and communication technologies that followed the industrial revolution have caused a fragmentation of the city, undermining its public spaces. Another cause of this fragmentation and loss of significance has been the social polarization that has followed the emergence of market economies and the privatization of space (Figure 7.10).

The causes of the privatization of space can be traced back to several changes in urban development processes. Throughout the twentieth century, the development companies have been growing in size and complexity. Small, locally based developers working closely with the local elite have given way to large developers whose headquarters are often based outside the locality and who command massive productive capacity. This change, alongside the changes in construction technology, has had major impacts on urban form (Whitehand, 1992). Furthermore, the financing of the development projects and ownership of property have undergone substantial change, as banks and financial institutions are increasingly operating at national and international, rather than local scale. As development companies are linked with broader capital markets, a growing disjunction can be detected between the development process and localities. If particular developments had some symbolic value for their developers in the past, it is now more the exchange value in the market that determines their interest. As space is stripped of its emotional and cultural value, which is only developed through people's use through time, it is treated as a mere commodity (Madanipour, 1996). What the investors are interested in is a safe return on their investment.

At the same time, the fear of crime has been a major reason for a withdrawal of people from the public space (Miethe, 1995). With the decline of the welfare state, the role of the public authorities in the cities has been undermined. The new additions to urban space are often developed and managed by private investors, as

7.10 The public spaces of the city have been increasingly developed and owned by private organizations (Los Angeles, USA)

the public authorities find themselves unable or unwilling to bear the costs of developing and maintaining public places. A combination of the need for safe investment returns and safe public environments has led to the demand for total management of space, hence undermining its public dimension. From shopping malls to gated neighbourhoods and protected walkways, new urban spaces are increasingly developed and managed by private agencies in the interest of particular sections of the population. It is in response to this privatization trend that the development of public realm is being promoted. Rather than exacerbating socio-spatial polarization through creating exclusive enclaves and nodes, the development of truly public spaces is expected to promote a degree of tolerance and social cohesion.

The lines that define the public spaces of the city are often the lines between public and private properties. The relationship between public and private spaces has shaped cities throughout history and has been at the centre of their social organization. However, since the critique of Aristotle against Plato, the role of private property in the city has been the subject of debate, as we saw in Chapter 2. After the rise of neo-liberalism in the West and the collapse of socialist regimes in the East, the balance between the public and the private space has entered a new phase, in which private development and control of cities have grown. As in the medieval cities, the contours of urban space are being carved out of a constant tension between public and private relationships. Urban designers can have a significant role in elaborating a public realm which mediates, and promotes a civilized relationship, between private interests with their spatial expressions, private domains, and the collective needs of the various groups and individuals that live together in cities.

PUBLIC SPACE FOR SOCIAL COHESION

The dispersion of cities has had severe social consequences. The rise of the industrial city in the nineteenth century uprooted large numbers of people from villages and small towns and concentrated them in cities, where the industries were located. But as we saw in Chapter 5, from early on, this led to social and spatial segregation among the middle and working classes. As Engels reported from Manchester in the 1840s, it was possible to live in the city and visit it everyday without coming into contact with the working class areas (Engels, 1993). From early on, however, this segregation was explosive and caused fear among the political and cultural elite. Socio-spatial segregation has remained a feature of the modern city to this day. It is still possible for citizens to live and work in the suburbs without ever visiting the troubled inner city. While the racial and social segregation of the American city is well known, the European city also suffers from increased threats of social polarization and segregation (Madanipour, Cars and Allen, 1998). Cities that were transformed once through industrialization are being transformed once again through deindustrialization and transition to service economy. As before, such transformation has caused fear and anxiety, as some established socio-spatial patterns have been destabilized.

Promotion of the public space has been seen as one of the vehicles of confronting this fragmentation and managing this anxiety (Figure 7.11). Promotion of some form of togetherness can be seen through various definitions of public space. For example, public space is seen as, 'the common ground where people carry out the functional and ritual activities that bind a community' (Carr et al., 1992: xi), or 'space we share with strangers . . . space for peaceful coexistence and impersonal encounter' (Walzer, 1986: 470). By creating areas in which different people intermingle, it is hoped that they can be brought together and a degree of tolerance be promoted. This is especially crucial at a time when the welfare state has come under threat of restructuring and social fragmentation has intensified.

7.11 Public spaces are promoted as a means of bringing people together, leading to tolerance and social cohesion (York, UK)

In this sense, the promotion of public space can be linked to a number of major themes of debate in social and political philosophy. One theme is the relationship between individualism and holism, or as is known in political debates, between libertarians and communitarians: whether the radical autonomy of individuals should be sought, or the wellbeing of a community as a whole. Promoting the public space as a meeting point of the atomized individuals clearly emphasizes the importance of togetherness. Another theme is the separation of the public and the private realms, which is one of the central themes of liberal political theory and was also promoted by other theorists of public sphere, such as Hannah Arendt (1958) and Jürgen Habermas (1989), as we saw earlier. A strong public sphere, where public life is conducted and which is clearly separated from the private realm, is seen to be essential for the health of a society. This line of thinking, however, has been criticized by Marxists, who saw this distinction as rooted in the private ownership of property and therefore leading to alienation, and by feminists, who saw this distinction as associating the private sphere with women and undermining their role in social life. It is also criticized by postmodernists who reject universal tendencies and see the withdrawal from public sphere as a sign of self preservation and dynamism of a society by developing new forms of communities.

The separation of the public and private spheres is one of the central themes of liberal political theory. It is therefore not surprising that it is challenged by a number of radical movements, among them Marxist and feminist criticism. The Marxist critique of public–private dichotomy rests on the concept of alienation, as discussed in Chapter 2. The private control of the means of production and the division of labour result in the alienation of workers from their work, their products and their fellow human beings. For Marx, the contradiction between the private and public, and in a broader sense between individual and society, belonged to bourgeois society. On the one hand, Marx and his followers did not believe in anything as being private in the sense of standing outside society or as prior to it. On the other hand, they believed that public power of the state would disappear after the establishment of rational, self-regulating communities. By the abolition of private property and the division of labour, alienation would be overcome and the public–private distinction disappear (Kamenka, 1983).

Challenging the dichotomy between the public and private is central to the political struggle of feminism, as we saw in Chapter 3. It is, as Pateman puts it, 'ultimately, what the feminist movement is about' (1983: 281). Men have been associated with the public realm and women with private sphere. The subjection of women to men, it is argued, is obscured by the dichotomy between the public and private and its apparently universal, egalitarian and individualist order. The problem this poses is that the public world, or civil society, is conceptualized and discussed as being separate from the private domestic sphere, which then becomes forgotten in theoretical discussion. The reality, however, is that these spheres are interrelated and the world of work cannot be understood as separate from the world of domestic life. Indeed, 'the sphere of domestic life is at the heart of civil society rather than apart or separate from it' (Pateman, 1983: 297). At the same time, as more women have joined the public realm of work and politics, the nature of public sphere and the forms of opposition to it have started to change (Banhebib, 1996).

Some critics of the separation of public and private spheres go back to the rise of industrial capitalism, which separated the realms of work and home from each other. Before the industrial revolution, the family was the unit of both production and reproduction, and social life was not split into separate, autonomous spheres. The separation of home and work created a male-dominated, public sphere of work, as opposed to a private sphere which was identified with women but which also trapped them. Withdrawal from community bonds and splitting of social life into public and private spheres, therefore, was not a voluntary commitment by many thousands of families that went through this transformation. Dividing the world into public and private spheres, or 'privatization', was 'an unanticipated consequence of industrialization' and can be one interpretation of the decline of community (Brittan, 1977: 56–8).

The withdrawal from the public sphere, however, others argue, is not necessarily a negative development. It is a sign of dynamism and self preservation of a society, of fighting against alienation and standing up to ideologies, teachings and claims to domination or even emancipation (Maffesoli, 1996: 46). Rather than lamenting the end of great collective values and the withdrawal into the self, the development of new small groups and existential networks should be evaluated as a positive step forward. It is a new form of organicism in which emotional communities, based on exchange of feeling, are emerging, a new version of *Gemeinschaft* or a new tribalism (Maffesoli, 1996).

Public space mediates between the private spaces that make up the bulk of the city and plays a role in confronting this process of socio-spatial fragmentation. Without it, the spatial movement across the city becomes limited and subject to obstacles in need of constant negotiation. As in the medieval factionalism of the Mediterranean city, where neighbourhoods were separated by walls and gates or in the gated neighbourhoods of today, passage across the space (and subsequently communication in social life) of the city is limited and compartmentalized.

PUBLIC SPACE AS A SOCIAL CAPITAL

Public spaces of the city have been considered as one of its assets, a social capital that can be used in the social integration of its residents (Figure 7.12). There is a wide range of definitions available for social capital. The use of the term goes back to the early twentieth century, first used by Lyda Hanifan, a school reformer in West Virginia in 1919. It was later used by Jane Jacobs in the 1960s in her seminal work, where she saw the neighbourhood networks forged by long-term residents as a city's irreplaceable social capital (1961: 138).

Some of the main figures who have discussed the concept in more detail, include James Coleman, Pierre Bourdieu and Robert Putnam. A brief look at these writings show how public space in particular, and public sphere in general, can be seen as a key contributor to social capital formation. Bourdieu defines social capital as 'resources based on connections and group memberships' (quoted in Calhoun, 1993: 70). It is, therefore,

> the aggregate of the actual or potential resources which are linked to possession of a durable network of more or less institutionalized relationships of mutual acquaintance and recognition – in other words to membership in a group – which provides each of its members with the backing of the collectively-owned capital. (Bourdieu, 1986: 248–9)

7.12 Public spaces are seen as part of a society's social capital, to be used in preventing social fragmentation and alienation (Alnwick, UK)

Bourdieu's social capital is one among a number of capitals that individuals accumulate and, once recognized and legitimized, turn into symbolic capital. As distinct from this phenomenological account of social capital, Putnam sees social capital as the

> norms and networks of civil society that lubricate cooperative action among both citizens and their institutions. Without adequate supplies of social capital – that is, without civic engagement, healthy community institutions, norms of mutual reciprocity, and trust – social institutions falter. (Putnam, 1998: v)

Michael Woolcock summarizes the position of the major contributors to theorizing social capital in generally defining social capital as 'the information, trust, and norms of reciprocity inhering in one's social networks' (1998: 153).

Many sentences that define social capital also include how it is being used. According to James Coleman, who was one of the earlier writers to use the term in its current sense,

> Social capital is defined by its function. It is not a single entity, but a variety of entities having two characteristics in common: They all consist of some aspect of social structure, and they facilitate certain actions of individuals who are within the structure. Like other forms of capital, social capital is productive, making possible the achievement of certain ends that would not be attainable in its absence. (1990: 302)

There is, therefore, a notion of function and direction inherent in most definitions, that social capital is an asset that is being used in a particular direction. Lang and Hornburg (1998: 4) for example, define social capital as referring to 'the stocks of social trust, norms, and networks that people can draw upon in order to solve common problems'. In this sense, most uses of the term have a practical, utilitarian emphasis, that is, the concept has the potential to perform useful political and organizational work.

This overlap of the contents of the concept with its direction of use can potentially cause confusion. It is also one reason why all shades of political opinion seem to be promoting it. Communitarians, for example, seek to re-establish the bonds of community that they see have been lost in the modern period. The notion of social capital, with its potential contribution to the strengthening of the local communities, therefore, plays a crucial role in this agenda. Public space is a key arena to promote this togetherness of the community. For the conservatives, it is considered as a means to re-establish the social order by strengthening moral values and social norms that were in crisis in the transition from the industrial age to the information age. This was seen as marked by a combination of technological innovation, large-scale entry of women into the labour market, the undermining of all forms of authority, rising crime and decline in social and family ties (Fukuyama, 1999). One of the main attractions of the concept for writers such as Fukuyama has been that it could be used to challenge and hence reduce the role of state and its intervention in social life. The reform of the welfare state, therefore, becomes associated with reducing reliance on the state, where development of social capital is closely related to self-help (Wann, 1995). Public space here is an arena which facilitates the development of trust and the possibility of action outside the state remit and control. The social democrats, on the other hand, see a positive relationship between social capital and state intervention. Rather than seeing the relationship between state and society as mutually exclusive, they emphasize the role the state can play in the accumulation of social capital and hence the development of a strong civil society. Public space, when provided by the state, is one instrument in this process. Social capital, therefore, has been seen as both a means to reduce the role of state and a way of asserting this role. This clearly establishes the importance of the way it is being used.

The ambiguity between the content and direction, and the fact that the concept of social capital is being promoted across the political spectrum, raises an important question: 'who uses it and who benefits from it?' One dimension of this question, as we saw, is the extent of the relationship between state and society. Another aspect is the nature of this relationship. If it is being used only as an instrument of management and social control, rather than a means of improving the quality of life, the notion can become problematic.

There is also an important question about the distribution of social capital among the networks and relations of a society. People living in poor areas often have very rich networks which enable them to survive, but these are often not considered as the appropriate 'social capital' for engagement in a dynamic local economy (Madanipour and Bevan, 1999). Used in this way, the concept may become a vehicle of blaming the poor for their lack of social capital as a prerequisite to achieve economic viability. It is in relation to the poor sections of the population that one of the most important criticisms is waged against the concept. In a polarizing society, how can we expect social capital to develop among unequal partners? How can reciprocity and group memberships cross the social and economic divide, rather than deepening it? How far does the development of social capital contribute to the establishment of new elites, rather than creating new opportunities for those who need them most?

Social capital is considered by some to play a clear economic role, with a 'a tangible dollar value' (Fukuyama, 1999: 14). One of the major criticisms against the notion of social capital, however, is that it uses the language of economics to talk about a social and cultural phenomenon. It is treated with suspicion, therefore, by sociologists, who see it as a take-over of the social sciences by economic concerns. On the other hand, economists find the concept difficult in that it cannot be empirically approached and measured.

Most uses of social capital seem to think of it as a 'thing', an asset that can be utilized in different ways; as indeed the term suggests a form of 'capital'. But it could be argued that social capital is also a process, one of constantly producing reciprocal norms and networks. Any group whose members stop investing in their mutual relationships is doomed to disintegrate, as the relationships of trust and reciprocity can collapse with neglect. In the same way that the internal dynamics of a group is essential in maintaining social capital formation, the external agencies play a major role. A part of public sphere that is not constantly used and maintained will collapse or be marginalized.

Any intervention from outside has the potential to develop further social capital formation in a group or a locality. The intervention by those seeking to help, to utilize resources or to legitimate an authority can, however, interrupt this process of social capital development and lead to a disruption, or even disintegration of social capital within a group or community. In this sense, the widespread use of the term among the policy community, as a tool that can be used in economic, social or political development, seems to border on carelessness or instrumentalism. Rather than a multi-dimensional, open-ended part of social life, public space is then seen as a means to achieving a limited target.

PUBLIC SPACE FOR ECONOMIC COMPETITIVENESS

The recent interest in the promotion of urban public spaces can be interpreted as a concern for the reintegration of fragmented cities. It can also be seen as a means of marketing localities. As localities and regions compete in the world economy to attract the increasingly mobile capital, they need to create safe and attractive environments for the investors and their employees (Hall, 1995) (Figure 7.13).

As a consultants' report on the regeneration of Newcastle city centre, for example, asserts,

> major public sector investment in enhancing the quality of the public realm will be a pre-cursor to building confidence in the private sector and the development of the City's tourism economy and to the attraction of private sector investment in property development activity. (EDAW, 1996: Para 41, Executive Summary)

7.13 As localities and regions compete in the world economy to attract the increasingly mobile capital, they promote their assets, including the quality of their infrastructure and public environments (Lille, France)

The return of aesthetics to city planning, therefore is seen as a sign of the return of capital to the city (Boyer, 1990). The new service sector and high technology industries are far less attached to localities than the heavy industries of the past. The shift of the economic base, from manufacturing industry into the service sector, means the role of cities is being redefined. Rather than concentrations of blue collar workers in industrial cities, the service cities are concentrations of white collar workers with their very different needs and expectations. This shift has under-mined large parts of the workforce, especially the unskilled male workers, and has led to a widening gap in income distribution and a deepening pattern of socio-spatial segregation and exclusion. It has also meant the availability of more resources for parts of the cities and the rise of a new interest in the city by high earners, who are reclaiming the city through gentrification and urban regeneration.

In addition to attracting investors and the jobs they create or the employees they bring with them, some local authorities are improving the quality of their envi-ronments to attract tourists. Cities that have been known first as industrial and then as run-down places, are now promoting themselves as tourist destinations. It is not, however, enough to have a number of impressive buildings and entertaining activities in a city. The public spaces which connect these buildings and activities are also important in the decisions of the tourists. Creation of new public spaces is, therefore, part of the larger process of creating spectacles in the cities. Waterfront developments, for example, are part of the process of erasing the already fading memory of manufacturing industry. New public spaces of the city are therefore one of the vehicles of changing the image of cities in a very competitive global market-place and a re-entry of a finite commodity, land, back into the local markets. It is also a vehicle of legitimacy for the local authorities, symbolizing their commitment and effectiveness in urban regeneration. Some also see it as a potential cure for the problems of crime, as the disenchanted youth who are blamed for many ills of the cities can find an arena for socializing and entertainment.

For much of the twentieth century, especially after the Soviet revolution and the Great Depression, Western societies have witnessed an increased level of intervention by the state in social life. This was a trend which came to its culmination after the Second World War, with emphasis on the Keynesian economics and the development of the welfare state. As this system started to suffer from a crisis since the mid-1960s, a new agenda emerged, one which questioned the extent of state intervention. The result was a contraction in the role of state in economic and social affairs. This has been in parallel with the shift out of industrial production. In the transition from the industrial city to the service city, there has been a transformation of the public sector and its role. The large-scale involvement of the private sector has created an imbalance in the development and management of cities, which is manifest in privatization of public space. Promotion of public space seeks to address this imbalance. The pressure to develop leisure facilities in cities as part of the transition to a service economy, where catering for the needs of the young professionals with their disposable incomes comes as a priority in economic development. This includes ideas about the 24-hour city, use of cultural industries in urban regeneration, and promoting a European style café culture in British cities. These can be analysed in the light of this transition, as necessary elements reclaiming the city from a manufacturing past for a service-based future.

However, there are clear tensions between these various roles of public space. An example of developing public space to confront socio-spatial divide is the city of Berlin, which was divided for more than a generation. Now it is being reintegrated through a new transport and communication infrastructure and the creation and enhancement of the public spaces and institutions along the lines of division between east and west, as in Potsdamer Platz. By deleting the marks of separation and by creating the possibility of communication and interaction, it is hoped to heal the spatial and ideological divide that shaped the city for most of the second half of the twentieth century. The reintegration of the city and its selection as the capital of the united Germany, however, has created new forms of divide. The introduction of market economy in the east and the end of some special subsidies in the west, as well as new waves of immigration into the city from around the country and around the world have created new challenges and new divisions. Confronting the economic and ethnic divisions that are emerging, however, does not seem to be a key concern in the creation of new public spaces. The public spaces, therefore, are not yet addressing the problems of an emerging divide in social groups that marks the city. As the city creates a new hierarchy of social groups, the behaviour of those at the lower levels are carefully watched (and controlled) in the public spaces. However, in a few initiatives, such as that by Kommunales Forum in the Wedding district of the city, marginal public spaces are the focus of attention for their use for disadvantaged communities, rather than as a spectacle (Figure 7.14).

CONCLUSION

We have seen in this chapter how the public spaces of the city have changed, alongside the evolution of small integrated towns to large sprawling metropolises. From a main core of most public activities, the public space has changed into an

7.14 In Wedding district, Kommunales Forum has focused the attention of regeneration of public spaces in a disadvantaged neighbourhood (Berlin, Germany)

attachment to the centres of activity, subordinated to the movement of fast vehicles. In all stages of this process, it has been a subject of contest between various agencies involved in urban development and management. This is why in the contemporary city the public space has been once again subject to privatization, and of a new emphasis by the public authorities as a means of attracting investment and as a social capital promoting social cohesion.

As we saw in Chapter 6, the metaspatial nature of public sphere in the contemporary society means that no single public space can become the container of all public sphere activities. This is at once a decline and an advancement. The decline lies in the fact that the fragmented large society is not able physically to be present in a single place and contribute to political processes, participate in ceremonies, and engage in economic exchange. The advancement lies in that the potential tyranny of a single place and a single event cannot rule the city, and as such allows more freedom for citizens.

Cities are threatened by social polarization and segregation, as expressed in suburbanization and inner city decay. As the state's sphere of control has contracted over the past three decades, as part of a general trend of societal change, the balance of control and production of urban space has favoured private interests. Combined effects of privatization of space and the threat of social fragmentation pose a serious threat for the future of the city. Urban design's contribution to this problem has been promoting urban public space as nodes for social integration. This fits well with the change of economic base from industrial to service sector, which requires new forms of production and consumption of space.

Throughout history, urban public spaces have always played a central role in the social life of cities. But they have lost their significance and are no longer the main nodes of all the social networks. Technological change, larger populations and specialization of activities have led to a fragmentation of functions and a despatialization of public sphere. Treatment of space as a commodity and stratification of society have led to socio-spatial segregation and privatization of space. Treating city design as merely providing an aesthetic experience is in line with marketing the cities and a new attention to cities by capital markets. In this context, public space can play once again an active role in urban life. Urban designers promote spatial enclosures which are positively defined and which accommodate a mixture of people and activities. Creating these inclusive nodes may be a positive step towards reducing the potential conflicts arising from different interpretations and expectations of urban space, and in promoting an urbanism of tolerance and social cohesion. At the same time, these places may be expected to serve the demands of economic competitiveness for the cities, undermining their possible role in promoting social cohesion and cultural richness.

Chapter 8
Public and private spaces of the city

So far, we have gone through the various spatial scales of the city, have seen how personal, interpersonal and impersonal spaces of the city are interpreted and used, and have studied how the public and private spaces of the city are constructed accordingly. This chapter will present an attempt to bring some of these themes together and present some concluding remarks.

THE EXCLUSIVE REALM OF THE SELF AND INTIMATE OTHERS

The most fundamental distinction between the private and the public is the distinction between the human subject's inner space of consciousness and the outer space of the world. The most private space of all is the space inside the body, where the contents of the mind can be kept hidden from others, or be revealed to them at will. The contents of the mind are shaped in a constant dialogue with the rest of the body, with other organs and the unconscious impulses and desires, as well as with the physical and social world outside the body. Biological and social forces from inside and outside the body influence and shape what we understand to be our innermost private sphere. The normative classical notion of autonomous human subjects in control of themselves and the world around them helped the development of the modern bourgeoisie to break free from nature and society, with its hitherto religious rules and traditions. This distinguished them from the socio-centric notion of individual that they found in their societies, which still prevails in many parts of the world. The modern critics, from empiricists to philosophers of language, psychoanalysts and others, have rejected this notion of the self. It has become clear that humans are in fact interdependent subjects who are thinking and acting through mediating and making connections between forces that are often beyond their control. Rather than a pure, disconnected and disembodied private sphere, human subjectivity is located at the intersection of biological and social forces and is constantly changing them and being shaped by them. The inner private space of the body and the public space of the world are, therefore, interpenetrating and interdependent.

Setting and maintaining boundaries between the private and the public starts when children begin differentiating between the self and others. As they grow into

adults, the space associated with the self finds different spatial layers. The immediate layer beyond the body is the personal space, an invisible small space around
the body that finds expression in social encounters, as it regulates the spacing of
individuals. This is an extension of the body and is considered to be a protective
bubble, a portable private space. Personal space locates individuals in physical
space and, together with other forms of territorial claims, positions them in social
space, enabling a sense of identity to be developed and rituals of communication
and recognition to take place. There are no physical boundaries around personal
space. Instead, it is demarcated through gestures, language and behaviour. It is
observed by the individual and others. Its size and degree of observation depend
on the circumstances of the social encounter and on the characteristics of those
engaged, such as age, gender, status and culture. It is a mechanism that people
acquire through socialization to regulate the individuals' privacy, as well as enabling
them to communicate with one another. It is a means of protection and communication, a vehicle of control over one's body in social encounters, establishing a power
relationship with the person's immediate environment.

Physical objects can be used to establish personal space, as for example the
glass and metal boxes of cars, or any other system of signs and symbols that
demarcate a territorial claim over space. The historically established, socially institutionalized form of private sphere, however, is private property, which ensures
exclusive access to space for known individuals.

Private sphere is a part of life that is under the control of the individual in a
personal capacity, outside public observation and knowledge or state and official
control. It is a sphere of freedom of choice for individuals, protected from the external gaze. Legal protection for privacy, to be free from arbitrary interference and
attacks, has been incorporated into the Universal Declaration of Human Rights. The
right to privacy has been interpreted by some as the right to be let alone. Private
space, therefore, is part of space that belongs to, or is controlled by, an individual,
for his/her exclusive use, keeping the others out. This may be established through
patterns of use, which create a sense of belonging and provoking territorial behaviour. This may also be institutionalized through a legal framework, which entitles
individuals to call parts of space their private property. As compared to personal
space, private property has fixed boundaries and is stationary.

Territoriality, it is argued, controls aggression in constructive directions, clari-
fies the relations of power and thus reduces tensions and conflicts. Private control
of property is an outlet for exertion of power and attachment of emotions. Private
property is seen as an embodiment of freedom through exertion of will over the
objects of the world, an expression of humanity in regulating concealment and
exposure. It is therefore a vehicle of psychological development, expression of

personal identity, and location and empowerment in social networks and, in the past, a condition for entering the public realm. It also is a commodity that is exchanged in the market and is regulated by the law, where the personal significance of private space finds an impersonal character.

What happens, however, when people are, either through force of others or due to their own characteristics and life trajectories, unable to exert these levels of control? The homeless, who are deprived of exclusive access, to space, and the poor, who have limited abilities to maintain such access, are themselves excluded from taming and developing their aggression, the development of their identity and a sense of location in society. The main problem with the notion of privacy as private control of space remains the distribution of this finite resource. Discussions about the positive and negative aspects of owning property go back to ancient times, and revolutionary movements or utopian thinking to redistribute resources can be found all throughout history. For communists in the nineteenth and twentieth centuries, the answer was in the abolition of private property, which alienated the workers from the fruits of their work. While conservatives and libertarians vigorously protected the boundaries, liberals and social democrats sought social justice through better distribution of resources, some arguing for connecting welfare rights to human rights. The boundary between the public and private spheres and the location of this boundary, therefore, has been a heated political and ideological battleground.

The spatial unit of private property is closely associated with the social unit of household. Exclusivity and intimacy are combined to find expression in the home, the symbol of private sphere. Historically it has been a socio-spatial unit where biological and social life processes have been nurtured and protected from the intrusion of others. As the origin of the modern family house, the medieval bourgeois house was a centre of sociability, a meeting place for a range of people and activities. From the eighteenth century on, it was transformed into a place of intimacy and privacy, which was reflected in the increasingly central role of children in the household. The house was now symbolizing an overall separation of the nuclear family from society, the private from the public sphere, to create a safe haven from the impersonal urban world outside. Inside the house, a hierarchical stratification was created, through separation of servants from masters, children from parents, women from men, visitors from family. This hierarchy was reflected in the transformation of the house from one dominated by a multifunctional large hall to a multiplication and specialization of rooms connected through corridors, in a sense using an urban morphology for domestic space. These introduced a range of private, semi-private, and even semi-public spaces around the house, to cater for a coexistence of individual, personal private spaces and household interpersonal spaces. Stratification coincided with a differentiation of house types, from the town-house to the terraced, semi-detached, detached houses and flats, reflecting the new social hierarchies. These characteristics of the domestic space were extended to larger sections of society through state intervention, by mass public housing schemes, and through the market mechanism of speculative volume building.

For communists, private property was illegitimate and unjustified, as it consolidated private gain and maintained privileges. Attacks on private property were closely associated with attacks on family. Marx and Engels asked for the abolition of the family, which was based on private gain and on capital. Feminists also argued against the modern family, where women were associated with the private sphere of domesticity, maternity and dependence, as distinct from a male public sphere of work, politics, breadwinning, autonomy and responsibility. This, and the general separation of public and private spheres, they argued, locked women in an inferior position.

These pressures from inside the private sphere from women (as well as from children), and the pressures from outside, through state intervention in education, health and welfare, as well as the rising new life styles and intimate arrangements, have transformed the intimate space of the home. Rather than a completely segregated safe haven, the intimate space of the home is changing through constant dialogue with other units of social organization. Two tensions have emerged from these dialogues, which are likely to influence the future of household as a social organization: one between the individual and the household, and the other between the external image of the family and its internal reality.

Private sphere, therefore, is simultaneously located in the privacy of the mind, is extended to personal space of the body, is superimposed on land in private property, and is associated with a unit of social organization in the home. The subjective space of consciousness, the socio-psychological personal space of the body, the institutionalized spaces of exclusive private property and the intimate home have formed the different layers of the private space. We have seen how the contents of each layer is subject to pressures from inside and outside, and is therefore constantly changing. We have seen how the private sphere is not pure or completely separate, but interdependent with the public sphere, as reflected in their boundary, which is expected to be clear but is often ambiguous and contested.

THE SHARED REALM OF EXPOSURE AND EXCHANGE

Rather than association with personal and intimate, public spaces of cities, almost anywhere and any time, can be described as places outside the boundaries of individual or small group control, mediating between private spaces and used for a variety of often overlapping functional and symbolic purposes. Descriptively, therefore, public spaces have been multi-purpose accessible spaces distinguishable from, and mediating between, demarcated exclusive territories of households and individuals. Normatively, these spaces are considered public if they have been provided and managed by public authorities, and have concerned the people as a whole, being open or available to them and being used or shared by all members of a community.

The concept of public space that is used today is rooted in the modern notions that emerged in the eighteenth century, which saw society as a realm of contract and exchange among strangers. This distinguished the modern commercial society from its predecessor, where individuals followed traditions and related to one another through involuntary ties of kinship and clan. Breaking these ties, however, required a new cultural framework, reflected partly in the promotion of good manners, to enable effective exchange among total strangers. For some, this was a transition to freedom, where social interaction was conducted through politeness and sympathy, resulting in a more tranquil, predictable and orderly social life. For others, this was no more than a big loss, with alienating, soul-destroying effects, creating inequality and injustice.

A tension that emerged in the nineteenth century was around determining the nature and framework of this exchange. While for the rationalists of the eighteenth century it was essential to create a free and neutral space of sociability, for the romantics and revolutionaries of the nineteenth century it was important to be able to express themselves freely. The question that needed answering was whether to see the city as a rational, impersonal realm of strangers linked through instrumental exchange regulated within clearly set rules of conduct, or to see it as a place where those strangers were engaged in meaningful expression of their emotions and individuality. The simple order of the public façades in one century and the extravagant decorations of the following century were some of the architectural reflections of this tension. This was a tension that once again was played out in the twentieth century between modernism and postmodernism, which were the new versions of rationalism and romanticism.

Furthermore, as the complexity of urban societies grew, exchange of ideas, goods and services among individuals became largely mediated through abstract impersonal media. Meanwhile, as cities have grown to house more than half of the world's population and globalization finds a faster pace, personal, face-to-face exchange remains the most important form of communication, whether rational and instrumental or expressive and meaningful, whether following the social forces from outside or bodily impulses from inside.

The interplay of external and internal forces create pressures from all sides that inevitably lead to tensions and imbalances of changing moods, energies and circumstances. The social encounter, however, requires a level of balance and stability. To manage this potentially turbulent and continuous change, therefore, individuals rely on masks, which are made of a socially mediated suppression of impulses, to stage a stable, relatively consistent performance. The mask is then an idealized self, a stable elaborate construct that human beings wear in social encounters to protect the self, hide its volatility and control the situation through staging a performance. The mask and the self may become intertwined, as these performances are inscribed on the performer's body, in patterns of belief and behaviour. Masks, nevertheless, are the boundaries between public and private spheres, and we change them to adjust to the public scenes and private moods. This is our social front, which is composed of setting, appearance and manner.

Public life, therefore, is seen as a performance, where symbols are presented and exchanged, and where masks are displayed, compared and reshaped. The city becomes a stage for this performance, a theatre made of these settings and appearances. When the street is not used as a stage and public life is not formed of playacting, some argue, civility declines. The constant work of human life, therefore, is the management of surfaces, creating a civilized social space through a balance between concealment and exposure, between public and private spheres, which is only possible through careful construction and maintenance of boundaries. These surfaces are essentially appearances, gestures and patterns of behaviour, but also include building façades, and all elements of the city that are displayed in its public spaces.

There are many parallels between city design and stage design, both showing two contrasting approaches. Tribal communities, early Greek theatres, medieval religious drama and secular Elizabethan drama united the stage and the auditorium, facilitating direct communication between audience and the performers. This was unlike the theatre of imperial Rome and the modern aristocratic and bourgeois theatre that have inserted a distance between the audience and the performers. Similar tendencies towards city design can be traced in these periods, whether seeing the city's public spaces as a place for participating in social life or as a monumental backdrop to grand spectacle. Both in city design and stage design, neutrality and flexibility of the stage and the possibility of participation of the audience in the performance have been essential for direct communication.

In the relationship between auditorium and stage, between backdrop and floor, between display and participation, we can identify two ways of treating space for performance. One approach keeps them separate and reduces their relation to mainly visual, the other brings the two together and creates participation and two-way communication. One treats public space as a backdrop, at best articulated to have a monumental effect, where display is the primary function. The other treats public space as a place for interpersonal communication and social encounter, where the setting has an active part in the performance.

There are, at the same time, significant differences between performance and social life, as performance does not address the first person narratives, the distinction between temporary and permanent, fiction and truth. There are, therefore, clear limitations in comparing cities with theatres. Representation and exchange are closely connected with the material conditions in which they take place. It limits the analysis if representation is separated from its context and is considered in abstraction. There are also several shortcomings with the dramaturgical model of public realm, such as its Cartesian separation of the self, its emphasis on the mask at the cost of the agent behind it, its social ahistorical emphasis, its trust of conventions, its lack of interest in normative questions, and its tendency to aestheticize social relations.

Public space is the institutional and material common world, the in-between space that facilitates co-presence and regulates interpersonal relationships. By being present in the same place with others, shared experience of the world becomes possible and a link is made with previous generations who experienced (or future generations who might experience) the same physical reality. This connecting role that bridges time endows public space with permanence. Shared experience also becomes possible by co-presence with others through the same institutions, such as rituals, performances and public opinion etc.

Public space is a place of simultaneity, a site for display and performance, a test of reality, an exploration of difference and identity, an arena for recognition, in which representation of difference can lead to an awareness of the self and others, and to an examination of the relationship between particular and general, personal and impersonal. It is a place where many-sided truths co-exist and tolerance of different opinions is practised. It appears that the modern city prevents this, as individuals use private cars to pass through public spaces, segregate themselves from others into areas and neighbourhoods, and connect to the others through the medium of complex, abstract, bureaucratized institutions. It is therefore essential that public space facilitates unmediated alongside mediated relations among human beings.

Some analyses of the public sphere have looked into the past and have idealized formative periods in which public sphere played a significant role in society. In ancient Greece, the public realm of the city-state was the realm of speech, action and freedom, as contrasted with the private realm of the household that was the realm of violence and necessity. The sharp distinction between freedom and violence indicates their interdependence, the two sides of the same coin. Only by the suppression of the majority of population (women, children, slaves, foreigners etc) could the heads of households participate as free equals in public sphere. The same was true in the rise of the modern bourgeois public sphere, where an elite could develop and function only by keeping the majority out and under control. As Arendt and Habermas have shown, interpersonal, face-to-face communication by the elite was the main feature of these forms of public sphere. However, as they fail to come to terms with, the extension of this participation in exchange to the larger society is both necessary and welcome, which requires developing new forms of communication and a multiplicity of interconnected public spheres.

As a major constitutional part of civil society, the public sphere is a collection of material and institutional common and inclusive spaces, in which the members of society meet, to share experiences, to present and exchange symbols and create meaning, and to deal with collective self-rule through seeking consensus as well as exploring difference. The public sphere therefore limits the power of state, but also contributes to the development of common political debate and cultural exchange, which informs and influences collective decisions, allowing for the negative and positive meanings of freedom simultaneously to develop.

The centrally located public spaces of towns integrated political, cultural and economic activities of the town, as exemplified by the Greek agora. However, they started to be multiplied and specialized as the towns grew in size and activities became more complex. The attitudes to public space also changed. In Greek and medieval cities, each building was the focus of attention and was an end in itself. In Roman and post-Renaissance cities, however, the notions of symmetry and harmony ruled, where public spaces became subordinate to dominant buildings and axial planning. The medieval city was a place of trade, where public and private interests competed constantly for space, shaping the city along this struggle. The city's location was often at the intersection of trading routes and its public spaces were elaborations of the roads and crossroads. Public spaces were treated as outdoor rooms, enclosed within lively and clear edges, closed vistas, embellished by public art, with a centre left open to be used for various activities. In complete contrast, the Renaissance and Baroque city was a centrally planned display, symmetrically laid out, restricting the private interests to conform to public display of the power of the royal court, the secular state and the emerging age of reason, whose symbols occupied the centre of space. In all periods, the public spaces were, as Alberti reminds us, variations on the theme of crossroad, which were articulated for utility and display.

In the Eastern city, this dialectic between utility and display can also be found in different periods and between organic development and imposition of abstract orders. The use of axial planning, geometrical order and political significance of the centre shaped the cities of the ancient times from Mesopotamia to China, where public spaces of commerce and religion, of sociability, display and exchange formed the heart of cities. In the medieval Middle Eastern city, public and private spaces had sharp gender associations, as mosques and markets were kept separate from the house through a hierarchy of roads and blank walls, which enwrapped introverted courtyards. The modern Eastern city, like its Western counterpart, is dominated by the motor car and increased complexity of socio-spatial patterns. In both Eastern and Western cities, throughout their histories, public spaces have remained contested places, through wars, revolutions and upheavals, as their control meant the control of the common symbols of power, the control of the city and of society.

Modernism introduced a new concept of space. The motor car took over the urban space, changing the relationship between human beings and buildings, between buildings and open spaces, between mass and void, abolishing enclosed public spaces such as streets and square as known before. This gave way to vast open spaces and flexible location of high-rise buildings, subordinating the void to the mass, undermining the spaces of sociability. After the static, enclosed public spaces of the past in both East and West, the modernist public spaces were to be free-floating, fast-moving and all-encompassing.

Scientific discoveries, technological development, urbanization and globalization have all transformed the speed and scale of events and hence the nature of cities and the relations between public and private spheres. The modern city has gone through a spatial and temporal process of dispersion, creating non-converging networks, in complete contrast to the cohesive nodal role of the public space in much of urban history. From the clear distinction of the integrated public and private spaces in the small settlements, cities have grown in size, scattered and fragmented along functional and social lines. Public and private spaces have both exploded and multiplied as part of this urban explosion, to accommodate change. Domestic space has moved from an integration of work, leisure and living to ever more precarious, mono-functional intimate and exclusive spaces of ever smaller households. The public space has also lost its integration of cultural economic and political significance, to be despatialized and become an instrumental tool to sell the city, although it is also expected to help promote social cohesion and cultural richness.

These explosive processes have had both positive and negative outcomes. The tyranny of a particular social organization, of a single place and a single event has given way to more freedom of choice and a plurality of arenas for social life. At the same time, it seems any attempt to overcome the narrowly instrumental use of space and bring the fragments together to construct meaningful places requires a monumental effort. This is especially so when the citizens of suburbanized and polarized cities find it difficult to acknowledge the significance of public infrastructure and common space for all.

Technological advances have despatialized and fragmented urban space. The emotional links with public space have been cut to be replaced with financial interest by non-local investors and large-scale developers. The only emotions left appears to be negative, resulting from fear of crime. Rather than a multi-dimensional, open-ended part of social life, public space is being used as an instrument to achieve a certain end. Chief among these ends has been the perceived need to increase the competitiveness of a place. As cities and regions compete in the global marketplace, safe and attractive environments are essential in attracting investors, workers and visitors. The city becomes an aesthetic display for sale and the public spaces become an integral part of this privatization and commercialization.

As transition into the industrial era caused anxiety and fear, moving out of this era has also created new fears and anxieties, resulting in uncertainty and lack of permanence. In this context, public sphere is considered to be a social capital, an important part of civil society, which can promote cohesion and prevent further fragmentation and atomization of the society. By the changing role of women in society, their challenge to the historically male-dominated nature of the public realm and the relationship between the two realms has started to be transformed. Others advocate the acknowledgement of energies that may result from a degree of withdrawal from the unfairly structured public realm, as self-preserving communities are created alongside.

Public spaces of the city are spaces of sociability, where social encounter can and does take place. These spaces of sociability, however, are not always accessible to all. For example, the formation of distinctive neighbourhoods, with a centrally located public space aimed at facilitating social interaction and integration, is one way of giving a distinctive flavour to the spaces of sociability. Neighbourhoods are promoted as a unit of city building, as an environmentally friendly urban form that reduces travel and energy consumption, and where impersonal urban space can be broken into interpersonal spheres of communities. Neighbourhoods are used as tools with which urban space can be subdivided into manageable parts, where ever-larger developers can engage in large-scale urban development projects. They are where systems of differentiation can be formed to establish spatial differences along ethnic, cultural and economic lines, and a refuge be created for protection from the anonymous world of the city and its constantly changing conditions and anxieties created by entry into and out of the industrial era. The role of public space then becomes, simultaneously, a medium of promoting pedestrian movement, a location for social interaction, a tool for urban management, a showcase, a selling point for the developer, a system of signs to assert different identities. In a sense, the establishment of neighbourhoods can extend the private realm by creating a semi-private, semi-public realm, where a smaller number of urban residents may be aware of each other and of their differences from the rest of the citizens. The public space here then serves a variety of purposes, all of which appear to create some distinction and interpersonal exchange in the midst of impersonal urban world, which can only be maintained by devising tools for the exclusion of those who do not belong. By their nature, therefore, these spaces are not meant to be accessible to all, and hence are less public than those in the impersonal city centres. As elite, marginalized or communitarian spaces, these are conditioned spaces, providing advantages for some and reducing access for others.

It is no wonder that those who have attacked the notion of society as an agglomeration of strangers (from Adam Ferguson onwards) have promoted the emotional safety of the old small towns. The interpersonal micro-urbanism was indeed a means of confronting the impersonal urban society of strangers engaged in soulless contracts. The public space, rather than an extension of the familiar places of communities, as a place of self-asserting ritual, became a neutral place of exchange among strangers. Assertion of local identity in the anonymity of urbanization may appear to be similar to the desire for local specificity in the midst of globalization. Both may appear to be based on fear of change, as politics of identity show. Rather than a community of communities, as communitarians hope, neighbourhoods can become sites of exaggerated difference, creating more fractures in society and leading to a neo-medievalism of factional strife among localities and communities, reducing the chances of coexistence and of the ability to negotiate for a set of common platforms and shared experiences.

URBANISM AND THE CHALLENGES OF THE BOUNDARY

One of the main themes that can be identified in the relationship between the public and private spheres is that they are *interdependent* and largely influence and shape each other. This is best exemplified in the relationship between the self and the other, which lies at the heart of public–private relationships. Another theme is that the separation of the public and private spheres and spaces is a continuous normative process. In practice, public and private spaces are a *continuum*, where many semi-public or semi-private spaces can be identified, as the two realms meet through shades of privacy and publicity rather than clearly cut separation.

The boundary between the private inner space of the self and the public space outside is the body itself. The articulation of this boundary takes place through many forms of communicative devices, some of which have been developing for long. From body transforming ornaments, such as piercing and painting the skin, to wearing outer layers such as functional items of clothing and symbolic performative items of jewellery, to body gestures, patterns of behaviour and language, the boundaries between the self and others, between private and public spheres are mediated and articulated for protection and communication. In this articulation, the role of the boundary becomes ambiguous, as it is simultaneously a part of the private and public spheres. It is the area where the two meet and are kept apart, shaped by the two spheres and shaping them at the same time. The treatment of this boundary gives meaning and significance to the distinction between the public and private spheres. It is here that the first-person and third-person views of the world meet, where the subject's authority rooted in an empirically distinguishable private realm meets the public realms of language, space and other institutions.

The significance of the boundary may be seen to be due to its materiality. Like any other social object, it is imbued with meaning through production and use by humans. Through mutual or collective agreement, we associate symbolic significance with the objects we use in our daily lives. For example, a small wooden structure can be called and used as a chair only through such agreed symbolization. The common world of things, therefore, helps bring people together and construct meaning. The boundary between public and private spheres is one such object, which we use in a symbolic capacity to characterize particular parts of our lives. The boundary, however, has an extra significance, as it lies between two spheres, in a mediating, defining role. It reflects a system of power relations, as it is a line drawn in space to separate the world into two spheres. Through creating barriers, it has been used to shape behaviour, control access and manage different social groups.

The wall that separates two neighbours, home from street, and city from countryside, lies at the heart of the notion of law and society. City building therefore is partly a boundary setting exercise, subdividing space and creating new functions and meanings, establishing new relationships between the two sides. The way boundaries are established, articulated and related to the private or public spheres often has a major impact on the character of each side, defining many characteristics of urbanism in general. The boundaries are simultaneously means of separation and communication. Colonnades, front porches, semi-public gateways and foyers, elaborate façades and courtyards are some of the ways the boundary between the public and private has been articulated to allow interaction and communication between the two realms.

This dialogue between the two realms, rather than rigid walls, promotes a civilized ambivalence, which can only enrich social life. At the same time, there are pressures to separate the two clearly, such as in the conduct of public officials who should keep their public duties apart from their private interests or in the need for the protection of a person's private sphere from public gaze. It becomes the task of a multiplicity of boundaries to express and shape this coexistence of ambiguity and clarity. The boundary no doubt reflects an expression of power and therefore there are those who benefit and those who suffer from it. But the ability to regulate concealment and exposure appears to be needed for all, as so few would wish to live in an undifferentiated common space. Rather than abolishing this ability, a dialogue is needed that ensures the parties can redraw the contested boundaries through negotiation, allowing for permeability and adjustment while protecting the basic need for regulation. This means combining legal and political clarity while allowing for practical and social flexibility, with a degree of permeability that would facilitate interaction and communication.

A central challenge in urbanism is to find a balance between the public and private realms. Two questions that need addressing simultaneously are: how can a realm be established that caters for the cultural and biological needs of a social individual to be protected from the intrusion of others? How can a realm be established that caters for the needs of all members of a society to be protected from the encroachment of individuals? In response, there are those who wish to expand individual freedoms at the expense of public needs, and those who promote the expansion of the public sphere by expanding the realm of the state and restricting the private sphere. Urbanism can be threatened both by those who undermine the public realm and by those who do not acknowledge the necessity of the private realm, as the two are interdependent and not mutually exclusive.

As the shape of the city and the characteristics of urban life are influenced by the way public and private distinction is made, the role of urban designers becomes ever more significant. By establishing the boundary between the two realms so that a civilized relationship can be promoted, the threat of encroachment by private interests into the public realm and the threat of public intrusion into the private sphere are both minimized and carefully managed. Rather than being caught in a battle between communitarian and libertarian approaches, which can be stifling, a porous and highly elaborate boundary which acknowledges and protects individual and collective interests and rights is what distinguishes a sophisticated urban environment from a harsh one.

Bibliography

Abercrombie, P., 1945, *Greater London Plan 1944*, HMSO, London.

Ahmadi, F. and Ahmadi, N., 1995, *Iranian Islam and the Concept of the Individual: On the non-development of the concept of individual in the ways of thinking of Iranians*, Uppsala University, Uppsala.

Alberti, Leon Battista, 1988 (originally 1450), *On the Art of Building in Ten Books*, The MIT Press, Cambridge, MA.

Al-Dossary, Mona, 2001, *A study of current residential buildings in Al-Khobar and the forces that shape them*, Unpublished PhD dissertation, School of Architecture, University of Bath.

Aldridge, Trevor, 1997, *Boundaries, Walls and Fences*, 8th edition, FT Law and Tax, London.

Alexander, C., Neis, H., Anninou, A. and King, I. 1987, *A New Theory of Urban Design*, Oxford University Press, New York.

Altman, Irwin and Ervin Zube, eds, 1989, *Public Places and Spaces*, Plenum Press, New York.

Altman, Irwin, 1975, *The Environment and Social Behaviour: Privacy, personal space, territory, crowding*, Brooks/Cole, Monterey, California.

Appleton, Ian, 1996, *Buildings for the Performing Arts*, Butterworth Architecture, Oxford.

Arberry, A.J., 1994 (originally 1958), *Classical Persian Literature*, Curzon Press, London.

Arendt, Hannah, 1958, *The Human Condition*, University of Chicago Press, Chicago.

—— 1998, *The Human Condition*, 2nd edition, The University of Chicago Press, Chicago.

Ariés, Philippe, 1973 (originally 1960 in French), *Centuries of Childhood*, Penguin Books, Middlesex.

Aristotle, 1992, *The Politics*, Penguin, London.

Bachelard, Gaston, 1994 (originally 1958 in French), *The Poetics of Space*, Beacon Press, Boston MA.

Baer, Nancy van Norman, 1991a, Design and Movement in the Theatre of the Russian Avant-Garde, in Baer 1991b, ed., *Theatre in Revolution,* Thames and Hudson, London, pp. 35–59.

—— 1991b, ed., *Theatre in Revolution: Russian avant-garde stage design: 1913–1935*, Thames and Hudson, London.

Barton, Hugh, 1996, 'Going green by design', *Urban Design*, No. 57, January 1996, pp. 13–18.

Bater, J.H., 1980, *The Soviet City*, Edward Arnold, London.

Bauer, Ernest, 1973, Personal Space: A study of blacks and whites, *Sociometry*, Vol. 36, No. 3, pp. 402–8.

Bell, Paul, Green, Thomas, Fisher, Jeffrey and Baum, Andrew, 1996, *Environmental Psychology*, 4th edition, Harcourt Brace College Publishers, Fort Worth.

Benhabib, Seyla, 1996, *The Reluctant Modernism of Hannah Arendt*, Sage, Thousand Oaks.

Benn, S.I. and Gaus, G.F., 1983, eds, *Public and Private in Social Life*, Croom Helm, St Martin's Press, London.

Bentley, Ian, Alcock, Alan, Murrain, Paul, McGlynn, Sue and Smith, Graham, 1985, *Responsive Environments: A manual for designers*, Butterworth Architecture, Oxford.

Berman, M., 1982, *All That is Solid Melts into Air: The experience of modernity*, Verso, London.

Bobbio, Norberto, 1990, *Liberalism and Democracy*, Verso, London.

Bonnes, Mirilia and Secchiaroli, Gianfranco, 1995, *Environmental Psychology: A psycho-social introduction*, translated by Claire Montagna, Sage, London

Borsi, Franco, 1975, *Leon Battista Alberti*, Phaidon, Oxford.

Bourdieu, Pierre, 1986, 'The forms of capital', in John Richardson, ed., *Handbook of Theory and Research for the Sociology of Education*, Greenwood Press, New York, pp. 241–58.

—— 2000, *Pascalian Meditations*, Polity Press, Cambridge.

Boyce, M., 1983, 'Iranian festivals', in E. Yarshaer, ed., *The Cambridge History of Iran, Vol. 3 (2), The Selucids, Parthian and Sasanian Periods*, Cambridge University Press, Cambridge, pp. 792–818.

Boyer, M. Christine, 1990, 'The return of aesthetics to city planning', in Dennis Crow, ed., *Philosophical Streets: New approaches to urbanism*, Maisonneuve Press, Washington, D.C., . pp. 93–112.

Boys, Jos, Bradshaw, Frances, Darke, Jane, Foo, Benedicte, Francis, Sue, McFarlane, Barbara, Roberts, Marion and Wilkes, Sue, 'House design and women's roles', in Matrix Group, 1984, *Making Space: Women and the man-made environment*, Pluto, London.

Brain, David, 1997, 'From public housing to private communities: The discipline of design and the materialization of the public/private distinction in the built environment', in J. Weintraub and K. Kumar, eds, *Public and Private in*

Thought and Practice: Perspectives on a grand dichotomy, The University of Chicago Press, Chicago, pp. 237–67.

Breheny, Michael, 1992, 'The contradictions of the compact city: A review', in M. Breheny, ed., *Sustainable Development and Urban Form*, Pion, London, pp. 138–59.

Breheny, M., Gent, T. and Lock, D., 1993, *Alternative Development Patterns: New settlements*, Department of the Environment, HMSO, London.

Briggs, Asa, 1968, *Victorian Cities*, Penguin, Middlesex.

Brittan, Arthur, 1977, *The Privatized World*, Routledge and Kegan Paul, London.

Buker, Eloise, 1999, 'Is postmodern self a feminized citizen?' *Critical Review of International Social and Political Philosophy*, Special Issue on Feminism, Identity and Difference, Vol. 2, No. 1, pp. 80–99.

Butterworth, George, 1977, ed., *The Child's Representation of the World*, Plenum Press, New York.

Calhoun, Craig, 1992, ed., *Habermas and the Public Sphere*, MIT Press, Cambridge, MA.

—— 1993, 'Habitus, Field, and Capital: The question of historical specificity', in C. Calhoun, LiPuma, Edward, Postone, Moishe, eds, *Bourdieu: Critical perspectives*, Polity Press, Cambridge, pp. 61–88.

Calthorpe, P., 1994, 'The region', in P. Katz, ed., *The New Urbanism: Toward an architecture of community*, McGraw Hill, New York, pp. xi–xvi.

Calthorpe, Peter, 1996, 'The Pedestrian Pocket', in Richard LeGates and Frederic Stout, eds, The City Reader, Routledge, London, pp. 468–74.

Canovan, Margaret, 1998, 'Introduction', in Arendt, Hannah, *The Human Condition*, 2nd edition, The University of Chicago Press, Chicago, pp. vii–xx.

Carr, S., Francis, M., Rivlin, L. and Stone, A., 1992, *Public Space*, Cambridge University Press, Cambridge.

Castoriadis, Cornelius, 1991, *Philosophy, Politics, Autonomy: Essays in political philosophy*, Odéon, Oxford University Press, Oxford.

Cave, Lyndon, 1981, *The Smaller English House*, Robert Hale, London.

CEC, 1990, *Green Paper on the Urban Environment*, EUR 12902, Commission of the European Communities, Brussels.

Coleman, James, 1990, *Foundations of Social Theory*, Harvard University Press, Cambridge, MA.

Coleman, Janet, 1996, 'Preface', in Janet Coleman, ed., *The Individual in Political Theory and Practice*, Clarendon Press, Oxford, pp. ix–xix.

College, M., 1977, *Parthian Art*, Paul Elek, London.

Colquhoun, Alan, 1989, *Modernity and the Classical Tradition*, MIT Press, Cambridge MA.

Cooper, David, 1999, ed., *Epistemology: The classic readings*, Blackwell, Oxford.

Copley, Stephen, and Edgar, Andrew, 1998, 'Introduction', in S. Copley and A. Edgar, eds, *David Hume: Selected essays*, Oxford University Press, Oxford, pp. vii–xxii.

Cottingham, John, 1992a, 'Introduction' in J. Cottingham, ed., *The Cambridge Companion to Descartes*, Cambridge University Press, Cambridge, pp. 1–20.

—— 1992b, 'Cartesian dualism: theology, metaphysics, and science', in J. Cottingham, ed., *The Cambridge Companion to Descartes*, Cambridge University Press, Cambridge, pp. 236–57.

County Council of Essex, 1973, *A Design Guide for Residential Areas*, County Council of Essex, Essex.

Cullen, G., 1971 (1994 reprint), *The Concise Townscape*, Butterworth Architecture, Oxford.

Davis, Mike, 1992, 'Fortress Los Angeles: The militarization of urban space', in M. Sorkin, ed., *Variations on a Theme Park*, Hill and Wang, New York, pp. 154–80.

de Planhol, X, 1968, 'Geography of settlement', in W.B. Fisher, ed., *The Cambridge History of Iran, Vol. 1, The Land of Iran*, Cambridge University Press, Cambridge, pp. 409–68.

—— 1970, 'The Geography of Setting', in *The Cambridge History of Islam, Vol. 2B, Islamic Society and Civilization*, Cambridge University Press, pp. 443–68.

Dennett, Daniel, 1993, *Consciousness Explained*, Penguin, London.

DoE (Department of the Environment), 1997, *Planning Policy Guidance Note 1, Annex A*, HMSO, London.

—— 1977 (first published 1961), *Homes for Today and Tomorrow* (Parker Morris Report), HMSO, London.

—— 1996, *Sustainable Settlements and Shelter: The United Kingdom National Report*, Habitat II, The Department of the Environment, HMSO, London.

Descartes, René, 1968 (originally 1637), *Discourse on Method and The Meditations*, Penguin, London.

Diffie, Whitfield and Landau, Susan, 1998, *Privacy on the Line: The politics of wiretapping and encryption*, MIT Press, Cambridge, Mass.

Doxiadis, C.A., 1972, *Architectural Space in Ancient Greece*, MIT Press, Cambridge, MA.

Duany, Andres and Plater-Zyberk, Elizabeth, 1994, 'The neighbourhood, the district, and the corridor', in P. Katz, ed., *The New Urbanism: Toward an architecture of community*, McGraw Hill, New York, pp. xvii–xx.

Dumont, Louis, 1970, *Homo Hierarchicus: The caste system and its implications*, Weidenfeld and Nicolson, London.

Dunne, Joseph, 1996, 'Beyond sovereignty and deconstruction: The storied self', in Richard Kearney, ed., *Paul Ricoeur: The hermeneutics of action*, Sage, London, pp. 137–58.

EDAW, 1996, *Grainger Town: Regeneration Strategy, Final Report*, Newcastle upon Tyne.

Engels, Friedrich, 1986 (originally 1884), *The Origin of the Family, Private Property and the State*, Penguin Classics, Penguin, London.

—— 1993 (originally 1845), *The Condition of the Working Class in England*, edited by David McLellan, Oxford University Press, Oxford.

English Partnerships, 1998, *Greenwich Peninsula: Investing in the 21st Century*, Greenwich Peninsula Development Office, London.

English, P., 1973, 'The Traditional City of Herat, Afghanistan', in L.C. Brown, ed., *From Madina to Metropolis*, pp. 73–89, The Darwin Press, Princeton New Jersey.

Epstein, Richard, 1998, *Principles for a Free Society: Reconciling individual liberty with the common good*, Perseus Books, Reading MA.

Ernst, Morris and Schwartz, Alan, 1962, *Privacy: The right to be let alone*, Macmillan, New York.

Essex County Council, 1973, *A Design Guide for Residential Areas*, Essex County Council, Essex.

Etzioni, Amitai, 1995, *The Spirit of Community: Rights, responsibilities and the communitarian Agenda*, Fontana Press, London.

European Commission, 1994, *Europe 2000+: Cooperation for European territorial development*, Office for Official Publication of the European Communities, Luxembourg.

Faghih, N., 1984, 'Esfahan, Shahri baraye Aber-e Piadeh', in A. Javadi, ed., *Me'mari-e Iran*, Vol, II, Mojarrad, Tehran, pp. 663–9.

Fishman, R., 1987, *Bourgeois Utopias: The rise and fall of suburbia*, Basic Books, New York.

Foley, Mark, 1994, *Dance Spaces*, The Arts Council of England, London.

Fraser, Nancy, 1989, *Unruly practices: Power, discourse and gender in contemporary social theory*, Minnesota U.P., Minneapolis

Freud, Sigmund, 1985, *Civilization, Society and Religion*, Penguin, London.

Frye, Richard, 1965, *Bukhara: The medieval achievement*, University of Oklahoma Press, Norman.

Fukuyama, Francis, 1999, *The Great Disruption: Human nature and the reconstitution of social order*, Profile Books, London.

Fyfe, Theodore, 1936, *Hellenistic Architecture*, Ares Publishers, Chicago.

Gale, Stanley, 1949, *Modern Housing Estates*, B.T. Batsford, London.

Garfinkel, Simon, 2000, *Database nation: The death of privacy in the 21st century*, O'Reilly & Associates, Sebastopol, CA

Gaube, H., 1979, *Iranian Cities*, New York University Press, New York.

Geertz, Clifford, 1988, *Works and Lives: The anthropologist as author*, Polity Press, Cambridge.

—— 1993 (originally 1972), *The Interpretation of Cultures*, Fontana Press, London.

Gibberd, Frederick, 1962, *Town Design*, Architectural Press, London.

Giddens, A., 1984, *The Constitution of Society: Outline of the theory of structuration*, Polity Press, Cambridge.

Giedion, Sigfried, 1967, *Space, Time and Architecture: The growth of a new tradition*, Harvard University Press, Cambridge, MA, 5th edition (first edition 1941).

Glotz, Gustave, 1929, *The Greek City and Its Institutions*, K. Paul, Trench, Trubner; A.A. Knopf, London.

Goffman, Erving, 1969, *The Presentation of Self in Everyday Life*, Allen Lane, The Penguin Press, London.

—— 1972, *Relations in Public: Microstudies of the public order*, Harper & Row, New York.

Gorman, Vanessa, 1995, 'Aristotle's Hippodamos', *Historia*, Band XLIV/4, Franz Steiner Verlag Wiesbaden GmbH, Sitz Stuttgart.

Gray, Edmund, 1994, *The British House: A concise architectural history*, Barrie and Jenkins, London.

Greed, Clara, 1993, *Introducing Town Planning*, Longman, Harlow.

Greenberg, C.I. and Firestone, I.J., 1977, 'Compensatory responses to crowding: Effects of personal space intrusion and privacy reduction', *Journal of Personality and Social Psychology*, Vol. 39, No. 9, pp. 637–44.

Greenfield, Susan, 2000, *The Private Life of the Brain*, Allen Lane, The Penguin Press, London.

Groseclose, E., 1947, *Introduction to Iran*, Oxford University Press, New York.

Guiton, Jacques, 1981, *The Ideas of Le Corbusier on Architecture and Urban Planning*, George Braziller, New York.

Guy, Clifford, 1994, *The Retail Development Process: Location, property and planning*, Routledge, London.

Habermas, Jürgen, 1984, *The Theory of Communicative Action*, Heinemann, London.

—— 1989 (originally 1962), *The Structural Transformation of the Public Sphere: An inquiry into a category of bourgeois society*, Polity Press, Cambridge.

—— 1993, 'Modernity: An incomplete project', in Thomas Docherty, ed., *Post-modernism: A reader*, Harvester Wheatsheaf, Hemel Hempstead, pp. 98–109.

Hall, Edward, 1959, *The Silent Language*, Doubleday, Garden City, New York.

—— 1966, *The Hidden Dimension: Man's use of space in public and private*, The Bodley Head, London.

Hall, Peter, 1973, *The Containment of Urban England*, Allen and Unwin, London.

—— 1995, 'Towards a general urban theory', in J. Brotchie, M. Batty, E. Blakely, P. Hall and P. Newman, eds, *Cities in Competition*, Longman Australia, Melbourne.

Hansen, Mogens Herman, 1995, 'The "autonomous city-state": Ancient fact or modern fiction', in M.G. Hansen and Kurt Raaflaub, eds, *Studies in the Ancient Greek Polis*, Historia, Franz Steiner Verlag, Stuttgart, pp. 21–43.

Harris, Bruce, James Luginbuhl, and Jill Fishbein, 1978, 'Density and personal space in a field setting', *Social Psychology*, Vol. 41, Issue 4 (December 1978), pp. 350–3.

Hayden, Dolores, 1996, 'What would a non-sexist city be like? Speculations on housing, urban design, and human work', in LeGates, Richard and Frederic Stout, eds, *The City Reader*, Routledge, London, pp. 142–57.

Hegel, F., 1967 (originally 1821), *Hegel's Philosophy of Right*, Oxford University Press, London.

✓ Hill, Lisa and McCarthy, Peter, 1999, 'Hume, Smith and Ferguson: Friendship in commercial society', *Critical Review of International Social and Political Philosophy*, Vol. 2, No. 4, pp. 33–49.

Honneth, Axel, 1995, *The Fragmented World of the Social: Essays in social and political philosophy*, State University of New York Press, Albany.

Howard, E., 1960, *Garden Cities of To-morrow*, Faber & Faber, London.

Howell, Sandra and Tentokali, Vana, 1989, 'Domestic privacy: Gender, culture, and development issues', in Setha Low and Erve Chambers, eds, *Housing, Culture, and Design*, University of Pennsylvania Press, Philadelphia, pp. 281–300.

Hume, David, 1998, *Selected Essays*, Oxford University Press, Oxford.

Inglis, Fred, 2000, *Clifford Geertz: Culture, custom and ethics*, Polity Press, Cambridge.

Irvine New Town Corporation, 1971, *Irvine New Town Plan*, (Irvine, Scotland).

Jacobs, J., 1961, *The Death and Life of Great American Cities*, Vintage Books, New York.

Jameson, Michael, 1990, 'Private Space and the Greek City', in Oswyn Murray and Simon Price, eds, *The Greek City: From Homer to Alexander*, Clarendon Press, Oxford, pp. 171–95.

Jenkins, Richard, 1996, *Social Identity*, Routledge, London.

Kamenka, E., 1983, Public/private in Marxist theory and Marxist practice, in S.I. Benn and G.F Gaus, eds, *Public and Private in Social Life*, Croom Helm, St Martin's Press, London, pp. 267–79.

Kant, Immanuel, 1993 (originally 1781), *Critique of Pure Reason*, Everyman, J.M. Dent, London.

Katz, Peter, 1994, ed., *The New Urbanism: Toward an architecture of community*, McGraw Hill, New York.

Keating, Dennis and Krumholz, Norman, 1999, eds, *Rebuilding Urban Neighbourhoods: Achievements, opportunities and limits*, Sage, Thousand Oaks, CA.

Keller, Suzanne, 1968, *The Urban Neighbourhood: A sociological perspective*, Random House, New York.

Kenworthy Teather, Elizabeth, ed., 1999, *Embodied Geographies: Spaces, bodies and rites of passage*, Routledge, London.

Knox, Paul, 1995, *Urban Social Geography: An introduction*, Longman, Harlow.

Koyré, Alexandre, 1970, 'Introduction', in E. Anscombe and P. Thomas Geach, eds, *Descartes: Philosophical Writings*, Thomas Nelson and Sons, Middlesex, pp. vii–xliv.

Krier, Rob, 1979, *Urban Space*, Academy Editions, London.

Kuipers, Dean, 2002, 'One is the loveliest number', *Calendar Live, Los Angeles Times*, 2 May 2002, Web Edition.

Kumar, Krishan, 1997, 'Home: The promise and predicament of private life at the end of the twentieth century', in J. Weintraub and K. Kumar, eds, *Public and Private in Thought and Practice: Perspectives on a grand dichotomy*, The University of Chicago Press, Chicago, pp. 204–36.

Landman, Karina, 2000, *An Overview of Enclosed Neighbourhoods in South Africa*, CSIR Building and Construction Technology, Pretoria.

Lang, Robert and Hornburg, Steven, 1998, 'Editors' Introduction: What is social capital and why is it important to public policy?', *Housing Policy Debate*, Vol. 9, Issue 1, pp 1–16.

Lapidus, I.M., 1967, *Muslim Cities in the Later Middle Ages*, Harvard University Press, Cambridge, Massachusetts.

—— 1969, 'Muslim Cities and Islamic Societies', in Lapidus, I.M. (ed), *Middle Eastern Cities*, pp. 47–79, University of California Press, Berkeley.

—— 1973, 'Traditional Muslim Cities: Structure and Change', in Brown, L.C. ed., *From Madina to Metropolis*, pp. 51–69, The Darwin Press, Princeton, New Jersey.

Latour, Bruno, 1993, *We Have Never Been Modern*, Harvester Wheatsheaf, New York.

Lawrence, A.W. and Tomlinson, Richard, 1996, *Greek Architecture*, Fifth edition, Yale University Press/Pelican History of Art, Harmondsworth, Middlesex.

Le Corbusier, 1927, *Towards a New Architecture*, The Architectural Press, London.

—— 1971, *The City of To-morrow, and its Planning*, The Architectural Press, London.

Lefebvre, Henri, 1991, *The Production of Space*, Blackwell, Oxford.

Liben, Lynn, 1988, 'Conceptual issues in the development of spatial cognition', in Stiles-Davis *et al.*, eds, pp. 167–94.

Liu, Laurence, 1989, *Chinese Architecture*, Academy Editions, London.

Lloyd, David, 1992, *The Making of English Towns: 2000 years of evolution*, Victor Gollancz, London.

Locke, John, 1976 (originally 1681), *The Second Treatise of Government*, Basil Blackwell, Oxford.

Logan, John and Molotch, Harvey, 1987, *Urban Fortunes: the political economy of place*, University of California Press, Berkeley.

Logan, John, 1993, 'Cycles and trends in the globalization of real estate', in P. Knox, ed., *The Restless Urban Landscape*, Prentice Hall, Englewood Cliffs, New Jersey, pp. 33–54.

Lynch, Kevin, 1960, *The Image of the City*, MIT Press, Cambridge, MA.

Lyotard, Jean Francois, 1992a, *The Postmodern Explained: Correspondence 1982–1985*, University of Minnesota Press, MN, Power Publications, Sydney.

—— 1992b, 'Answering the Question: What is Postmodernism?', in Charles Jencks, ed., *The Post-Modern Reader*, Academy Editions, London, pp. 138–50.

Madanipour, A., 1993, 'Principles of urban design in the British New Towns', *Open House International*, Vol. 18, No. 3, pp. 32–47.

—— 1996, *Design of Urban Space: An inquiry into a socio-spatial process*, John Wiley, Chichester.

—— 1998a, 'Social exclusion and Space', in A. Madanipour, G. Cars and J. Allen, eds, *Social Exclusion in European Cities*, Jessica Kingsley, London.

—— 1998b, *Tehran: The making of a metropolis*, John Wiley, Chichester.

—— 1999, 'Why are the design and development of public spaces significant for cities?', *Environment and Planning B: Planning and Design*, Vol. 26, pp. 879–91.

—— 2001, 'How relevant is "planning by neighbourhoods" today?', *Town Planning Review*, Vol. 72, No. 2, pp. 171–91.

Madanipour, A. Cars, G. and Allen, J. 1998, eds, *Social Exclusion in European Cities*, Jessica Kingsley and Regional Studies Association, The Stationery Office, London.

Madanipour, A. and Bevan, Mark, 1999, *Walker: A Neighbourhood in Transition*, CREUE Occasional Paper Series, No. 2, School of Architecture, Planning and Landscape, University of Newcastle upon Tyne.

Madanipour, A., Hull, A. and Healey, P., 2000, eds, *The Governance of Place: Space and planning processes,* Ashgate, Aldershot.

Maffesoli, M., 1996, *The Times of the Tribes*, Sage, London.

Marx, Karl and Engels, Friedrich, 1930 (originally 1847), *The Communist Manifesto of Karl Marx and Friedrich Engels*, edited by D. Ryazanoff, Martin Lawrence Ltd, London.

—— 1985 (originally 1848), *The Communist Manifesto*, Penguin Classics, Penguin, London.

Marx, Karl, 1974 (originally 1859), *Capital: A critical analysis of capitalist production*, Vol. 1, Lawrence and Wishart, London.

McCarthy, Thomas, 1978, *The Critical Theory of Jürgen Habermas*, Hutchinson, London.

Miethe, Terance, 1995, 'Fear and withdrawal from urban life', *Annals, AAPSS*, No. 539, May 1995, pp. 14–27.

Ministry of Health, 1944, *Design of Dwellings*, (Dudley Report) Report of the Design of Dwellings Sub-Committee of the Central Housing Advisory Committee, HMSO, London.

Moghaddam, Fathali, 1998, *Social psychology: Exploring universals across cultures*, W.H. Freeman, New York.

Molinari, Cesare, 1975, *Theatre through the Ages*, Cassell, London.

Moudon, A.V., 1991, ed., *Public Streets for Public Use*, Columbia University Press, New York.

Morris, Brian, 1994, *Anthropology of the Self: The individual in cultural perspective*, Pluto Press, London.

Mumford, Lewis, 1954, 'The neighbourhood and the neighbourhood unit', *Town Planning Review*, Vol. 24, pp. 256–70.

Muncie, John and Sapsford, Roger, 1995, 'Issues in the study of "the family", in J. Muncie, M. Wetherell, R. Dallos and A. Cochrane, eds, *Understanding the Family*, Sage Publications, London, pp. 7–37.

Muncie, J., Wetherall, M., Dallos, R. and Cochrane, A., 1995, eds, *Understanding the Family*, Sage Publications, London.

Muthesius, Stefan, 1982, *The English Terraced House*, Yale University Press, New Haven.

Nagel, Thomas, 1995, 'Personal rights and public space', *Philosophy and Public Affairs*, Vol. 24, No. 2 (Spring 1995), pp. 83–107.

—— 1998a, 'Conceiving the impossible and the mind-body problem', *Philosophy*, Vol. 73, No. 285, pp. 337–52.

—— 1998b, 'Concealment and exposure', *Philosophy and Public Affairs*, Vol. 27, No. 1 (Winter 1998), pp. 3–30.

Narveson, Jan, 1995, 'Social Philosophy', in Robert Audi, ed., *The Cambridge Dictionary of Philosophy*, Cambridge University Press, Cambridge, pp. 747–8.

Nasser, Noha, 2000, *Urban design principles of a historic part of Cairo: A Dialogue for sustainable urban regeneration*, Unpublished PhD dissertation, School of Architecture, University of Central England, Birmingham.

Nast, Heidi and Pile, Steve, eds, 1998, *Places Through the Body*, Routledge, London.

Neill, Sir Brian, 1999, 'Privacy: a challenge for the next century', in Basil Markesinis, ed., *Protecting Privacy*, Oxford University Press, Oxford, pp. 1–28.

Nolan, Lord, 1995, *Standards in Public Life: Volume 1: Report*, HMSO, London.

Norris, Clive, 1999, *The Maximum Surveillance Society: The rise of CCTV*, Berg, Oxford.

Nozick, Robert, 1974, *Anarchy, State, and Utopia*, Blackwell, Oxford.

Olsen, Donald, 1986, *The City as a Work of Art: London, Paris, Vienna*, Yale University Press, New Haven.

Parent, W.A., 1983, 'A new definition of privacy for the law', *Law and Philosophy*, Vol. 2, pp. 305–38.

Park, Robert, 1950, *Race and Culture*, The Free Press, Glencoe, Illinois.

Parsons, David, 2001, 'Personal becomes public', *The Guardian: Media,* Monday 18 June 2001, p. 10.

Pateman, 1983, 'Feminist critiques of the public/private dichotomy', in S.I. Benn and G.F Gaus, eds, *Public and Private in Social Life*, Croom Helm, St Martin's Press, London, pp. 281–303.

Pevsner, Niklaus, 1968, *An Outline of European Architecture*, Penguin, Harmondsworth, Middlesex.

Pile, Steve, 1996, *The Body and the City*, Routledge, London.

Plato, 1993, *Republic*, Oxford University Press, Oxford.

—— 1994, *Gorgias*, Oxford University Press, Oxford.

Platt, Colin, 1976, *The English Medieval Town*, Secker and Warburg, London.

—— 1990, *The Architecture of Medieval Britain: A social history*, Yale University Press, New Haven.

Politis, Vasilis, 1993, 'Introduction', in Immanuel Kant, *Critique of Pure Reason*, Everyman, J.M. Dent, London, pp. xxvii–lii.

Post, Robert, 1989, 'The social foundations of privacy: Community and the self in the common law tort', *California Law Review*, Vol. 77, No. 5, pp. 957–1010.

Pratt, Andy and Ball, Rick, 1994, 'Industrial property, policy and economic development: the research agenda', in R. Ball and A. Pratt, eds, *Industrial Property: Policy and economic development*, London, Routledge, pp. 1–19.

Putnam, Robert, 1998, 'Foreword', *Housing Policy Debate*, Vol. 9, Issue 1, pp. v–viii.

Quarrie, Joyce, 1992, ed., *Earth Summit 1992: The United Nations Conference on Environment and Development*, The Regency Press, London.

Rasmussen, David, 1996, 'Critical theory and philosophy', in D. Rasmussen, ed., *The Handbook of Critical Theory*, Blackwell, Oxford, pp. 11–38.

Roberts, Marion, 1991, *Living in a Man-Made World: Gender assumptions in modern housing design*, Routledge, London.

Robertson, D.S., 1969, *Greek and Roman Architecture*, 2nd edition, Cambridge University Press, Cambridge.

Robinson, Julia, 1989, 'Architecture as a medium for culture: Public institution and private house', in Setha Low and Erve Chambers, eds, *Housing, Culture, and Design*, University of Pennsylvania Press, Philadelphia, pp. 253–80.

Roelofs, Joan, 1999, 'Building and designing with nature: Urban design', in David Satterwaite, ed., *The Earthscan Reader in Sustainable Cities*, Earthscan, London, pp. 234–50.

Roger, D.B. and Mjoli, Q.T., 1976, *Journal of Social Psychology*, Vol. 100, No. 1, pp. 3–10.

Rosenau, Pauline Marie, 1992, *Post-Modernism and the Social Sciences*, Princeton University Press, Princeton, New Jersey.

Roth, Philip, 1998, *American Pastoral*, Vintage, London.

Rousseau, Jean-Jacques, 1968 (originally 1762), *The Social Contract*, Penguin, London.

Rybczynski, Witold, 1986, *Home: A short history of an idea*, Viking, New York.

Saalman, Howard, 1968, *Medieval Cities*, Studio Vista, London.

Sangregorio, Inga-Lisa, 1995, 'Collaborative housing: The home of the future?', in L. Ottes, E. Poventud, M. van Schendelen and G. von Banchet, eds, *Gender and the Built Environment*, Van Gorcum, Assen, The Netherlands, pp. 101–14.

Sapsford, Roger, 1995, 'Endnote: Public and Private', in J. Muncie, M. Wetherell, R. Dallos and A. Cochrane, eds, *Understanding the Family*, Sage Publications, London, pp. 317–22.

Saunders, Peter, 1990, *A Nation of Home Owners*, Unwin Hyman, London.

Schmitt-Pantel, P., 1990, 'Collective activities and the political in the Greek city', in

O. Murray and S. Price, eds, *The Greek City: From Homer to Alexander*, Clarendon Press, Oxford, pp. 199–213.

Schrift, Alan, 1996, 'Nietzsche's French legacy', in Bernard Magnus and Kathleen Higgins, eds, *The Cambridge Companion to Nietzsche*, Cambridge University Press, Cambridge, pp. 323–55.

Schubert, Dirk, 2000, 'The Neighbourhood Paradigm: From garden cities to gated communities', in Robert Freestone, ed., *Urban Planning in a Changing World: The twentieth century experience*, E&FN Spon, London, pp. 118–38.

Schutz, Alfred, 1962, *Collected Papers I: The problem of social reality*, Martinus Nijhoff, The Hague.

Scruton, Roger, 1996, *Modern Philosophy*, Mandarin, London.

Searle, John, 1995, *The Construction of Social Reality*, Penguin, London.

—— 1999, *Mind, Language and Society: Philosophy in the real world*, Wiedenfeld & Nicolson, London.

Selman, Paul, 1996, *Local Sustainability*, Paul Chapman Publishing, London.

Sen, Amartya, 1999, *Development As Freedom*, Alfred Knopf, New York.

Sennett, Richard, 1994, *Flesh and Stone,* Faber & Faber, London.

—— 1976, *The Fall of Public Man*, Cambridge University Press, Cambridge.

—— 2000, 'Reflections on the public realm', in Gary Bridge and Sophie Watson, eds, *A Companion to the City*, Blackwell, Oxford, pp. 380–7.

Sert, Jose Luis, 1944, *Can Our Cities Survive?, An ABC of urban problems, their analysis, their solution*, Harvard University Press, Cambridge, MA.

Silver, Allan, 1997, 'Two different sorts of commerce – friendship and strangership in civil society', in *Public and Private in thought and Action: Perspectives on a grand dichotomy*, Weintraub, J. and Kumar, K., eds, Chicago University Press, Chicago, pp. 43–74.

Simmel, Georg, 1978 (originally 1907), *The Philosophy of Money*, Routledge and Kegan Paul, London.

—— 1997 (originally 1903), 'The metropolis and mental life', in Leach, Neil, ed., *Rethinking Architecture: A reader in cultural theory*, Routledge, London, pp. 69–79.

Sinha, S.P. and Mukerjee, N., 1990, 'Marital adjustment and personal space', *Journal of Social Psychology*, Vol. 130, No. 50, pp. 633–9.

Sitte, Camillo, 1986 (originally 1889), 'City Planning According to Artistic Principles', in George Collins and Christiane Collins, *Camillo Sitte: The birth of modern city planning*, Rizzoli, New York.

Social Exclusion Unit, 2001, *A New Commitment to Neighbourhood Renewal: National Strategy Action Plan*, Cabinet Office, London.

Sommer, Robert, 1969, *Personal Space: The behavioural basis of design*, Prentice-Hall, Englewood Cliffs, New Jersey.

Sorokin, Pitirim, 1957, 'Foreword', in Ferdinand Tönnies, *Community and Society*, translated and edited by Charles Loomis, Harper and Row, New York, pp. vii–viii.

Southall, Aidan, 1998, *The City in Time and Space*, Cambridge University Press, Cambridge.

State of Western Australia, 1997, *Liveable Neighbourhoods: Community Design Code*, Western Australian Planning Commission, Perth.

Stiles-Davis, Joan, Kritchevsky, Mark and Bellugi, Ursula, 1988, eds, *Spatial Cognition: Brain bases and development*, Lawrence Erlbaum Associates Publishers, Hillsdale, New Jersey.

Strachey, James, 1985, 'Sigmund Freud: A sketch of his life and ideas', in Albert Dickson, ed., *Civilization, Society and Religion*, Penguin Books, London, pp. 11–26.

Stratton, Lois, Tekippe, Dennis and Flick, Grad, 1973, Personal space and self-concept, *Sociometry*, Vol. 36, No. 3, pp. 424–9.

Taylor, Charles, 1979, *Hegel and Modern Society*, Cambridge University Press, Cambridge.

—— 1989, *Sources of the Self: The making of the modern identity*, Cambridge University Press, Cambridge.

—— 1995, 'Liberal politics and the public sphere', in Amitai Etzioni, ed., *New Communitarian Thinking: Persons, virtues, institutions and communities*, University Press of Virginia, Charlottesville, pp. 183–217.

Taylor, Nicholas, 1973, *The Village in the City*, Temple Smith, London.

Tibbalds, Colbourne, Karski and Williams, 1990, *City Centre Design Strategy, Birmingham Urban Design Studies, Stage 1*, City of Birmingham.

Tomlinson, R.A., 1995, *Greek and Roman Architecture*, British Museum Press, London.

Tönnies, Ferdinand, 1957 (originally 1887), *Community and Society (Gemeinschaft und Gesellschaft)*, translated and edited by Charles Loomis, Harper and Row, New York.

Trancik, Roger, 1986, *Finding Lost Space: Theories of urban design*, Van Nostrand Reinhold, New York.

Urban Task Force, 1999, *Towards an Urban Renaissance*, E&FN Spon, London.

Urban Villages Forum, 1998, <*http://www.urban-villages-forum.org.uk*>.

Valdés, Mario, 1991, 'Introduction: Paul Ricoeur's poststructuralist hermeneutics', in M. Valdés, ed., *A Ricoeur Reader: Reflection and imagination*, Harvester Wheatsheaf, Hemel Hempstead, pp. 3–40.

Vance, J.E., 1977, *This Scene of Man*, Harper's College Press, New York.

Veitch, Russell and Arkkelin, Daniel, 1995, *Environmental Psychology: An interdisciplinary perspective*, Prentice Hall International, New Jersey.

Vitruvius, 1999, *Ten Books on Architecture*, translated by Ingrid Rowland, Cambridge University Press, Cambridge.

Wacks, Raymond, 1993, 'Introduction', in R. Wacks, ed., *Privacy, Volume 1, The International Library of Essays in Law and Legal Theory*, Dartmouth, Aldershot, pp. xi–xx.

Waldron, Jeremy, 1993, *Liberal Rights*, Cambridge University Press, Cambridge.

Walsh, B., Craik, K. and Price, R., 1999, *Person-environment Psychology: New directions and perspectives*, L. Erlbaum, Mahwah, New Jersey.

Walzer, M., 1986, 'Pleasures and costs of urbanity', *Dissent, Public Space: A discussion on the shape of our cities,* (Fall 1986), pp. 470–5.

Wann, Mai, 1995, *Building Social Capital: Self help in a twenty-first century welfare state*, Institute for Public Policy Research, London.

Ward-Perkins, J.B., 1974, *Cities of Ancient Greece and Italy: Planning in classical antiquity*, George Braziller, New York.

Watson, O.M. and Graves, T.D., 1966, 'Quantitative research in proxemic behaviour', *American Anthropologist*, Vol. 74, pp. 83–90.

Weintraub, Jeff, 1997, 'The theory and politics of the public/private distinction', in Weintraub, J. and Kumar, K., eds, *Public and Private in Thought and Action: Perspectives on a grand dichotomy*, Chicago University Press, Chicago, pp. 1–42.

White, Rodney, 1994, *Urban Environmental Management: Environmental change and urban design*, Wiley, Chichester.

Whitehand, J.W.R., 1987, *The Changing Face of Cities*, Blackwell, Oxford.

—— 1992, *The Making of the Urban Landscape*, Blackwell, Oxford.

Willetts, David, 1998, 'Tackling Social Exclusion', *Social Sciences*, No. 40, p. 3.

Wittkower, Rudolf, 1971, *Architectural Principles in the Age of Humanism*, W.W. Norton and Company, New York.

Woolcock, Michael, 1998, 'Social capital and economic development: Towards a theoretical synthesis and policy framework', *Theory and Society*, Vol. 27, pp. 151–208.

Yang, Martin, 1945, *A Chinese Village: Taitou, Shantung Province*, Columbia University Press, New York.

Young-Bruehl, Elisabeth, 1982, *Hannah Arendt: For love of the world*, Yale University Press, New Haven.

Zaretsky, E., 1976, *Capitalism, the Family and Personal Life*, Pluto Press, London.

Žižek, Slavoj, 1999, *The Ticklish Subject: The absent centre of political ontology*, Verso, London.

Index

Note: Figures are indicated by *italic* page numbers